W9-BGM-593

Roots of Civic Identity

International Perspectives on Community Service and Activism in Youth

Miranda Yates and James Youniss have brought together an international collection of essays that describe the state of community participation among the world's youth. Authors from around the globe use fresh empirical data to present portraits of contemporary youth constructing their civic identities through such means as community service and political activism. The image of "generation X" as socially disconnected and apathetic is contradicted by young people's efforts to comprehend the complexities of society and to work toward the realization of social–moral ideals. The findings contribute to a theory of political socialization that bases youth's understanding of political aspects of society and citizenship on participation in community and civic activities rather than on the intake of abstract pieces of formal information. To this end, youth seek to resolve ideological tensions, such as in Northern Ireland, Israel, and Palestine; to overcome corrupting political practices, such as in Italy and Taiwan; to deal with disillusionment, such as in Palestine and the emerging Eastern European nations; and to bridge barriers against youth's meaningful participation in the working of society, such as in Canada, Japan, the United Kingdom, and the United States. Special conditions, such as the diminution of the welfare state, for instance, in former West Germany, and the rapid turn toward democracy in former East Germany offer insight into the process through which youth try to establish meaningful person–state relationships, both individually and collectively defined.

Miranda Yates is Project Director at the Menninger Foundation, after serving as Postdoctoral Fellow at the Center for the Study of Race and Ethnicity in America at Brown University. She is the coauthor, with James Youniss, of *Community Service and Social Responsibility in Youth* (1997). In 1996, Dr. Yates was honored by the Society for Research on Adolescence with the Hershel Thornberg Dissertation Award. Her articles have appeared in the *Journal for Research on Adolescence*, *Journal of Adolescent Research*, *American Behavioral Scientist*, and *Social Development*.

James Youniss is Director of the Life Cycle Institute and Professor of Psychology at The Catholic University of America. His previous books include *Parents and Peers in Social Development* (1980), *Adolescent Relations with Parents, Fathers, and Friends* (1985), and *Community Service and Social Responsibility in Youth* (1997). He has edited *Psychological Responses to Social Change* (1995) and *After the Wall: Family Adaptations in East and West Germany* (1995). Dr. Youniss is the recipient of awards from the Humboldt Foundation in Germany and from the Japanese Society for the Promotion of Science.

Roots of Civic Identity

International Perspectives on Community Service and Activism in Youth

Edited by

Miranda Yates   James Youniss

 **CAMBRIDGE**
UNIVERSITY PRESS

CAMBRIDGE UNIVERSITY PRESS
Cambridge, New York, Melbourne, Madrid, Cape Town, Singapore, São Paulo

Cambridge University Press
The Edinburgh Building, Cambridge CB2 2RU, UK

Published in the United States of America by Cambridge University Press, New York

www.cambridge.org
Information on this title: www.cambridge.org/9780521622837

© Cambridge University Press 1999

This publication is in copyright. Subject to statutory exception
and to the provisions of relevant collective licensing agreements,
no reproduction of any part may take place without
the written permission of Cambridge University Press.

First published 1999
This digitally printed first paperback version 2006

A catalogue record for this publication is available from the British Library

Library of Congress Cataloguing in Publication data

Roots of civic identity : international perspectives on community service and
activism in youth / edited by Miranda Yates, James Youniss.
p.   cm.
Includes bibliographical references.
ISBN 0-521-62283-2 (hardbound)
1. Young volunteers in social service – Cross-cultural studies.
I. Yates, Miranda.   II. Youniss, James.
HV40.42.R66   1998   98–20714
361.3'7'083 – dc21   CIP

ISBN-13 978-0-521-62283-7 hardback
ISBN-10 0-521-62283-2 hardback

ISBN-13 978-0-521-02840-0 paperback
ISBN-10 0-521-02840-X paperback

To Stephanie Ahlers, Katie Murphy, Ellen O'Connell, and other people who encourage youth to struggle for justice and peace in their daily lives

Contents

Preface

This volume originates from a symposium held in Boston at the biennial meeting of the Society for Research on Adolescence (SRA) in February 1996. The symposium brought together researchers from several countries who were investigating community service and civic engagement in youth. Along with us, the participants, who also became contributors to this volume, were Connie Flanagan, Manfred Hofer, and Debi Roker. Lothar Krappmann of the Max Planck Institute in Berlin, Germany, served as the discussant for the symposium and offered insight by tying the papers together and setting forth future research questions. The symposium was well attended and generated enthusiasm among the participants and audience. We subsequently learned that several members of the audience, including Hans Oswald, Mark Pancer, Mike Pratt, Rachel Seginer, and Keiko Takahashi, were also doing research in this area, and the idea germinated to bring our work together in an edited book.

But our goal was not just to present an international array of empirical research on youth's community service and activism. We also believed that this cross-cultural sampling of research offered insight into an emerging theoretical perspective on the development of civic identity in youth. This perspective emphasizes the formative influence of youth's participation in service and civic activities on their political understanding and future civic engagement. The chapters show several ways that this process is carried out in varying social–historical contexts.

In addition to the participants in the SRA symposium, we are grateful to the other contributors in the book. All of the authors tackled their chapters with great energy and imagination and were highly conscientious in responding to our seemingly endless queries and deadlines. We are also indebted to Julia Hough at Cambridge University Press for her consistent enthusiasm and apt suggestions. Bill Grundy was extremely helpful in the volume's production.

Our initial work in this area was made possible by the support of the William T. Grant Foundation, and we are grateful to its officers, Beatrix Hamburg and Lonnie Sherrod. Miranda Yates's work on this book was also funded by a postdoctoral fellowship at Brown University's Center for the Study of Race and Ethnicity in America. This award was generously arranged by Fayneese Miller and Vartan Gregorian.

Other colleagues and friends have played key roles in aiding the development of our ideas. They are Mary Ann Clark, Bill Damon, Lynn Davey, Mike Foley, Rachel Forsyth, Dan Hart, Otto Hentz, Robert Hoderny, Barbel Kracke, John McCarthy, Peter Noack, Mary Jo Pugh, Gisela Trommsdorff, and JoLee Webb. Woinishet Negash provided assistance in the preparation of the manuscript. Lastly, we thank our families for their patience and encouragement.

Contributors

Irina Averina
Russian Academy of Sciences
Moscow, Russia

Brian K. Barber
Center for the Study of the Family
Brigham Young University
Provo, UT 84602, USA
[email: barber@acd1.byu.edu]

Lucia Boccacin
Centro Studi e Richerche sulla
    Famiglia
Universita Cattolica del S. Cuore
Largo Agostino fra Gemelli
1-20123 Milano, Italy
[fax: 39 2 7234 2642
email: crfam@mi.unicatt.it]

Luba Botcheva
Sapio Research Foundation
Sofia, Bulgaria

Jennifer Bowes
Macquarie University
Sydney, Australia

John Coleman
Trust for the Study of Adolescence
23 New Road
Brighton BN1 1WZ, UK
[fax: 01273 679907
email: tsa@mailhost.pavilion.co.uk]

Beno Csapo
Attila Joszef University
Szeged, Hungary

Connie Flanagan
The Pennsylvania State University
323 Agricultural Administration
    Building
University Park, PA 16802, USA
[fax: 814 863-4753
email: cflanagan@psu.edu]

Giyoo Hatano
Department of Human Relations
Keio University
2-15-45 Mita, Minato-ku
Tokyo 108, Japan
[fax: 81 33789 7480]

Manfred Hofer
Department of Education
University of Mannheim
D-68131 Mannheim, Germany
[email: fp54@rummelplatz.uni-
    mannheim.de]

Britta Jonsson
Institute of Education
Stockholm, Sweden

Peter Macek
Masaryk University
Brno, Czech Republic

Elena Marta
Centro Studi e Richerche sulla
   Famiglia
Universita Cattolica del S. Cuore
Largo Agostino fra Gemelli
1-20123 Milano, Italy
[fax: 39 2 7234 2642
email: serizzi@jekyll.it12.bull.it]

Hans Oswald
School of Education
Postfach 601553
D-14415 Potsdam, Germany
[email: oswald@rz.uni-potsdam.de]

S. Mark Pancer
Department of Psychology
Wilfred Laurier University
Waterloo, Ontario
Canada N2L 3C5
[fax: 519-746-7605
email: mpancer@mach1.wlu.ca]

Katie Player
Trust for the Study of Adolescence
23 New Road
Brighton BN1 1WZ, UK
[fax: 01273 679907
email: tsa@mailhost.pavilion.co.uk]

Michael W. Pratt
Department of Psychology
Wilfred Laurier University
Waterloo, Ontario
Canada N2L 3C5
[fax: 519-746-7605
email: mpratt@mach1.wlu.ca]

Debi Roker
Trust for the Study of Adolescence
23 New Road
Brighton BN1 1WZ, UK
[fax: 01273 679907
email: tsa@mailhost.pavilion.co.uk]

Giovanna Rossi
Centro Studi e Richerche sulla
   Famiglia
Universita Cattolica del S. Cuore
Largo Agostino fra Gemelli
1-20123 Milano, Italy
[fax: 39 2 7234 2642
email: crfam@mi.unicatt.it]

Rachel Seginer
School of Education
University of Haifa
Haifa 31905, Israel
[fax: 972 4 8240911
email: redc316@uvm.haifa.ac.il]

Elena Sheblanova
Russian Academy of Sciences
Moscow, Russia

Perri Strawn
Department of Anthropology
Yale University
New Haven, CT 06520, USA
[email: Perrijo@aol.com]

Keiko Takahashi
Department of Psychology
University of the Sacred Heart
4-3-1 Hiroo, Shibuya-ku
Tokyo 150, Japan
[fax: 81 33407 1986
email: a88610@m-unix.cc.u-
   tokyo.ac.jp]

Jean Whyte
Clinical Speech and Language Studies
Trinity College
Dublin 2, Ireland
[email: jwhyte@tcd.ie]

Miranda Yates
Covenant House California
1325 North Western Avenue
Hollywood, CA 90036, USA
[email: myates@covcorp.org]

Contributors

James Youniss
Life Cycle Institute
The Catholic University of America
Washington, DC 20064, USA
[fax: 202-319-6267
email: youniss@cua.edu]

Introduction: International Perspectives on the Roots of Civic Identity

JAMES YOUNISS AND MIRANDA YATES

This book presents a series of portraits of youth's involvement in community service and activism from various cultures and nations. One purpose of this global sampling is to gain an estimate of the political and moral development of contemporary youth insofar as it signifies what to expect from the next generation of citizens as we approach the twenty-first century. An equally important goal of this sampling is to learn more about the ways in which diverse governmental structures and formal socializing institutions affect youth's construction of political–moral identities.

Perhaps because we are approaching the end of the millennium, much hesitancy has been expressed about the present generation of youth and its ability to carry on and help reform our political and moral traditions. Some commentators have bemoaned the universal spread of the modern "youth culture" of MTV, jeans, and fast food around the globe. They also have criticized a rising interest in material possessions, coupling it with a fear that youth have placed hedonistic pleasure ahead of social obligation.

Without denying facts, many of us who study youth professionally believe that the evidence needs to be viewed carefully and that negative cases surely should not be generalized to youth at large. For example, in the United States, crimes against property, by far the largest category of juvenile crime, have held at a steady rate over the past 25 years (Siegel & Senna, 1994), and, although violent juvenile crime has increased in recent years, it still involves a small proportion of all youth (Siegel & Senna, 1994). Jones and Krisberg (1994), for example, report that the proportion of the U.S. youth population arrested for violent crime increased from 0.3% in 1982 to 0.5% in 1992.

Our viewpoint also takes into consideration youth's positive behavior, which the bleak accounts tend to overlook. The overwhelming majority of U.S. youth claim to have close and respectful relationships with their

1

parents (Barber & Olsen, 1997; Grotevant, 1998), are seriously engaged in schoolwork and related activities (Berliner & Biddle, 1995), and say that religion is important in their lives (Youniss, Yates, & Su, 1997). Moreover, several national surveys show that 60% or more of U.S. youth are involved in volunteer community service at least a few times a year, and that about 25% are involved on a monthly, weekly, or daily basis (Youniss & Yates, 1997).

What is often forgotten in negative caricatures is that the vast majority of youth live normal lives, striving to be successful students, caring about family and persons around them, and feeling responsible for the well-being of their peers and the broader community. What is also forgotten is that youth are frequently connected to normative society through numerous institutions, including the school; related clubs, civic associations, churches, organizations such as the Scouts, YMCA, sports leagues, and 4-H; and groups designed to foster specialized talents in music and the arts. As Larson (1994) has observed, the role of these norm-bearing institutions has tended to be neglected in our appraisals of youth at the peril of overlooking the full range of socialization processes, which extends well beyond the nuclear family and functions to integrate youth deeply into our social traditions.

Much discussion of contemporary youth has been focused on the United States, if only because it is thought to be the seminal starting point for the global youth culture. However, recent changes in the structure of social science and in political awareness have shown the need to broaden our perspective so that it encompasses youth internationally. In terms of social science, foreign governments, such as Germany and Japan, have consciously promoted interaction between scholars in their universities and scholars in the United States. Foundations such as Alexander von Humboldt in Bonn, Johan Jacobs in Zurich, Max Planck Institute in Berlin, and Japanese Society for the Promotion of Science have sponsored academic exchanges that bring researchers together to share professional experiences and form collaborative projects. After 20 years of such efforts, it is now common at professional meetings that some symposium panels include expert presenters from more than one nation. Indeed, the seeds for this book were planted in such a symposium in Boston at the 1996 meeting of the Society for Research on Adolescence and in Quebec at the 1996 meeting of the International Society for the Study of Behavioral Development.

International exchange has been accompanied by a new political awareness that is rapidly affecting the way that we think about youth.

It is difficult to cite all of the key events, but we will list a few that seem to have had an obvious impact. One was the decline in manufacturing jobs in Western nations, and the correlated rise in youth unemployment in the 1970s (Lewko, 1987). Books such as Willis's (1977) *Learning to Labor*, Fine's (1991) *Framing Dropouts*, and Macleod's (1995) *Ain't No Makin' It* have addressed the continuing effects of these economic changes on youth's prospects and their development.

Another event of consequence was the abrupt ending of the cold war with the consequent breakup of the socialist bloc in Eastern Europe. Youth from the former East Germany through the inner depths of the Soviet Union all of a sudden found themselves cast into a new political and economic context that their elders did not understand and, therefore, could not help them learn. After 50 years of living under socialist rule, adults themselves had to give up familiar ways of thinking to adapt to the novel structures of democracy and capitalism. This required abandonment of political principles and the attainment of totally unfamiliar political practices such as voting in free elections, assembling in public, protesting against government decisions, or simply discussing politics with one's neighbors without fear of reprisal. As will be shown, these political practices constitute the meaning of democracy. Without these practices, democracy, as a formal system, has no meaning for people's lives (Noack, Hofer, & Youniss, 1995).

Youth's involvement in civil strife and war was equally important in the broadening process. Television reports from Rwanda, Northern Ireland, Bosnia, and Central America, for example, highlighted youth with firearms and sometimes in the center of terrorist activities. Meanwhile, in Palestine, youth were shown throwing stones at Israeli tanks and soldiers. To make the image even more vivid, these activities, known as the *Intifada*, were a key part of the popular revolution that proved to be instrumental in significantly enhancing the political base of Palestine and in leading to serious negotiations for peace and hopes for the establishment of a Palestinian state (Barber, chapter 9, this book).

A further event, which is still in process, is the worldwide pattern of immigration of large populations from rural areas to cities and, for example, from Eastern and Southern Europe and North Africa to Western Europe; from South and Central America to the United States; and from Asia to several points west. The facts of immigration have forced researchers to pay attention to the difficulties many youth face in having to adjust to a new culture as they are experiencing the throes of adolescence. Further, these youth can hardly rely on parents or older siblings to provide clues and strategies because they also are novices in the midst of negotiating the same new culture (e.g., Nauck, 1995; Zivkovic, 1995).

In summary, negative images and overgeneralized caricatures of the present youth generation are unsupported by empirical data and only deflect attention from youth's many assets and strengths. In addition, our perspective on youth is becoming more international as we see the variable conditions in which youth are actually growing up. As we attend to changing political circumstances, civil strife, immigration, and the like, we see that the present generation of youth comprises a complex variety of persons having to adapt to a range of political and economic conditions that are staggering in breadth and complexity. If we want an honest assessment of this generation, we must go outside our narrow and familiar niche to sample youth living in varied circumstances in a variety of nations and cultures. Unless we expand our perspective, our theories are likely to offer narrow accounts of American middle class youth and miss the larger target of youth in general, with all the complexity and diversity that concept entails.

A New Approach to Socialization

A few decades ago, the study of political and moral development was dominated by an approach to socialization that today seems quite inadequate; it defined society, with its norms and values, in somewhat formal terms, made them homogeneous within society, and assigned them consensus status. With this starting point, the task was to show how adults, who understood society, communicated what they knew to the youth generation in a convincing manner. The process of communication began in the family, was formalized in school, and was reinforced by institutions that most closely dealt with youth. With these elements in place, all that remained was for youth to internalize what they had been presented, and, once this was accomplished, society was assured of being perpetuated from one generation to the next.

Here, we review reasons why this approach is now seen as inadequate and describe the approach that is needed to replace it. This is preparatory to showing how studies of youth in the various nations and cultures can contribute positively to the construction of a new approach.

It is now well understood that putting "internalization" at the end of the socialization process implied that youth were passive in receiving wisdom from adults. In the area of moral judgment, Kohlberg (1969) led researchers to see that youth constructed moral concepts by using reasoning to reflect on, rather than simply internalize, experience. In the field of political socialization, a similar insight was achieved by Rosenberg (1988), who pointed to the active use of reasoning in forming political concepts. There is little disagreement that the socialization approach we seek must assume that youth are active in using available cognitive competence to organize and make sense of the input adults and institutions provide.

Second, as already noted, researchers have become sensitized to the complexities that real societies present to the task of adolescent development. The traditional approach implicitly assumed that society was based on a homogeneous consensus and, thus, could be passed along through a consistent volley of messages. But even a brief look around the world shows that societies often comprise varying or competing views. If youth were to internalize society as it is, they would possess unpalatable concoctions of differences and contradictions. Consider, for example, any of the nations, from Northern Ireland through Afghanistan, that are currently involved in civil warfare between factions that hold to incompatible world views. These examples demonstrate the complex makeup of societies. They reveal the weaknesses of the internalization model by illustrating the importance of cognition to youth's making sense of the conflictual realities in which they live.

Third, as noted, parents and adults are not always in a position to hand youth a clear and authoritative view of what society is or ought to be. Consider the example of the Eastern European states in which parents lived their entire lives under socialist political and economic rule. It is safe to say that today these adults are still struggling to learn how to adapt to democracy and capitalism for the very practical reason that their marriages, work, and recreational lives have been affected by new rules of the market and new political frames (e.g., Walper, 1995). Adults who are still figuring out the rules of the system are hardly in a position to teach their children in an authoritative manner. Adult uncertainty similarly prevails for immigrant families in which parents' experiences in their initial culture do not prepare them for the culture to which they have moved. Indeed, in some cases, youth become the experts who serve as mediators to help their parents adjust to the new culture (Nauck, 1995).

Fourth, the prior two points raise the larger question of what society is or how it should be defined. One of the major problems with the old approach was its failure to define the precise content of socialization. More often than not, we were left with the notion that society consisted in formal knowledge and abstract principles (Bernstein, 1976) – the macrostructure in Parsonian functionalism. The field of microsociology has helped break through this barrier to an adequate theory by providing an epistemology that serves the needs of a new approach. Giddens (e.g., 1993) argues that, whereas society can be defined in formal and abstract terms, for example, democracy as a set of rights and obligations, formal knowledge must ultimately be turned into practices if it is to have meaning for people's lives.

The case of the Eastern European socialist states is illustrative of Gidden's position. These regimes came to their end in 1989 when citizens refused to behave in accord with the formal structures of government. People in Leipzig, Germany, peaceably assembled at St. Nicolai church to carry lighted candles to the center of town in protest against an exploitative government. Similarly, Czech citizens in Prague gathered at Wenceslaus Square to jingle their keys in the face of threatening tanks and soldiers. Instead of walking individually to their apartments, the Czech people stood forcefully in opposition to the military, which never retaliated. These cases illustrate Gidden's (1993) central argument that actual practices reconstitute formal structures, and, when alternative practices replace them, the formal structures are undermined. The primary content of socialization must consist in practices that recapitulate and literally redefine formal structures. Structures, thus, depend on practices without which they remain mere abstractions that await definition through people's actions.

Fifth, a specific kind of socialization follows from the preceding points. It is a socialization that is grounded *in doing* and leads again to *habitual practices*. Verba, Schlozman, and Brady (1995) have captured this well in their study of factors that determine contemporary adults' participation in democratic processes. They first define adults' involvement in terms of actions such as voting, working in political campaigns, and joining social movements. They then look back into the youth of these adults to search for factors that predicted positive socialization. The most potent predictor of adult participation was involvement in student government during high school, providing a clear example of how democratic practices acquired during youth were related to democratic participation in adulthood. This finding is almost identical to that reported by Hanks and Eckland (1978), who found that involvement in extracurricular activities, including school government during high school, was the clearest predictor of positive political engagement at age 30. According to Verba et al. (1995), these results demonstrate that effective socialization

consists in "hands on training for future participation" and direct "opportunities to practice democratic governance" (p. 425).

Boyte (1993) and Kahne and Westheimer (1996) have expanded on this
viewpoint in their analyses of civic education. They question the value
of teaching democracy through the acquisition of pieces of information
such as the 6-year election terms for senators or via field trips to national
monuments. They propose that effective teaching of citizenship requires
hands on participation in democratic activities such as debating real
views regarding, for example, affirmative action and environmental policy, views that have multiple sides, are not easily reconciled, and merit
serious discussion. Boyte (1993) describes how community service would
be one effective device for prodding middle class youth to "reflect on
the complex dynamics of power, race, and class," which they would
confront when they got out of their neighborhoods and attended to real
needs (p. 766). For Boyte, the goal of service is to provide training for
the practices of democratic behavior and instilling of *habits* "of political
participation that sustain a person, a community, and a nation" (p. 766).

Fortunately, there are prospective data that support and clarify this
position. For example, two recent studies have looked at adults who,
during their youth, actively participated in the U.S. Civil Rights Movement of the 1950s and 1960s (Fendrich, 1993; McAdam, 1988). These researchers asked whether 25 years after their participation, these persons
were at all distinguishable in their political behavior from nonpartici-
pants. The answer is yes. Both studies employed comparison groups of
persons who either applied to participate, but for various reasons could
not, or attended the same universities. Twenty-five years later the participants were significantly more active in local political activities, voted
at higher rates – over 90% voted regularly – and participated in public
movements such as promoting local causes or protecting the environment. These studies provide strong evidence for the notion that political
practices acquired during youth can effectively result in identity-forming
political habits that, thus, become part of the individual's self-definition
and shape the individual's relationship to society.

Confirming evidence of another sort comes from studies of persons
who show extraordinary moral commitment. Hart and Fegley (1995)
found that adolescents who contributed unusual amounts of service to
their community of Camden, New Jersey, had incorporated the practice
of service into their self-concepts. They did not see their actions as heroic
but viewed them as part of their identities. Colby and Damon (1992)
found the same to be true of adults whom experts had judged to be

exemplars of moral commitment. These adults, however, did not view themselves as being unusual or meriting special recognition. The daily practice of help for others in need had become so ingrained that it was understood simply as a part of their identity, in the sense that I am a person who habitually does these actions without need for praise or comment.

In summary, the second goal of this book is to advance a new concept of socialization that recognizes (a) the role of cognitive activity, in contrast to "internalization," and (b) the complexity of knowing what society is or should be, in contrast to positing a homogeneous and consensus array of knowledge and granting authoritative status to adults, qua adulthood. (c) It is further important to think of social structures in terms of the practices that define, reconstitute, and support them. The preceding points, then, lead to a reconceptualization of socialization that gives priority to the acquisition of practices that may be habitual insofar as they are long lasting and become integral to one's identity. Rather than viewing practices as discrete behaviors, however, they are more appropriately construed as habitual ways of acting that are part of a person's self-concepts or, more accurately, essential components of a person's identity.

Socialization and Social Contexts

Although this sampling across several nations will provide information about the present youth generation, our larger aim is to learn more about the ways in which variations in social contexts affect socialization opportunities and the socialization process. We do not pretend to have gathered a systematic sample of nations. Rather we sampled opportunistically in order to produce strategic comparisons that will highlight connections between the socialization of youth and social structure.

In chapter 1, Yates's analysis of community service in the United States is presented within the framework of a long tradition of voluntary and private social services. Although the government provides some services and has since the Civil War (Skocpol, 1992), the country has always relied on private and religious philanthropy. The United States also has a history of advocating the pedagogical value of service participation in youth (Wade & Saxe, 1996). Youth who participate in service today can be seen as partaking in a cultural tradition that coexists as well as substitutes for the restricted services that government offers. This analysis is paired with data from Pancer and Pratt, in chapter 2, on youth in

Canada, which has a different tradition of volunteerism because of a history of government provision of services as a social right. For example, Canada provides universal health coverage and supplies aid to education for all children, whether in private or public schools. These chapters offer national data on youth service as well as case study findings focused on illuminating developmental processes. These chapters allow some comparisons in terms of types of youth who serve, what they do, what the roles of family or institutions are in involving youth, and what the consequences of services might be.

Chapter 3 by Roker et al. on the United Kingdom and chapter 4 by Marta et al. on Italy provide another kind of comparison. The United Kingdom and Italy are similar modern welfare states that are closely allied with European nineteenth- and twentieth-century political and church history (Hobsbawm, 1993). But these states differ markedly in terms of their current legitimacy. In Italy, a well-publicized series of government scandals has created a crisis of trust that challenges youth idealism with a rightful skepticism. Also in Italy there is a widening rift between church doctrine and state policy exemplified in recent disputes over divorce laws and by the fact that this Catholic country has Western Europe's lowest birth rate. In the United Kingdom, there is less of a crisis of confidence in government and there is more focus on economic policy that can keep the nation on par with the rest of the European Economic Community. Debate is confined mainly to the two traditional parties that offer ideological alternatives toward government and individual responsibility. Further, the power of the church has been diminished to that of persuasion through a long process of church–state separation and secularization of society. As with the United States and Canada, the contrast between these two states is made in terms of community service, in particular, the kinds of service that are common and their probable effects on participants.

The comparison of youth in the former (East) German Democratic Republic (chapter 5 by Oswald) and the (West) Federal German Republic (chapter 6 by Hofer) offers a different type of contrast. For half a century, Germans in the West have lived under democratic rule in a capitalist system that was part of the Western economic order. During most of the same period, Germans in the East lived under socialist rule within the Soviet bloc. In 1989, the socialist era ended abruptly and the former East Germany was absorbed into West Germany under the latter's political and economic system. It is clear that youth in these two parts of the present Germany now face entirely different challenges in their socialization. As Oswald makes clear, youth in the eastern states must learn how to become politically active citizens within a democratic system. This task must be accomplished without parents and neighbors serving as adult models because these adults, themselves, need to acquire the same political habits anew. These adults must learn how to vote, how to assemble in interest groups, how to tolerate different views, and how to participate in other basic democratic processes that German citizens in the West have been participating in since 1949. Meanwhile, the challenge for youth in the West is to develop a sense of social responsibility in a welfare state that has promoted individualism and privacy under the assurance of universal health care and financial security in old age, among other things. They also must come to terms with the inclusion of former East German citizens and with the financial costs and shifts in employment that have been a part of this process.

The problem of youth's having to learn how to function in a novel political and economic milieu is taken up more fully in chapter 7 by Flanagan et al., which compares political attitudes in the former socialist countries of Bulgaria and Czechoslovakia with the Scandinavian democratic welfare states of Sweden and Denmark. Flanagan et al. emphasize the influence of national context on youth's interpretation of *the social contract* that they are being asked to adopt. The contrast between states is enhanced by the novel political–economic structures that Bulgarian and Czech youth encounter and the incipient uncertainty that is emerging about the form of social welfare found in Scandinavia. These latter states reached the epitome of their present structure after World War II, during what Hobsbawm (1993) calls the *Golden Era* of the twentieth century. Current world economic conditions and the recent demographic coupling of low birth rates with an increased and aging population have generated actuarial concern that the social contract, which was entered freely and sincerely, cannot be fulfilled even in the near future. Hence, one might expect to find youth in these settings to be going in opposite directions, Bulgarian and Czech youth adjusting expectations upward with hopeful idealism and Scandinavian youth adjusting standards downward with cautious realism.

Chapter 8 by Whyte also contains its own contrast. She reports political outlooks and political knowledge of Catholic and Protestant youth in Northern Ireland and in Dublin. Youth in the North have lived in continuing sectional acrimony that is political and religious in origin. It would be difficult for any Irish adolescent not to know about the social inequalities, the ever-present prospects of terrorism, and the tension they breed. These youth are growing up in a context that offers clear political and moral options. One is to take a side and become a combatant. Another is to retreat to neutrality in an effort to escape the tension of fighting for or against a position. A third is to seek resolution between the sides through nonviolence, compromise, and hope.

Chapter 9 by Barber is a unique study of young adults who during their adolescence participated in the Intifada movement in the present state of Palestine. As has Northern Ireland, Palestine has endured through a condition of siege and political uncertainty for several generations. It has sought through military and diplomatic means to free itself from the Israeli occupation. A major part of the impetus for peace negotiations came from the Intifada, in which adolescents played a pivotal role. The question posed in this chapter is how the former youth activists, now young adults, have developed psychologically and socially after spending their adolescence in conditions of intense and pervasive political strife and violence.

Another chapter that discusses a topic not considered elsewhere (chapter 10 by Seginer) reports on Israeli youth who have completed mandatory military service. Israel also is a state that has existed in a constant condition of vigilance under potential threat from surrounding states. Mandatory military service for youth, in part, fulfills a need for armed preparedness, but it also may serve other functions such as enlisting national loyalty. It is possible, then, that mandatory service is a device that helps solidify national identification during the developmental era of youth when identity issues are paramount.

The last comparison can be made between youth in Japan (chapter 11 by Takahashi and Hatano) and in Taiwan (chapter 12 by Strawn). These countries provide samples of Asian youth in two quite different contexts. Japan is somewhat equivalent to Germany in being a democratic modern welfare state in which the government, reorganized after 1945, was structured according to principles current at that time. Thus, the formal structure protects labor, provides extensive social services for health and welfare, and guarantees to meet the needs of the elderly. One expects that Japanese youth would have attitudes toward the state and society similar to those of German youth.

Taiwan, in distinction, is a state whose status is under continual question relative to the Republic of China. Youth are growing up in a context of ambiguity with regard to the future and to whether Taiwan should remain an autonomous country or unite with the Republic of China through some form of incorporation. Government schools provide youth with formal indoctrination supporting Taiwan's autonomy, but this so-cialization is accompanied by different messages that recommend alter-natives. Youth's socialization, then, must engage cognitive effort to resolve the complex choices between opposing ideologies and visions of the future.

In summary, these contrasting contexts, which are grounded in his-torical events and shaped by current internal and international tensions, are designed to inform the socialization processes outlined in the pre-vious section. In working toward an adequate theory of socialization, we need to take into account the contexts in which youth are living, the structural conditions that shape their horizons, and the institutions that guide their development. Collectively, the chapters in this book show that youth cognitively construct the political and moral understandings that form their identity and that different societal contexts offer varied opportunities and options that affect the socialization process and shape its outcome. In addition, each chapter makes a unique contribution in focusing on important aspects of the socialization process and its context.

The present sample of nations provides a strategic, although incom-plete, array of representative contexts in which youth today are actually living. This array allows us to estimate the role of context in the various forms just described. By comparing states that guarantee services and states that do not, and states where government is trusted and where it is distrusted, we hope to learn more about the ways context affects the power of community service to engender personal political agency and moral–social responsibility. In comparing youth in newly established democratic states with youth in welfare states that are advanced or per-haps in decline, we hope to learn more about youth's ability to grasp new political opportunity or, perhaps, develop a sense of skepticism at initial failures of this new system to deliver on its promise.

Three different countries offer us data on youth who are growing up in contexts of warfare and siege. In one, youth led an insurrection that had profound effects on helping to establish national autonomy. In an-other, youth do mandatory military service as a national manpower ne-cessity and as a potential rite of passage into adult citizenship. In the third, youth live in a context of cycling warfare and truce with negoti-ations. In all three cases, the need for decision making is the prerequisite for internalization. Youth must choose whether to sustain the historical conditions on which the tensions are based, to become apolitical, or to seek a resolution that will lead to a peaceful future.

We adopt the perspective that youth, as a generation, *make history*

(Flacks, 1988; Toren, 1993). Just like adults, youth must make sense of the world around them. This does not mean that each generation of youth must create society anew. Although there are occasions when this is called for and possible, the more likely case is that youth will draw from available traditions to form coalitions with adults in forging the future. It is wrong to think of society as a static structure that always deserves to be sustained. The making of history is a normal task that entails starting with the material one is given and working toward a meaningful future. The past plays a key role because youth draw from it both useful information and ideological inspiration.

This introduction has consciously blurred the lines between the political and the moral in process and in outcome. This caution is warranted, we believe, especially in a study of the present sort in which various cultures are under study. Consider a concept such as social responsibility that could be interpreted in either a political or a moral sense. One could be responsible to the community by fulfilling civic duties such as voting in an informed manner. Or one could be responsible in a moral sense by putting the community's well-being before one's personal interests. We do not address which criteria to use in deciding between the political and moral, and, moreover, we recognize the power of ideology to make the politically preferred position appear as if it were a moral necessity. Given these problems, we believe it is best to allow the terms to be used interchangeably or alternately across these cultural variations. In the long run, however, we leave it to youth to strive for a synthesis that would allow them to transcend ethnic and national political rivalry in a morally justified universal outlook.

References

Barber, B. K., & Olson, J. A. (1997). Socialization in context: Connection, regulation, and autonomy in the family, school, and neighborhood, and with peers. *Journal of Adolescent Research, 12,* 287–315.

Berliner, D. C., & Biddle, B. J. (1995). *The manufactured crisis: Myths, fraud, and the attack on America's public schools.* Reading, MA: Addison-Wesley.

Bernstein, R. J. (1976). *The restructuring of social and political theory.* New York: Harcourt, Brace, Jovanovich.

Boyte, H. C. (1993). Community service and service education. *Phi Delta Kappan, 72,* 765–767.

Colby, A., & Damon, W. (1992). *Some do care: Contemporary lives of moral commitment.* New York: Free Press.

Fendrich, J. (1993). *Ideal citizens.* Albany: State University of New York Press.

Fine, M. (1991). *Framing dropouts: Notes on the politics of an urban public high school.* Albany: State University of New York Press.

Flacks, R. (1988). *Making history: The American left and the American mind*. New York: Columbia University Press.

Giddens, A. (1993). *New rules of sociological method: A positive critique of interpretative sociologies*. Stanford, CA: Stanford University Press.

Grotevant, H. D. (1998). Adolescent development in family contexts. In W. Damon (Ser. Ed.) & N. Eisenberg (Vol. ed.), *Handbook of Child Psychology. Vol. 3. Social, Emotional, and Personality Development* (5th ed.) (pp. 1097–1149). New York: Wiley.

Hanks, R., & Eckland, B. K. (1978). Adult voluntary associations. *Sociological Quarterly, 19*, 481–490.

Hart, D., & Fegley, S. (1995). Prosocial behavior and caring in adolescence: Relations to self-understanding and social judgment. *Child Development, 66*, 1347–1359.

Hobsbawm, E. (1993). *Age of extremes*. New York: Pantheon.

Jones, M. A., & Krisberg, B. (1994). *Images and reality: Juvenile crime, youth violence, and public policy*. Washington, DC: National Council on Crime and Delinquency.

Kahne, J., & Westheimer, J. (1996). In the service of what? The politics of service learning. *Phi Delta Kappan, 74*, 593–599.

Kohlberg, L. (1969). Stage and sequence: The cognitive developmental approach to socialization. In D. A. Goslin (Ed.), *Handbook of socialization theory and research* (pp. 347–480). Chicago: Rand McNally.

Larson, R. (1994). Youth organizations, hobbies, and sports as developmental contexts. In R. Silbereisen & E. Todt (Eds.), *Adolescence in context: The interplay of family, social, peers, and work in adjustment* (pp. 46–65). New York: Springer-Verlag.

Lewko, J. H. (Ed.) (1987). *How children and adolescents view the world of work*. San Francisco: Jossey-Bass.

McAdam, D. (1988). *Freedom summer*. New York: Oxford University Press.

MacLeod. J. (1995). *Ain't no makin' it*. Boulder, CO: Westview Press.

Nauck, B. (1995). Educational climate and intergenerative transmission in Turkish families: A comparison of migrants in Germany and non-migrants. In P. Noack, M. Hofer, & J. Youniss (Eds.), *Psychological responses to social change* (pp. 67–86). New York: De Gruyter.

Noack, P., Hofer, M., & Youniss, J. (1995). *Psychological responses to social change*. New York: De Gruyter.

Rosenberg, S. W. (1988). *Reason, ideology, and politics*. Princeton, NJ: Princeton University Press.

Siegel, L. J., & Senna, J. J. (1994). *Juvenile delinquency: Theory, practice, and law*. New York: West Publishing.

Skocpol, T. (1992). *Protecting soldiers and mothers: The political origins of social policy in the United States*. Cambridge, MA: Belknap Press.

Toren, C. (1993). Making history: The significance of childhood cognition for a comparative anthropology of mind. *Man. 28*, 461–478.

Verba, S., Schlozman, K. L., & Brady, H. E. (1995). *Voice and equality: Civic volunteerism in American politics*. Cambridge, MA: Harvard University Press.

Wade, R. C., & Saxe, D. W. (1996). Community service-learning in the social studies: Historical roots, empirical evidence, critical issues. *Theory and Research in Social Education, 24*, 331–359.

Walper, S. (1995). Youth in a changing context: The role of the family in East and West Germany. In J. Youniss (Ed.), *After the Wall: Adaptations in East and West Germany* (pp. 3–21). San Franciso: Jossey-Bass.

Willis, P. (1977). *Learning to Labour.* Aldershot: Gower.

Youniss, J., & Yates, M. (1997). *Community service and social responsibility in youth.* Chicago: University of Chicago Press.

Youniss, J., Yates, M., & Su, Y. (1997). Social integration into peer and adult society: Community service and marijuana use in high school seniors. *Journal of Adolescent Research, 12,* 245–262.

Zivkovik, I. (1995). Adaptation patterns of parents and their children in the U.S. and Canada. In P. Noack, M. Hofer, & J. Youniss (Eds.), *Psychological responses to social change* (pp. 87–104). New York: De Gruyter.

1. Community Service and Political–Moral Discussions among Adolescents: A Study of a Mandatory School-Based Program in the United States

MIRANDA YATES

This chapter focuses on community service involvement among school-age adolescents in the United States. It discusses renewed interest in community service as a means of promoting prosocial development in participants. It then presents a theoretical approach for understanding the influence of service experience on participants. This approach connects service to identity formation in adolescence and is illustrated by a case study of a group of predominantly Black middle class adolescents who participated in a mandatory service program at an urban parochial high school. The theoretical, methodological, and social policy implications of this study's findings are discussed.

Current Interest in Community Service in the United States: Its Historical Roots and Rationale

The United States in the 1990s has witnessed a resurgence of interest in community service. This interest has taken several forms. First, Presidents Bush and Clinton both passed legislation to increase service opportunities for youth. Second, the state of Maryland as well as several cities and school districts made service hours a requirement for graduation from public high schools. A survey published in December 1995 reported that 15% of the nation's 130 largest school districts currently require service. This finding translates into required participation by some 1.2 million students (National and Community Service Coalition,

This work was supported by a grant from the William T. Grant Foundation to James Youniss and Miranda Yates.

1995). Third, several national organizations and education groups such as the National Service–Learning Cooperative/Clearinghouse were established to promote the integration of service into school and university curricula. Fourth, major business corporations such as IBM funded community service programs and initiatives. Another corporate example is the Prudential Insurance Company of America, which sponsored a program in 1995 to acknowledge outstanding service commitment of school-age youth.

One reason that promoting service participation in youth has broad appeal in the United States is that for many it evokes the nation's founding spirit (Kahne & Westheimer, 1996). Rhetoric on community service often cites Alexis de Tocqueville's observations on the importance of voluntarism in a democracy. Recent efforts to pass service legislation have been justified by a sense of decline in this core value of voluntarism and in political interest of youth (Commission on National and Community Service, 1993; People for the American Way, 1988).

The goal of promoting participatory citizenship in youth has driven school-based service learning efforts since the beginning of this century. Wade and Saxe's (1996) account of the historical roots of service learning in social studies connects the conceptualization of service learning to significant population shifts from rural to urban societies at the turn of the century. Within this changing context, the goal of eminent educators such as Arthur Dunn (1916) was to foster participatory citizenship through collective projects that connected the classroom to the needs of the community. Kahne and Westheimer (1996) also describe the enthusiasm for service learning of past curriculum theorists and educational reformers such as John Dewey, William Kilpatrick, George Counts, and Paul Hanna. Dewey, for example, is well known for promoting a vision of democratic education that advocated project-based instruction as a means of fostering academic growth and collective commitment.

At the end of the twentieth century, why has there been resurgent advocacy for community service in youth? Youniss and Yates (1997) point to several societal parallels between contemporary conditions and those at the turn of the century. They specify such conditions as an exacerbated split between the wealthy and poor, a peacetime outlook with a low possibility of military draft, burgeoning immigration, and dramatic changes in the labor market. These conditions have contributed to a general sense of social unease, tension, and questioning about the future in the United States. Within this societal context, it is not surprising that contemporary youth are often portrayed as disconnected from society and as in crisis (Giroux, 1996; Males, 1996). Nor is it surprising that educators and social policymakers feel a sense of urgency about providing youth with opportunities for meaningful participation in the workings of society.

Although the goal of expanding opportunities for youth may be laudable, negative stereotypes of contemporary youth as hedonistic and politically apathetic can be challenged. Findings from recent national surveys bring into question whether there exists a crisis of apathy in youth. These surveys indicate a consistent level of regular service participation among a substantial number of school-age adolescents. For example, a 1995 national survey of 9th through 12th graders reported that 20% volunteered over 20 hours per year and an additional 47% volunteered less than 20 hours (Wirthlin Group, 1995). In another example, a Gallup survey of 14- to 17-year-olds indicated that 48% had volunteered in the past month and 59% had volunteered in the past 12 months (Independent Sector, 1997). Youth in both studies specified participating in a range of school- and community-based activities, including tutoring younger children, visiting the elderly, distributing food and clothing at homeless shelters, and cleaning up parks. A third example comes from a historical survey conducted annually from 1972 to the present ("Monitoring the Future"), which reported a consistent level of participation among 12th graders with approximately 22% indicating weekly/monthly participation and approximately 45% indicating yearly participation (see Table 1.1; Yates & Youniss, 1996b). Given these levels of participation, current efforts to expand service opportunities should be framed as building upon youth's demonstrated strengths rather than counteracting their deficits (see Youniss & Yates, 1997, for a further discussion of this issue).

Research on Community Service

Despite the history of enthusiasm for community service learning in the United States, it has never made the transition from theory to widespread practice within the school curriculum. Wade and Saxe (1996) postulate that the sparseness of empirical evidence for its benefits partly accounts for this phenomenon. In the absence of compelling evidence, the complexities and time commitment of service learning programs, in contrast to more traditional, passive instruction, have hindered its implementation within formal curriculum.

Current service advocates have recognized the need for rigorous pro-

Table 1.1. *Percentages of High School Seniors Who Participate in Community Affairs or Volunteer Work, 1976–1992*

Responses	1976–7 (%)	1978–9 (%)	1980–1 (%)	1982–3 (%)	1984–5 (%)	1986–7 (%)	1988–9 (%)	1991–2 (%)
Never	34	31	31	33	31	32	34	33
Weekly/monthly	44	46	46	45	46	45	44	43
Yearly	22	23	23	22	23	23	22	24

Source: Data from "Monitoring the future."

gram evaluations and research on the effects of service on participants (Corporation for National and Community Service, 1994). However, much of the evaluative research conducted in the 1980s and 1990s reflects an atheoretical stance in which a potpourri of psychosocial measures are implemented with a pre- to posttest design (e.g., Newmann & Rutter, 1983). These studies typically have included measures of self-esteem, efficacy, political behaviors, and social attitudes. Not surprisingly, the results from these studies have often been disappointing. Despite the testimony of participants recounting the positive influence of service on their lives, quantitative findings have been modest or nonsignificant. Hamilton and Fenzel (1988) have attributed these results to ceiling effects and the use of global measures that fail to address the specific benefits of a program.

Theoretical Approach

Two current challenges of research on community service are to connect this experience to a theoretical understanding of social and moral development during adolescence and to implement appropriate methodologies that are sensitive to changes associated with service (see Yates & Youniss, 1996b, for a more detailed review of the community service literature). One theoretical approach, influenced by the writings of Erikson (1968), is to investigate service in relation to identity formation. This approach examines identity as a process in which youth struggle with questions of how they fit into a social world extending beyond the immediacy of friends and family. The focus is on how adolescents develop in their understanding of who they are within a societal framework with its history, ideologies, and traditions.

This approach connecting service and identity is supported by findings from interviews with adults who performed service in youth. For example, the retrospective testimony of individuals who participated in the U.S. Civil Rights Movement in the 1960s indicates that these individuals consider their involvement in service to have been critical in defining their sense of identity in adolescence and later adulthood (Fendrich, 1993; McAdam, 1988). According to these participants, service experience performed several functions important to the process of identity formation. First, it increased their awareness of societal problems. Second, it gave them the opportunity to try to alleviate these problems. A sense of efficacy or empowerment does not fully capture what participants gained from the experience. Participants also emphasize that part of the experience of service entailed developing a "realistic" assessment of the capacity of an individual to produce change (Coles & Brenner, 1965). Third, service helped participants to form connections with community organizations and other individuals, particularly of their own generation, committed to social reform.

Turning to community service in the 1990s, it may seem that comparing the diversity of activities that come under the general heading of "community service" to participation in the Civil Rights Movement is a bit of a stretch. It does seem unlikely that many of the service experiences in which school-age youth presently engage will recapture the historic drama of that movement. Nonetheless, the purpose of the comparison is to show the relevance of framing service as a potentially identity defining experience. Community service experiences can be understood as encouraging youth to grapple with social, moral, and political issues and to reflect on their own role in society (Yates & Youniss, 1996a). Interviews and journal entries from studies of school-based service participants support this conclusion by showing participants reflecting on issues of responsibility (Newmann, 1989), social relatedness, and self-awareness (Hedin & Conrad, 1991).

Methodological Approach

A review of research on community service indicates that the vast majority rely on survey instruments as single methods of data collection. However, as the data from the Civil Rights Movement participants and the studies of school-based participants suggest, a productive way of investigating service may be the use of qualitative data in the form of focus groups, interviews, and journal entries. In fact, several community service researchers have recommended this methodological approach, suggesting that evaluators may have been too quick to jump to quantitative procedures without properly understanding the processes under investigation (Hamilton & Fenzel, 1988; Newmann & Rutter, 1983).

As an added benefit, these types of qualitative data that are collected for research can also be conceived of as opportunities for reflection and integrated into the service program curriculum. A number of service researchers have recommended essay reflections as a way of accentuating the influence of service experience (Hamilton & Fenzel, 1988; Hart, Yates, Fegley, & Wilson, 1995). Further, moral education research from the 1970s and 1980s indicates that peer discussion groups may encourage upward shifts in moral reasoning (Higgins, 1995). These groups may be effective because with their peers, participants are able to evaluate several viewpoints. An important aspect of service research is that youth write about and discuss personal experiences, rather than hypothetical ones. Youth, therefore, may become more engaged in these types of reflections and more likely to offer insight about how they connect moral and political issues to their own emerging sense of identity.

A Case Study of Service Participation

An example of a study of community service from the perspective of identity formation and use of both qualitative and quantitative methods is presented here. The goal is to show how service experience may serve as a vehicle for engaging youth in moral and political issues as well as encouraging them to reflect on their own role in enacting change. Here, it is shown how conversations with peers about service at a soup kitchen entailed both exchanges on specific service experiences as well as attempts to fit those experiences within a larger sociohistorical framework.

The investigation focused on high school students who were required to serve a meal at least four times (minimum 20 hours) at an inner-city soup kitchen for the homeless, as part of a year-long course in social justice. Over the 1993–1994 school year, an array of methods were implemented, including focus groups, essays, participant observations, and surveys.

Sample

The students were 11th graders (third out of four years of high school) at a Washington, D.C., area school affiliated with the Catholic church from middle and lower-middle class families. The student population was 95% Black, 1% White, and 4% other minority. Students were 54% female and 46% male with the majority of students (71%) age 16 at the beginning of the study. The most frequently represented religious backgrounds were Catholic (35%) and Baptist (35%); 50% attended religious services on a weekly basis and 26% never attended. Forty-five percent of the students had participated in service before the beginning of the year. Of those students with prior service experience, most said that they had participated less than a year (45%) or 1 to 2 years (21%), and only 17% indicated that they were currently doing service outside school.

Data

Data from the focus groups are reported here. Students met with M.Y. in a focus group after each assigned trip to the soup kitchen (4 times, a total of 40 focus groups). The groups were held for 50 min during class hours, and the purpose was to talk about experiences at the soup kitchen. To facilitate conversation, groups comprised 10–15 students who met in a free room and sat in chairs around a rectangular conference table. The first meeting began with M.Y.'s asking students to respond to the question "In what ways was your experience at the soup kitchen different from what you expected?" The discussion then proceeded with the students responding to each other's comments. In the second through fourth meetings, M.Y. made a brief opening remark about the students' having recently completed an assigned trip, and then the students elected a peer to lead the conversation. With the permission of students, the groups were audiotaped and tapes later transcribed verbatim.

During each of the focus groups, students typically started off talking about their most recent trip to the soup kitchen. They offered impressions of people they served and with whom they worked. They often compared their most recent visit to the previous ones. Comments about work at the soup kitchen usually led to discussion of issues extending beyond specific service experiences such as welfare reform, drug use, and the responsibilities of public figures.

Analysis

The focus groups were analyzed though the collaboration of the two P.I.s and four research assistants. The research group read through all the transcripts and identified recurrent themes of conversation. They found that in talking about the soup kitchen, students often initiated discussions on stereotypes of the homeless, Black identity, moral responsibility, and political agency. Extended discussions, defined as exchanges among three or more students, were coded for these four topics (Cohen's kappa .81 for stereotypes, .76 for Black identity, .81 for moral responsibility, and .74 for political agency). A single excerpt could be coded for more than one topic.

Examples of each of these themes are offered to show how conversations about service evolved into more general conversations about society and self in relation to society. These excerpts also illustrate students' engagement in political–moral issues. Engagement is reflected in two ways. First, the topics recurred across focus groups and on multiple occasions (at least 10 times). Second, students addressed these themes in some of their complexity and contradiction, by taking into consideration several perspectives and drawing upon the sources of personal experience, opinions of family and friends, and information from the classroom and the media.

As a final note, although some of the examples cited here include quotes only from females, these were chosen because they best depicted the themes in a brief form. An examination of the focus group transcripts does not indicate a gender difference in focus group participation or reflectivity.

Who Are the Homeless? A central question that students addressed throughout the year was, Who are the homeless? Although the majority of students lived in neighborhoods with clear signs of poverty, it was not uncommon for them to indicate that they had never given food to or had a one-on-one conversation with a homeless person. Experiences at the soup kitchen led students to reevaluate ideas about homeless individuals, often by comparing their own lives to a homeless person's.

One example from the beginning of the year focused on reactions to the food served. A male student observed, "Some of the people would, like, look at the soup and they'd say, 'I don't want it.'" A female then observed: "I mean, if they were really. If they were coming to the soup kitchen. I don't know whether or not I saw a lot of pickiness, or it was like, 'What is that?' or 'I don't want that.'" Another female student then interjected: "Can I say something? Just because they were coming in there doesn't mean that they don't have no taste." The first female responded: "They come in there, 'Ya'll have anything else?' You're thinking this is what we have, this is what we're offering. I was kind of shocked that they were picky." A third female then entered the conversation: "Yeah it's terrible. Like if you go home and see leftovers in the refrigerator and your mother's not cooking nothing else. And you're like, 'Don't you have anything else?' I guess it's the same with them."

In another example from the beginning of the year, students focused on the clothing of those served. A female student commented: "I thought it was going to be a lot of older people coming in. OK, let me just tell you what I saw. I saw people with beepers and nice clothes. One man had on a new pair of Nikes. The other man had on a three-piece suit." Another female student concurred: "I saw maybe the same thing. I saw a security guard, like a post office worker . . . I thought it would be people in dirty grungy clothes and all." A third female then tried to explain these observations: "That could be the only outfit they had. Like they worked as a security guard and they just keep wearing it every day."

Being a Black American in the 1990s. Students also addressed ideas about race and what it means to be a Black American in the 1990s. Referring to specific experiences at the soup kitchen, students evaluated racial stereotypes of homelessness while revealing increased sensitivity to the vulnerability of minorities, particularly Black youth, to poverty and homelessness.

The following is an example from the beginning of the year in which students directly connected treatment of homeless people to treatment of Blacks. Earlier, students had been talking about the efforts of some local businesses to move the soup kitchen from its downtown location. A female student said: "I mean not with just homeless people. It happens with everybody. Like Georgetown [an upscale D.C. neighborhood] was a residential Black place. Then they moved all the Black people out. So it's White people. Now it's what you call a preppie town right in the middle of DC, right? It's the same thing. They're going to move the homeless out, upscale it." A second female student asked the first, "So where they going to move the homeless to?" A first female replied: "I don't know. It's just going to keep on reversing back-and-forth." A third female then said: "That's why I like this class because . . . it informs us about all the situations. So now we kinda know right?"

In another example from the middle of the year, students brought up racial stereotypes. This exchange began when a female student described some volunteers from out of town who were at the kitchen on her day of service. She recounted: "When I went, there was [a group of student volunteers] from North Carolina. . . . I was serving soup with the teacher. She seemed sort of racist to me. . . . A few White people came in and, like, she was saying, like she could understand how Black people could do something like this . . . It was like 'Oh, you're better than this.' " A second female student asked: "Do you think that's because she didn't know? It's just that she hadn't thought that a White person shouldn't be homeless or something like that? Do you think that it's something you're taught, or do you think it's something that, you know, she just thought of?" The first student responded: "I just think she thought it was going to be Black people. She acted really surprised when she saw White people." At this point, a third female entered the conversation and tried to generalize from what had been said: "I think a lot of people don't realize that homelessness is not a situation of color. It's a situation that needs to be dealt with."

Moral Responsibility. Conversations about moral responsibility included debates about the application of moral principles to real life situations. One recurring moral issue concerned whether one should distinguish between homeless individuals who deserve help and those who do not: the worthy and less worthy. Some students had experiences at the kitchen that made them question whether all the people served really needed a free meal. In expressing this view, they often brought up the individual's responsibility to abstain from drug and alcohol abuse and they indicated concern about the fine quality of some people's clothing. Despite this unease, the majority of students argued against judging another and often articulated some form of the religious maxim that "only God can decide."

An example of this topic comes from a beginning of the year focus group in which one female student said: "When you see someone in need, and you have something that you can give them, you shouldn't just stand there. You should give them something." Another female student replied: "It bothers me. Why give it to them if they buy liquor or drugs?" A third female entered the conversation: "I think, I mean, if they need it bad enough, I hope it does them good. Cause I mean that's their business. And I'd give it to them and what they do with it, that's on them." A male student concurred: "I mean it's up to the individual. You can't rehabilitate a person if they don't want to be rehabilitated. They're going to make that decision."

Another example occurred later in the year, a few days before the Thanksgiving national holiday. The students had been comparing their anticipation of the holiday with the bleak prospects that homeless people faced. When one student was especially sympathetic to their plight, a male student disagreed by saying, "Ain't telling them to be no drunk, no drug addict." A female said, "Sometimes they don't have a choice." But a second female disagreed, "If you were a crack baby [you might not have a choice]." This discussion continued back-and-forth until a second male student concluded with the following: "[Many homeless people] don't start out being drug addicts and alcoholics. It's ... the street that turns them into it. That's their only pleasure. If you don't have nothing else. ... They say they first start drinking just to keep warm. You know, liquor makes you warm inside. ... Then after that it becomes addictive. They can't help it. A lot of people you gave money to were probably drug addicts; you never know. Ain't nobody gonna say, 'I'm a drug addict, help me out.' So I'm saying, either way, you're helping their cause."

Political Agency. In trying to understand homelessness, discussions often turned to political processes. Many students attributed homelessness at least partly to government policies and advocated government reform as a way of decreasing social problems. These conversations did not characterize government as an abstract or distant entity. Rather, students sought to define what government comprises, how it can be changed, and what their own role is in enacting change.

The following example occurred at the beginning of the year when students began talking about government corruption. A male student entered the conversation by asking, "How did we get from homeless people to the whole government?" Another male student replied, "Because we went from what the government do for the homeless." A female student then stated: "There's one thing I can't figure out. How to get the government to do something. Something right, positive, good." A male student replied: "To tell the truth, I think it's not going to take the government. Maybe, it going to take, I mean, people with a whole lot of money." A second female student countered: "I think it's the government. I think it's mostly the government." A third female then stated: "The government's not going to do it. It's going to take a whole lot of good individuals just to change. I mean you can't change the whole world. You can never do that, but you can change parts of it."

A second example took place later in the year when students debated the extent of their own political power as teenagers. A female student said: "We are sitting here talking about issues, but what are any of us really doing? That's the question I have for all of you." A second female responded: "We are taking one step; we are discussing it. Discussing it.

That's taking the first step." A third female elaborated upon the second student's comment: "We ourselves, 16, 17 years old, we don't necessarily have to do something right now because we don't have . . . power. If we get enough teenagers together, adults will listen to us, but if it's like five of us, adults are not going to listen." The first female replied: "I'm not saying that you go to an adult. . . . I'm saying that just like that man sitting on the corner, it doesn't kill me to take a dollar out of my pocket and hand it to him. That doesn't kill me." The third female tried to defend her position by telling her, "I'm not saying that," but the first female cut her off, declaring, "I have power at 16; I do."

Summary

Examples from focus groups have been provided in order to show how service experience may encourage adolescents to examine the connection between social, moral, and political questions and their own lives. The students' service experience shares some of the characteristics that Civil Rights Movement participants emphasized as identity-defining. First, over the course of the year, students became increasingly aware of the problem of homelessness and grew in understanding of its complexity. Second, many students thought about their own role in enacting social change. They had the positive experience of being respected and appreciated for helping another. They also tried to balance idealistic and pessimistic viewpoints in order to form a more realistic appraisal of what they can accomplish. Third, the service experience helped to connect the students to activists running the kitchen and also to fellow students who were informed and concerned about homelessness. The focus groups exemplify this idea by showing students trying collectively to understand the meaning of their service experiences. Interviews with alumni 5 and 10 years after participating in this program indicate that these aspects of the program are important. Alumni believe that the awareness and involvement that the experience inspired have been pivotal in guiding their actions and defining their sense of who they are as adults.

Methodologically, the findings from this study are strengthened by the use of multiple methods of data collection and multiple coders. The conclusions drawn from the focus groups regarding the students' transcendent interpretations of their service experiences were cross-validated by findings from service essays (see Yates & Youniss, 1996b, for details on this analysis) and from alumni interviews (Youniss & Yates, 1997).

Furthermore, by using several methods, the study took into account some parts of the service program's context, including the social justice curriculum, the pedagogical approach of the teacher/program organizer, and the school ambience and traditions. The focus group excerpts show that students do not unquestioningly accept their school's social justice ideology. Rather, they debate and struggle to make sense of the ideas with which they are presented in school. In order to understand better the coconstruction of ideas among the students, other promising forms of analyses of the focus group transcripts include an examination of the dynamics of exchange among the students (e.g., back-and-forth, elaborative consensus) as well as an account of the resources that students drew upon to justify their views (e.g., personal experience, classroom, opinions of parents, friends, and media).

The issue of context also brings up questions concerning the importance of the program curriculum relative to the actual service experience at the soup kitchen and the importance of the program's mandatory nature. Taking up the first question, this program's curriculum and service experience cannot be evaluated separately; each functioned as an integral part of the other. The curriculum offered students information about the historical, moral, political, and religious issues salient to the problem of homelessness in the United States. Students considered and debated this information in relation to their own previous experiences and those of their peers and family as well as in relation to their immediate experience at the soup kitchen. In turn, serving at the soup kitchen provided the opportunity for concrete and personalized application of the ideas discussed in class and emotionally engaged the students in a way that they might not have been engaged in the classroom.

The second question concerns whether the program's mandatory nature detracts from the students' experience of service. The program's design can be seen as doubly mandatory. Students are required to perform not only a requisite number of service hours, but also a specific type of service at a predetermined location. Critics of mandatory programs have argued that voluntary participation is a fundamental aspect of service and questioned whether imposing service on youth can lead to meaningful experiences (Bullock, 1996; Lange, 1996). Some advocates of service have urged that youth should be given a choice of service activities so that the experience matches personal needs and dispositions (e.g., Kropp, 1994). The data from this program suggest that required participation can be meaningful when the service is conceptualized and carried out as an integral part of a school's or other community institution's overarching mission. In this case, performing service cohered with the school's central goal of enacting a Catholic vision of social action. Students knew that service at the soup kitchen was part of a tradition at the school and described it as equivalent to a rite of passage. Furthermore, although there is obvious value to recognizing that individuals differ in being suited for particular kinds of tasks, any advantage from that should be weighed against the additional benefit that comes from having students work together on a common project. This program's students viewed their service at the soup kitchen as part of a common project. Having students come together and share their experiences in group discussions no doubt reinforced this notion. In the discussion sessions, students talked about the junior year as being the right time for them to go to the soup kitchen because they believed that they were now mature enough as a class to handle its challenges and make a contribution. Reflecting the importance of this event, alumni portrayed the soup kitchen and social justice course years later as a defining moment in their high school experience and adolescence (see Seginer, chapter 10, this volume, for a related discussion on mandatory youth service and the development of solidarity in Israel).

Conclusion

The 1990s has seen increased interest in community service participation by youth. At the federal policy level, educators, politicians, and assorted interest groups have engaged in a fierce debate over implementation and government funding (see Waldman, 1995). Whether or not significant federal funding continues and whether or not school-based programs are implemented on a wide scale, it seems likely that locally organized service participation by U.S. youth will continue (McAdam, McCarthy, & Zald, 1996).

Research on community service can help in the implementation of service programs. This research can also contribute to theoretical understanding of the process of identity formation in adolescence. Specifically, service data offer insight into the interconnections between self-understanding and moral and political development. Moral and political theorists have long argued for such basic interconnections, but empirical work, particularly on adolescents, has been sparse (Flanagan, 1991; Flanagan & Gallay, 1995; Youniss & Davidson, 1993). An improved understanding of these interconnections may be essential to moving forward in our knowledge of how youth become engaged in society and its political processes.

References

Bullock, S. G. (1996, May 16). Public service, or else. *New York Times*, p. A25.

Coles, R., & Brenner, J. (1965). American youth in a social struggle: The Mississippi summer project. *American Journal of Orthopsychiatry, 35*, 909–926.

Commission on National and Community Service (1993). *What you can do for your country*. Washington, DC: Author.

Corporation for National and Community Service (1994). *Principles for high quality national service programs*. Washington, DC: Author.

Davidson, P., & Youniss, J. (1993). Which comes first, morality or identity? In W. Kurtines, & J. L. Gewirtz (Eds.), *Handbook of moral development and behavior* (Vol. 1, pp. 105–121). Hillsdale, NJ: Erlbaum.

Dunn, A. W. (1916). *Social studies in secondary education*. Washington, DC: Government Printing Office.

Erikson, E. (1968). *Youth: Identity and crisis*. New York: W. W. Norton.

Fendrich, J. (1993). *Ideal citizens*. Albany: State University of New York Press.

Flanagan, C., & Gallay, L. (1995). Reframing the meaning of "political" in research with adolescents. *Perspectives on Political Science, 24*, 34–41.

Flanagan, O. (1991). *The varieties of moral personality*. Cambridge, MA: Harvard University Press.

Giroux, H. A. (1996). Hollywood, race, and the demonization of youth: The "kids" are not "alright." *Educational Researcher, 25*, 31–35.

Hamilton, S., & Fenzel, M. L. (1988). The impact of volunteer experience on adolescent social development. *Journal of Adolescent Research, 3*, 65–80.

Hart, D., Yates, M., Fegley, S., & Wilson, G. (1995). Moral commitment among inner-city adolescents. In M. Killen & D. Hart (Eds.), *Morality in everyday life: Developmental perspectives* (pp. 317–341). Cambridge: Cambridge University Press.

Hedin, D., & Conrad, D. (1991). Service: A pathway to knowledge. *Journal of Cooperative Education, 27*, 73–84.

Higgins, A. (1995). Educating for justice and community: Lawrence Kohlberg's vision of moral education. In W. M. Kurtines & J. L. Gewirtz (Eds.), *Moral development: An introduction* (pp. 49–81). Boston: Allyn & Bacon.

Independent Sector (1997). *Volunteering and giving among teenagers 14 to 17 years of age*. Washington, DC: Author.

Kahne, J., & Westheimer, J. (1996). In the service of what? The politics of service learning. *Phi Delta Kappan, 74*, 593–599.

Kropp, A. J. (1994, April 20). Kids need responsibility. *USA Today*, p. 12A.

Lange, K. (1996, March 10). Mandatory community service is spreading to public schools across the country, despite student reluctance and withdrawals. *Chapel Hill Herald*. p. 1.

Males, M. (1996). *The scapegoat generation: America's war on adolescents*. Monroe, Maine: Common Courage Press.

McAdam, D. (1988). *Freedom summer*. New York: Oxford University Press.

McAdam, D., McCarthy, J. D., & Zald, M. N. (1996). *Comparative perspectives on social movements: Political opportunities, mobilizing structures, and cultural framings*. New York: Cambridge University Press.

National and Community Service Coalition (1995). *Youth volunteerism: Here's what the surveys say*. Washington, DC: Author.

Newmann, F. (1989). *Adolescents' participation in a developmental activity: A method of assessment*. Madison: Wisconsin Center for Education Research.

Newmann, F. M., & Rutter, R. A. (1983). *The effects of high school and community service programs on students' social development*. Madison: Wisconsin Center for Education Research.

People for the American Way (1988). *Democracy's next generation: A study of youth and teachers*. Washington, DC: Author.

Wade, R. C., & Saxe, D. W. (1996). Community service–learning in the social studies: Historical roots, empirical evidence, critical issues. *Theory and Research in Social Education, 24*, 331–359.

Waldman, S. (1995). *The bill: How legislation really becomes law: A case study of the national service bill*. New York: Penguin.

The Wirthlin Group (1995). *The Prudential Spirit of Community Youth Survey*. Camden, NJ: Prudential Life Insurance Company of America.

Yates, M., & Youniss, J. (1996a). Community service and identity development in adolescents. *Journal of Research on Adolescence, 6*, 271–284.

Yates, M., & Youniss, J. (1996b). A developmental perspective on community service in adolescence. *Social Development, 5*, 85–111.

Youniss, J., & Yates, M. (1997). *Community service and social responsibility in youth*. Chicago: University of Chicago Press.

2. Social and Family Determinants of Community Service Involvement in Canadian Youth

S. MARK PANCER AND MICHAEL W. PRATT

The year was 1688. A major fire had destroyed the homes and belongings of scores of citizens in New France. The town of Quebec was swollen with the destitute, many of whom were forced to beg in the streets, having lost all they owned in the fire. The citizens of Quebec, concerned about the plight of their less fortunate compatriots, formed what was probably the first voluntary agency in Canada, the Bureau des Pauvres. This agency, managed and run by volunteers and supported by donations from the community, provided clothing, food, housing, and money to those in need. The Bureau des Pauvres continued to operate, providing relief to the poor, incapacitated, and elderly, until about 1700, at which time its functions were taken over by religious charities (Lautenschlager, 1992).

Volunteering in Canada: Some Historical Highlights

It was the churches that initiated most of the first organized social services in Canada. The Roman Catholic church founded the Hotel Dieu in Quebec in 1658, and La Maison de Providence in Montreal in 1688, to provide relief to the sick, incapacitated, and destitute, and education and training to those who could not afford to pay for them. Charitable organizations (called Societies) associated with the Roman Catholic church,

The research reported in this chapter was supported by a Wilfrid Laurier University Senior Research Fellowship to S. Mark Pancer and a grant from the Social Sciences and Humanities Research Council of Canada to Michael W. Pratt, Joan Norris, and Mary Louise Arnold. The authors are very grateful to Janet Lautenschlager of the Voluntary Action Directorate for the many resource materials she provided, and to Richard Shillington for his assistance in conducting supplementary analyses of the 1987 Survey of Voluntary Activity in Canada. We would also like to thank the agencies, families, and youth who gave so generously of their time to participate in this research.

such as the Society of Vincent de Paul, continued to provide support for the sick and indigent in Quebec through the eighteenth century and continuing into the nineteenth and twentieth centuries. Lay volunteers working with the Societies visited the sick and disabled, helped the unemployed find work, and ran clothing depots. They also began to take on social justice issues, advocating on behalf of disadvantaged groups in the community.

Similar societies soon spread to other parts of Canada. By the mid-1800s, "benevolent societies" had been established throughout Canada. Although many of these were associated with religious or ethnic groups, others were the creation of community residents. In Halifax, for example, the Poor Man's Friend Society was founded by a group of local businessmen to provide food, money, and comfort to the poor, sick, and disabled members of their community. These and other societies throughout the four founding provinces of Canada were becoming increasingly necessary with the large influx of immigrants from Europe during the middle and latter part of the nineteenth century. Toward the end of the century, as settlement expanded westward, immigration increased, and more and more of the population became concentrated in the cities, the number of charitable organizations burgeoned to address the social problems that arose with the changing character of the population.

Many of the organizations that are familiar to Canadians today began in the last decades of the nineteenth century. These include voluntary organizations that were concerned with health care (e.g., the Canadian Red Cross, established in 1896), child welfare (e.g., the Children's Aid Society of Toronto, founded in 1891), and social services (e.g., the YMCA and YWCA, begun in the mid to late 1800s). In the area of social services, for example, the YWCA took a leading role in improving the lot of Canadian women by running social and fitness clubs for women, providing training and employment counseling, and establishing homes and training centers for women who ran afoul of the law. Other organizations that began during this period took on the task of bringing about social change. These included labor groups who advocated for benefits for retired citizens and organizations such as the National Council of Women, who fought for improved legal rights for women.

In the early part of the twentieth century, concerned citizens worked through a host of voluntary organizations that had multiplied rapidly and could be found in every city, town, and village. Increasing urbanization and industrialization, however, brought problems that could not be managed by voluntary agencies alone. Reacting to labor unrest, such as gave rise to the Winnipeg General Strike of 1919, and to the Great Depression, the Canadian federal government took its first steps toward transforming the country into the modern social welfare state it has become today. Financial aid programs were established for war veterans unable to find employment; allowances for needy elderly people were introduced; and during the Depression, both federal and municipal governments established programs to create jobs and provide relief to the unemployed. After the Second World War, the provincial and federal governments, responding to volunteer advocacy groups, began to assume a much greater responsibility for social welfare, taking on many services that had formerly been provided by volunteers working with private organizations. An unemployment insurance program was established in 1940. The Family Allowance program was initiated in 1945, providing a monthly allowance to families to help support their young children. Publicly funded health care began in the provinces of Saskatchewan and British Columbia in the late 1940s and was eventually adopted across the country by means of a federally supported medical insurance program in 1968. The Canada Pension Plan was introduced in 1966 to support individuals who were retired or widowed or who suffered from permanent disability.

The entry of the government into the area of social welfare, however, did not mean a reduction in the work of volunteers and voluntary agencies. Established volunteer agencies continued to grow and expand, and many new organizations came into being to deal with current social and health issues. Voluntary organizations in health care, such as the Canadian Diabetes Association (founded in 1953), the Canadian Heart Foundation (founded in 1957), and, later, a wide range of acquired immunodeficiency syndrome (AIDS) organizations, were established to act as advocates for those who were afflicted and to provide support and information to the ill and their families. The organization known as Greenpeace began in Vancouver in 1970 to fight against the proliferation and testing of nuclear weapons and grew to become one of the most effective environmental advocacy groups in the world. A wide range of ethnic and cultural groups came into being, to fight racism and discrimination and to promote intercultural understanding. The Canadian Ethnocultural Council, founded in 1980, is an umbrella organization of nearly 40 member organizations, such as the Canadian Jewish Congress, the Chinese Canadian National Council, and the United Council of Filipino Associations of Canada, working for equality of rights for Canadians of all backgrounds. Other organizations, such as the Canadian Save the Children Fund, concerned themselves with helping developing countries. In addition to these groups, there is a host of organizations that provide volunteer assistance during disasters and emergencies; in the areas of recreation, sport, and music; and in almost every aspect of life in Canada.

Current Volunteering in Canada

In October 1987, the Department of the Secretary of State of Canada sponsored the National Survey of Volunteer Activity in Canada, the most comprehensive study of volunteer activity in Canadian history (see Duchesne, 1989; Ross & Shillington, 1989). In an initial screening questionnaire, approximately 70,000 Canadians 15 years of age and older were asked whether they had been involved in formal volunteering during the previous year. *Formal volunteering* referred to instances in which respondents gave of their time and skills to various groups and organizations without receiving pay to do so. Individuals who indicated that they had served as volunteers during the previous year were then sent a follow-up questionnaire asking for more detailed information about their volunteer experiences.

In the 12-month interval covered by the survey, approximately 5.3 million Canadians, representing 26.8% of the population, volunteered their time through a formal group or organization. These individuals contributed an average of 3.7 hours a week to their volunteer activities, equivalent to over 190 hours a year per volunteer. Eight percent of those surveyed contributed 500 hours or more per year – more than 10 hours a week – to formal volunteer activities.

What do Canadian volunteers look like? Canadians of all ages are active as volunteers, although, in general, volunteer participation increases with age until midlife, when it begins gradually to decline. The highest rates of volunteering occur in the 35- to 44-year age group, where about one-third participate in formal volunteer activity. Women are somewhat more likely to volunteer than men, with participation rates of about 30% among women and 24% among men, although men tend to put in more hours per week, on average, than do women (3.8 hours for men vs. 3.5 for women). The rate of volunteer participation tends to increase with the level of education and household income; however, the total number of volunteers is almost evenly divided between below- and above-average income households. The volunteer rates for those who are employed, unemployed, and not in the labor force are approximately equal. The resultant picture of the Canadian volunteer, then, is a diverse one – Canadian volunteers are men and women of any age, from every part of the country, and with varying levels of education and family income.

What do Canadians do as volunteers? Canadian volunteers provide a wide range of services, through a diverse array of organizations. About 17% of volunteer experiences described by survey respondents were through religious organizations, involving activities that ranged from assisting with religious services and education to running summer camps or providing food or shelter for the homeless. Approximately 16% of volunteer experiences were in the areas of leisure, recreation, and sports. These activities included maintaining playgrounds and parks, assisting in special community events such as rodeos and marathons, and coaching sports teams. The third largest area of volunteer activity related to education and youth development, accounting for about 14% of all volunteer experiences. Activities in this area included working with youth organizations such as Girl Guides and Boy Scouts and helping with artistic programs such as choirs and theater groups. About 10% of volunteer experiences involved health-related activities such as working as "candy-stripers" in hospitals or helping the physically and developmentally disabled, and 9% of volunteer experiences were in the social services field, working with groups such as the homeless, abused women, and troubled youth. The remaining categories of volunteer service include the thousands of Canadians who are involved in activities ranging from environmental conservation to international development to cultural endeavors.

How important are volunteer experiences to those who volunteer? When asked, "Of all the things you did in the past year, how important were your volunteer activities to you?" 93% of the respondents indicated that their volunteer activities were either very or quite important, and less than 1% indicated that they were not important at all. In addition, 90% of volunteers stated that they were satisfied with their volunteer experiences, and 73% indicated that they would give more time to their organizations if requested. Volunteers reported deriving a number of benefits from their activities; for example, 80% indicated that they had acquired new skills and knowledge as a result of their experiences, primarily in the area of interpersonal skills, communication skills, and organizational or managerial skills.

Volunteering among Canadian Youth

The National Survey of Voluntary Activity in Canada also provides a detailed picture of youth involvement as volunteers in their communities (Cumyn, 1989). Though Canadian youth, defined by Statistics Canada as those aged 15 to 19, participate in volunteer activities at a somewhat lower rate (23.2%) when compared to the average (of 26.8%), they contribute more person hours per year per organization (115.8) than do older volunteers (110.5). Demographically, they look much like their older counterparts: They show the same diversity in regional participation rates and income distribution. However, it appears that young women in this age category contribute significantly greater amounts of time to volunteering (an average of 3.9 hours per week) than do young men (an average of 2.8 hours per week).

Although Canadian youth perform many of the same activities that nonyouth volunteers do, the organizations through which they perform their work are somewhat different. Nearly a third (32.3%) of youth volunteers work with organizations involved in education and youth development, compared to a rate of 13.1% for nonyouth in these kinds of activities. Participation rates of youth in the areas of religion, leisure and recreation, and health are similar to those of older volunteers, but are somewhat lower in the area of social services (4.2% for youth compared to 9.4% for nonyouth).

One of the questions asked of respondents to the survey was how they first became involved with the organizations for which they volunteer. The most common ways in which youth aged 15 to 19 became involved with their organizations were by being approached by someone in the organization (36.3% became involved this way, compared to the Canadian average of 48.7%), by approaching the organization themselves (20.9% compared to Canadian average of 16.9%), or by being chosen by coworkers, classmates, or other group members (11.1% compared to the Canadian average of 5.8%). Differences in the volunteer rates between youth and nonyouth may well be a reflection of the smaller range of personal contacts possessed by youth compared to older individuals (Cumyn, 1989). For both youth and older Canadians, personal contact appears to be the key in engaging new volunteers. Media advertising and volunteer bureaus were relatively unimportant in attracting new volunteers (accounting for 3.5% of youth volunteers and 3.8% of nonyouth volunteers) when compared to more personal approaches.

Youth volunteers had an even more positive attitude toward their volunteer experiences than did their older counterparts. Nearly 90% (compared to 80% of nonyouth) indicated that they had acquired skills or knowledge as a result of their volunteer experiences, and more youth (42.2%) than nonyouth (27.0%) indicated that they would volunteer more time on a regular basis to their organization if asked.

The Determinants of Socially Responsibile Thinking and Behavior

It is clear from the Survey on Volunteer Activity that Canadian youth who participate as volunteers gain a great deal from their involvement. They report high levels of satisfaction with their activities; they indicate that they have acquired new skills and knowledge; and many have begun to think of themselves as lifelong volunteers. The results of the survey regarding the benefits that these Canadian youth derive from their volunteer work are consistent with the research literature, which suggests that young people can gain considerably by engaging in these kinds of socially responsible activities (Hamilton & Fenzel, 1988; Yates & Youniss, 1996).

Our own research in this area has focused on the determinants of socially responsible thinking and behavior in young people. A socially responsible individual, according to our own working definition, is someone who feels a sense of connection to those outside her or his circle of family and friends. Such an individual feels an obligation to help those in the community, nation, or society-at-large who are in need, and to share skills and resources with those who are less fortunate. This definition of social responsibility derives from two sources: the educator Robert Havighurst's (1972) ideas concerning "developmental tasks" and social psychological theory relating to a "norm of social responsibility." According to Havighurst (1972), one of the key developmental tasks of adolescence is participation as a "responsible adult" in one's community, region, or nation. Social psychological notions about a "norm of social responsibility" posit that there exists a social norm, felt in varying degrees by different individuals and cultures, that compels individuals to help those in society who are in need (Berkowitz & Daniels, 1963; Berkowitz, 1972; Miller, Bersoff, & Harwood, 1990).

How do adolescents come to think and behave in a socially responsible manner? How do they become involved in the life of their country and their community? Why is it that some young people become more socially responsible than others? The initial idea that we explored in our research was that the social milieus provided by family and peers are key elements in engaging young people in thinking about and becoming involved in community life. In contrast to the survey research we reviewed earlier in this chapter, our own research has employed a more narrative and qualitative approach to understanding how and why socially responsible behavior develops. In what follows, we describe two studies, one based on a narrative approach, involving interviews with 40 Canadian adolescents and their parents about their personal values, and the other, a qualitative study of exemplary young volunteers who were nominated by the community agencies with whom they worked.

Family Influences on Adolescent Values: Narrative Research Evidence

As part of a larger longitudinal study of family influences on adolescent moral development (Pratt, Arnold & Hilbers, 1998), we interviewed and observed 40 Canadian families at two different times, once when adolescents were age 14 and again when they were 16. Our families, primarily of European descent, live in a moderate-sized Canadian city or its surrounds. Parents reported "some university education" as their average educational attainment. We recruited the families through an ad in the local newspaper, asking for volunteers to study the development of "values and communication" in teenagers and their parents.

Mothers, fathers, and youth themselves were interviewed about the personal values, both moral and nonmoral, that they believed were most important for the adolescent (chosen from a standard set of 10; see Table 2.1). At both times of assessment, each family member was asked to provide a narrative about a specific time when parents had tried to teach an important value to the youth. These "socialization narratives" are the materials of primary interest here. Observational measures of parenting styles and family communication practices were also obtained (Pratt & Arnold, 1995), as well as indices of adolescents' moral reasoning development.

In an attempt to clarify the ways in which parents can influence adolescent outcomes generally, Darling and Steinberg (1993) proposed a model that captures some of the complexity of parent socialization effects. The three distinctive components of parenting in this model are *parent goals and values, parenting styles,* and *parenting practices.* The model assumes that parents may differ in each of these components; they may have distinctive values and aims for child rearing, they may create different styles or broad communication "climates" as contexts for family

Table 2.1. *Parent and Youth Value Choice Ratings and Agreement (Family Study)*

Value	Parent rating[a]	Child rating[a]	Parent–child correlation	
			Time 1	Time 2
Moral values				
Honest	1.70	1.13	.21	−.05
Kind, caring	0.92	0.69	.38[b]	.30[b]
Fair, just	0.60	1.02	.26	−.10
Trustworthy	0.65	0.77	.15	.11
Sharing	0.10	0.04	—[c]	—[c]
Nonmoral values				
Ambitious	0.53	1.12	.10	−.11
Independent	0.72	0.60	.19	−.05
Open	0.59	0.36	−.08	−.31[b]
Polite	0.40	0.10	—[c]	—[c]
Careful, cautious	0.20	0.05	—[c]	—[c]

[a]Rated on a 0 (not chosen)–3 (most important) scale.
[b]Significant correlation of parent and child choices, $p < .05$.
[c]Chosen too infrequently to calculate correlation.

socialization, and they may vary in the specific activities or practices they choose to implement their aims in particular learning situations. As we review findings from our narrative study, we focus on each of these categories of parenting in turn.

Parent Goals. Personal goals and values play a central role in the development and maintenance of altruistic behavior over time. Colby and Damon (1992), in their study of a number of adult "caring exemplars," noted that these individuals were marked by a strong integration of moral goals and aims into their personal identities. Such extraordinary integration of moral values into the self-concept seemed to result from a variety of transforming social influences that occurred across the life span (Colby & Damon, 1992).

Certainly one of these social influences, particularly for adolescents, can be parents. Hart and Fegley (1995), studying exemplary altruistic adolescents in Camden, New Jersey, found that these teenagers were characterized by self-ideals that were much closer to those of their parents than a matched comparison sample of their less altruistic peers. A number of earlier studies also reported retrospective evidence from historically compelling adult exemplars who resisted Nazi occupiers or were actively involved in the civil rights struggles in the United States in the 1960s (Oliner & Oliner, 1988; Rosenhan, 1970). These exceptional moral leaders frequently remarked on the role of their own parents as models and exemplars of personal commitment for them.

In our sample of Canadian youth and their families, we noted a pattern quite similar to these more extraordinary examples. We found that in families where adolescents' personal identities at age 14 predominantly included moral goals for the self (such as honesty, kindness, and fairness, rather than nonmoral goals such as ambition, politeness, or independence; see Table 2.1), parents' values for their youth were in fact more concordant with the adolescents' own value choices for themselves at both 14 and 16. This finding of adolescent–parent value congruence around moral goals in our data set was particularly clear for the altruistic value, among our choices, of "kind and caring." As shown, this was the second most important value chosen by parents (after honesty) overall. Parental emphasis on "kindness" as a value was mirrored by the adolescents' own choice of this value for themselves at both times of testing (as revealed in the parent–child value choice correlations in Table 2.1). As an example of this concordance, one 17-year-old girl described her family's teaching about kindness:

> My sister was recently in a minor accident, and the job that she usually has with a handicapped kid after school she can't do. And so my mom and my sister convinced me to work hours for her until the therapist says she can go back to it. And this child, you really have to care for her to work with her. She's a really sad case, she was in a car accident and her brain was damaged. You have to not lose your patience with her. . . . My mom's a really caring person and she has a really strong bond with this little girl. . . . She and my sister *should* be able to rely on me to help out on this.

Parents' child rearing values thus seemed to be important in youth development, particularly with respect to altruistic ideals that might predispose youth to be involved in service activities.

Parenting Styles. The most influential recent views on parenting style are those of Diana Baumrind (e.g., 1971). Baumrind described ideal types of parenting styles, based on variations in two dimensions of parenting, demandingness and responsiveness. Most successful is the authoritative style, which is characterized by high levels of maturity expectations (demands) as well as high levels of concern for the child's needs and individuality (responsiveness). In particular, Baumrind found high levels of social responsibility in children associated with such authoritative parenting. In contrast, authoritarian parenting (characterized by high demands with low levels of concern for the child's needs), and especially permissive parenting (characterized by low maturity demands), were both found to be less successful in encouraging children's social responsibility development.

Greater sophistication of moral reasoning has been previously linked to authoritative parenting (Boyes & Allen, 1993). Families characterized by high demands for maturity by parents, in the presence of greater responsiveness to the child as well, had adolescents who reasoned about dilemmas of justice and fairness issues at higher stage levels based on the standard Kohlberg system for scoring moral reasoning. In somewhat parallel fashion, Santolupo and Pratt (1994) found that Canadian families who were more authoritative in parenting had adolescents who reasoned about social and political issues such as the causes of unemployment in their communities in more sophisticated ways.

In our current study, we focused both on standard assessments of moral reasoning based in Kohlberg's theory and on new measures of thinking about altruistic issues. Skoe (in press) has recently studied thinking about the "ethic of care." As originally described by Gilligan (1982), this involves levels of sophistication in reasoning about the needs of others and the self in more or less balanced ways. Skoe (1998) found that young adults who were more advanced in these levels of care reasoning were more likely to be involved in service activities for the community and for others. In our adolescent sample, we found that a more authoritative parenting style was indeed associated with greater sophistication on Skoe's developmental "ethic of care" measure, when children's ages were controlled. A similar pattern characterized the relations between parenting style and the standard Kohlberg moral reasoning measures; higher stage reasoning was related to more authoritative parenting (Pratt & Arnold, 1995).

Thus, our findings point to the potential role of an engaged but structuring parenting style or climate in fostering more developmentally sophisticated thinking about service issues in youth. Of course, there is no simple link between the sophistication of individuals' moral or social thinking and their actual behavior (e.g., Blasi, 1995). People can think in complex ways and yet not behave consistently with this thinking. Direct research would be needed to establish the relation between parenting style and adolescents' actual community service activity.

Parent Practices. A wide range of parenting practices has been shown to be related to children's sociomoral development, often in complex ways (e.g., Eisenberg, 1995). It is through these specific practices that parents implement their socialization goals for the adolescent (Darling & Steinberg, 1993). Given this, what parenting practices were described by our youth in their narratives of parental teaching about altruistic values? One widely studied process is modeling. It is well established that generosity and altruistic behaviors are strongly influenced by the presence of a positive model, often a parent (e.g., Bryan & Walbeck, 1970). Further, models are most influential when their practices are consistent with their moralizing statements. Adults who "preach" about altruism, but fail to practice it, are less likely to have an impact (Bryan & Walbeck, 1970). Several youth in our sample described altrusitic models in their narratives about parents:

> I think they [parents] mostly taught me by example for kindness. Whenever I had a problem I could usually tell my mother . . . and she would listen and be caring when I needed it, so there wasn't one example where they taught me, but I learned it by example from them.

The research evidence on "simple" practice effects on children's caring behavior is also quite consistent. Being assigned or encouraged to care for others seems to promote prosocial tendencies, sometimes perhaps by encouraging children to think of themselves in new ways, as "helpful" people (Eisenberg, Cialdini, McCreath, & Shell, 1987). An example of this was provided by a 16-year-old boy:

> [When did your parents teach you about kind and caring?] . . . Like taking my allowance and giving it to a charity or the church or something, that maybe another person needed more than I did. . . . When I was younger, my mom would let me clean the house for her on weekends and I would get paid a little bit of allowance, and my mom would say "Well, if I pay you this money, you've got to give ten percent to the church offering because it will help others that need it more than you do." And that was really hard for me, but I did and that was an example. They [parents] forced me almost into a situation where I would be able to feel really happy that I had succeeded in helping another person.

Another example involved a 15-year-old girl, whose parents supported her community work through the church:

> OK, I went to Florida on a missions trip. We drove down and we were working with homeless people and street kids and crack ba-

bies.... We were working in soup kitchens and a homeless community. It just affected me a lot because it's right across from these huge high rises and hotels.... It was just pretty weird. I was sad for the people because a lot of them couldn't work because they had mental problems and a lot of them didn't have family who cared about them.... When I came back, my parents noticed a difference. They were really glad that I went, and they think that I should go back because they really thought that I changed and was probably less complaining and stuff.

About 15% of our adolescent sample, when asked to describe a critical moral incident in their lives, reported some sort of community-oriented helping activity like the one just discussed. Clearly, then, parents sometimes saw and promoted the values of such community service activities for their children's development.

Our findings suggest a range of ways in which parenting may influence adolescent motivation, thinking, and behavior in the direction of community service. Darling and Steinberg (1993) point out the complexity of direct and indirect pathways through which these various components (values, styles, practices) of their model may affect adolescent socialization outcomes. Moreover, as several of the examples from our sample have shown, it was noteworthy to us that the parent's role during this crucial developmental period was frequently to act in collaboration with other socializing agents (the church, the school, clubs) as a kind of "manager" of the socializing experiences provided to youth (Bronfenbrenner, 1979). Youth participation and learning from such community service can be initiated and supported, or undermined, by parental reactions.

A Qualitative Study of Youth Volunteers

The family values study we have described, in conjunction with other research on the transmission of moral values, indicates that parents can have a major impact on the way in which their children think about their responsibilities to help others. Thinking in a socially responsible manner, however, may or may not translate into engaging in socially responsible behavior. In what follows, we describe a study of adolescents who have been heavily involved in such behaviors, having contributed many hours serving as volunteers for organizations within their communities.

The fact that nearly one in four Canadians between the ages of 15 and 19 works as a volunteer suggests that involvement in community life often begins at an early age. How do these youths first come to be involved with community organizations? What motivates their involvement, and what keeps them involved? Although the research literature gives us some insight into the way in which specific factors such as parental behaviors (Hart, Yates, Fegley, & Wilson, 1995) and personal predispositions (Omoto & Snyder, 1995) might be important in the initiation of volunteer behavior in young people, it fails to provide a comprehensive picture of the many ways in which youths are initiated into the experience of volunteering, the factors that serve to maintain their involvement, and the wide range of impacts that these experiences can have on youth.

In order to begin to construct a more comprehensive theory about the development of volunteering, we decided to use a qualitative research methodology. Qualitative methods are particularly well suited to the development of theory. Typically, they involve the collection of detailed information about a particular subject from relatively few individuals. The wealth of information generated by such procedures allows the researcher to identify and consider a wide range of variables that relate to the behavior of concern. In contrast, quantitative methods typically involve the administration of standardized measures of fewer variables to a larger number of respondents, in an attempt to make generalizations about how the population-at-large will behave in a given situation. Qualitative methods are also well suited to the discovery and identification of the many different paths that can lead to behaviors such as volunteering.

In contrast to the random sampling procedure employed in quantitative methods, qualitative methods most often employ a purposeful sampling process in which respondents are selected in terms of their likelihood of yielding important information about the behavior under consideration. We used the "criterion sampling" method of purposeful sampling (Patton, 1990), employing commitment to volunteering as our criterion. Our reasoning was that youths who had demonstrated a strong commitment to volunteering would be able to provide us with a great deal of insight into how people come to be volunteers. Consequently, we approached community agencies in the health and social services area that typically employed large numbers of volunteers and asked them to nominate individuals between the ages of 16 and 20 whom they considered to be very committed to their volunteer work. These individuals were then contacted and asked to participate in a detailed interview concerning their volunteer activities.

Twenty youths between the ages of 16 and 20 were identified by this selection process and agreed to be interviewed. The youths certainly met the criterion of being committed volunteers. All had contributed large amounts of time in working on an unpaid basis for the organizations that had nominated them. In addition, most had previously worked or were currently working in a volunteer capacity with other community organizations. Although some had begun their volunteer activities relatively recently (i.e., within the previous year), others had begun formal volunteer work as young as 12 or 13 years of age. Their work spanned a diverse range of activities; they sorted and distributed food at the local food bank, visited the sick and elderly, sold products made in developing countries, tutored peers from their schools in a variety of subjects, provided emotional support to people attending court, mentored abused children, acted as "big brothers" or "big sisters" to children from single-parent families, taught music or Sunday school, and worked with developmentally delayed children and adults, among other activities.

In the interview, respondents were asked for a detailed history of their volunteer involvement – when they first started volunteering, how many agencies or organizations they had volunteered with, what they did as volunteers, how much time they spent volunteering, and how they first started as volunteers. We then asked about what first interested them about volunteering, and about family members, teachers, and friends who might have had an impact on their decision to volunteer. Respondents were also asked what they liked and did not like about volunteering, what they had learned from their experiences, and whether they felt they had changed as a result of their volunteer work. In the latter stages of the interview, we asked our young volunteers to move outside their own experiences and to comment on the responsibility that they thought people in general should have to help needy individuals from their community.

In analyzing the information from the interviews, we attempted to identify key themes or factors that appeared to be significant in initiating and sustaining volunteer activity. We then organized these themes into a theoretical model that described the process by which youth first became involved in volunteer work, the factors that maintained their involvement, and the outcomes, both short- and long-term, that they experienced as a result of their involvements. This model is presented in Figure 2.1.

Factors Important in Initiating Volunteer Involvement. How and why do young people first become interested in volunteering? We identified

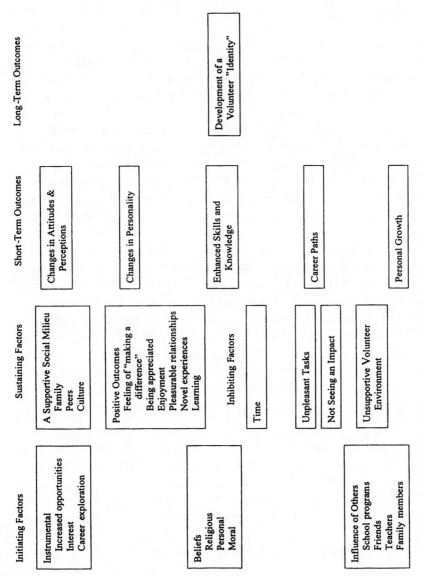

Figure 2.1. Model of volunteer involvement.

three major classes of *initiating factors* that prompted the youths' first contacts with the agencies with whom they worked; we labeled them "instrumental," "religious, personal, and moral beliefs," and "social influence" factors. Many of our respondents initiated the first contacts with the agencies on their own. For some, the purpose of the contact was "instrumental," in that they hoped to gain something from their work as volunteers – an opportunity to explore career options; improve their chances for scholarships, jobs, or entry to university; or merely have fun:

> There are the practical things that it [volunteering] gives me as well
> . . . it definitely looks good on a resume to have done a lot of these
> things.

> I think at an early age I realized that . . . I would like to go into
> a medicine related field, and I figured the best way to see what
> was actually going on in the hospital was to become a volunteer.

Others who contacted organizations on their own did so out of a sense of commitment to their personal, religious, or moral values:

> I think that behind everything has been my faith . . . I want to do
> things because Christ did so much for me and because that's what
> he's told us to do and to use our gifts . . . with other people and so
> . . . working in the community and helping other people has come
> really out of my Christian background and my faith.

> If you have spare time, you should go out and do something in-
> stead of just sitting and just lazing around and doing nothing . . .
> because you never know how much time you're gonna be here, so
> I just decided, like if I have spare time, then I'll do something . . .
> and so that's why I started [volunteering].

Consistent with the findings of the Survey of Voluntary Activity, many of these young volunteers began their work as a result of the urging or suggestions of others, such as friends and teachers:

> The hospital was my first [volunteer experience] . . . it was my
> teacher. It was grade six, I think it was, and . . . we'd talk and stuff
> and there was a group of my friends and she [the teacher] said you
> know, this would be great for you guys to do this, so then . . . I
> went and applied and got in and started volunteering there.

> I wasn't really into sports, so I was looking for something to do in
> school, so my mom, we were just talking about school groups and
> the Sunnyside group [a group of students volunteering at a local
> nursing home], and . . . she was encouraging me to try and get in-
> volved in that group, since I wasn't really into sports.

We also included volunteer programs in the "social influence" category of initiating factors, since we saw these types of initial volunteer contacts as originating more from outside than within the person. These kinds of programs were also a significant factor in starting a number of our respondents on their first volunteer jobs. One interviewee, for example, had taken a sociology course, which included 15 hours of volunteer work as a course requirement, in her final year of high school. Another had become a volunteer at court through a law program she had taken at her school.

Factors That Sustain Volunteer Involvement. Although factors such as the desire to improve one's chances for a scholarship or opportunities provided by school programs may have been important in initiating youths' first volunteer experiences, other factors were important in sustaining their involvement. Two kinds of factors were significant in this regard – the presence of a supportive family or social network and early positive outcomes that the youth experienced from their volunteer work.

Almost all the respondents were part of a social environment that supported their volunteer activities and provided models of community involvement; they had parents, family members, or friends who were themselves active in community life:

> My dad, you know, he's only been a member [of a service organization] for a few years, but he made me realize I guess that there are people out there that are less fortunate than we are and that you know, we should be lucky for what we have and thankful for what we have.

> My family ... has definitely had a big influence on me ... especially my father's family. He comes from a Mennonite background and he had fifteen brothers and sisters. ... I have an aunt and uncle in Mexico who are missionaries, I have an aunt and uncle who are going back and forth to the Ukraine with a mission there ... and a cousin who was doing prison ministry ... he had a group that went and sang and worked with people in prisons ... that family is just an amazing family and very giving ... it's a way of life, it's, you know, it's just understood that you do these kinds of things.

> I have one friend who volunteers at the Sunbeam Centre for children who are mentally challenged and physically as well. And then there's the Red Cross. I have friends who volunteer through the

Red Cross and some at the hospital. And I have one who does work with the Multicultural Women's Association.

Some of the interviewees belonged to groups that had been organized to provide help to their communities. Two of the youths, for example, were members of a "Concerned Citizens" group at their high school, which comprised students interested in working with community agencies, as well as addressing issues such as smoking and the environment.

Probably the most significant factors in sustaining volunteer involvement were the many positive outcomes that respondents reported experiencing as a result of their work. Among other things, they talked about the powerful feelings of satisfaction they derived from "making a difference" in people's lives, the feeling of belonging and appreciation they experienced in working with a service organization, and the relationships they had formed in the course of their work:

Just to see the reactions on their face . . . it's amazing, like if you give them flowers because they just delivered a baby or whatever . . . it's so nice to see.

It's kind of neat to go in there [drop-in center] and people know you . . . when you walk in they say hi, or when they walk in you know their name and you can have a conversation with them.

There's one resident who I'm really close to right now . . . it's been just over a year that I started visiting with her every week, so I've become really close with her . . . she doesn't really have any family of her own now, and she kind of sees me as like her granddaughter. . . . So, it kind of gives me a good feeling that she can see me as like a friend.

Factors That Inhibit Volunteer Involvement. Not all of the experiences described by the interviewees had been positive. Many (though not all) had had difficulty finding the time to volunteer, and some had worked on frustrating or uncomfortable tasks, in unfriendly environments. These factors tended to inhibit their desire to volunteer:

During school, it's extremely hard because in some courses you have like almost four hours of homework and then to go up and volunteer can be really hard.

When I did the hunger week, I was in [a grocery store] and I had to go up to people and ask for money – that I don't like to do because I find that very awkward and people are really mean.

There's times . . . especially working with the developmentally challenged . . . when you're putting a lot out and not getting a lot back and not seeing anything happen and you know, it's things like that that can . . . make it more difficult to keep doing it . . . when you're really trying hard to do something for other people and you're not seeing results and it's not happening, and that can be frustrating.

Staff plays a really important part in volunteer work, because if the staff isn't friendly, and they treat you more like [you're] a nuisance than helping, you don't really feel like going anymore.

Outcomes. To a person, the youths we interviewed described profound changes that they had undergone in several aspects of their lives as a result of their volunteer experiences. They reported developing a greater understanding of those they had helped and an appreciation for their own good fortune; they described changes in their personalities, such as becoming more patient and caring; they recounted the many skills they had developed and things they had learned as volunteers; and many stated that their volunteer work had had a significant influence on their choice of career:

I've learned to definitely think more of others and to appreciate what I have. Because you know, I realize that I have a lot compared to what some people have you know . . . some people don't have anything.

I think through volunteering . . . I gained a lot of confidence in myself and just what I can tackle and the challenges that I can take on in my life and . . . I guess I just totally . . . feel like I can take on any challenge now because of my experiences.

There's just innumerable things that I've learned, like little things about working with people and . . . even how people think and how people work and how people will respond and what's the best way for me to respond when things happen.

It's been one of the most draining volunteer work that I've done but I loved it the most, I've learned so much . . . and working with them [disabled children] is actually what has helped me decide on what I want to do for the rest of my life.

An Identity of Social Responsibility. It was clear from respondents' answers to the final questions of the interview that their volunteer experiences had had a profound influence on their way of thinking about themselves and the importance of making a contribution to social welfare. Nearly all of the respondents indicated that they not only would be continuing their present volunteer involvements, but also were considering others, despite their often demanding school and work schedules. Moreover, most respondents believed that more people should be volunteering, both for their own personal growth and because of the responsibility they bore for the welfare of their communities. It was evident that their experiences had helped to instill a sense of civic-mindedness and social responsibility in these young volunteers and had become a core element of their self-identity:

> A lot of times the . . . reason that you're in a position to help is just luck, you know, nothing that you've done to deserve to be . . . in a different position . . . and you know, things could change . . . in the blink of an eye and something could be different, and definitely people have a responsibility to be volunteering and doing things in their community. It's what makes it a community.

Implications and Applications

The results of our investigations into the determinants of socially responsible thinking and behavior suggest a number of ways in which to initiate young people into the world of community service, and to foster the development of a "socially responsible" identity that will carry on into adult life.

Both of the studies we have described point to the importance of the family in the adoption of socially responsible thinking and behavior. Parents can influence their children in many ways: They transmit moral values and goals to their children, they serve as models of altruistic and caring behavior, they provide opportunities for their children to care for others and often contribute to initiating their children's first volunteer experiences, they help their children assimilate their experiences into a framework of values, and they serve as a support to their children while they are engaged in community work. These family influences might be helpful both in attracting more young people into volunteer service and in making the experience more meaningful for them. The Survey of Voluntary Activity in Canada indicated that a significant proportion of volunteers began their activities through personal contact of some sort. However, youth, who have fewer (and certainly less diverse) contacts than adults, have fewer opportunities to become engaged in volunteer activity. It would be a simple matter for organizations that employ volunteers to encourage the adults who work as volunteers to bring along their children, and to provide appropriate and meaningful activities for children to engage in alongside their parents. This would not only serve to initiate youth into community service, but would provide common experiences for parents and children to discuss with one another, thereby encouraging the assimilation of volunteer experience into an identity of social responsibility.

Social milieus other than the family, such as schools and religious institutions, also appear to be important in initiating youths into volunteer activity, and in sustaining these activities once they begin. Programs offered through schools and religious institutions appear to serve two major functions. Often they provide opportunities for youth to gain their first experiences as volunteers. In addition, because youth are working alongside their peers while being involved in such programs, these programs provide for a supportive social milieu for such volunteering as well. This, then, suggests an expanded role for such volunteer programs in schools, religious institutions, and other community organizations. Schools, in particular, could contribute by a wider adoption of community service as part of the regular curriculum for children in their early teens. As well, greater coordination of school and community programs with the family as a whole can only be beneficial, as noted.

Our findings suggest that the nature of the volunteer experience can also be an important determinant of whether or not youth volunteers maintain their interests in volunteering and go on to develop an identity of social responsibility. The most powerful experiences recounted by the youths we interviewed were those that involved direct contact with those who were being helped, were enjoyable, helped develop useful skills, and, most importantly, allowed the youths to feel that they had "made a difference" in the lives of those with whom they worked. This suggests that careful consideration needs to be given to the kinds of work that youths are given to do when they volunteer their time. Regular monitoring of the youths' volunteer experiences would be critical in determining how they feel about their work, and the extent to which it meets their needs.

Canadian society provides a wealth of opportunity for individuals to become involved in the lives of their communities through volunteer service. Our research indicates that youth are ready – at a very young age – to benefit from such involvements. Programs that draw on the potential within families, schools, and religious and other organizations to initiate youth into volunteering, and to provide them with rewarding volunteer experiences can do much to develop a sense of social responsibility, and to establish the kind of caring society to which all nations aspire.

References

Baumrind, D. (1971). Current patterns of parental authority. *Developmental Psychology Monographs, 4*, 1–103.

Berkowitz, L. (1972). Social norms, feelings and other factors affecting helping behavior and altruism. In L. Berkowitz (Ed.), *Advances in experimental social psychology* (Vol. 6). New York: Academic Press.

Berkowitz, L., & Daniels, L. R. (1963). Responsibility and dependency. *Journal of Abnormal and Social Psychology, 66*, 429–436.

Blasi, A. (1995). Moral understanding and the moral personality. In W. Kurtines & J. Gewirtz (Eds.), *Moral development.* (pp. 229–254). Needham Heights, MA: Allyn & Bacon.

Boyes, M., & Allen, S. (1993). Styles of parent-child interaction and moral reasoning in adolescence. *Merrill-Palmer Quarterly, 39*, 551–570.

Bronfenbrenner, U. (1979). *The ecology of human development: Experiments by nature and design.* Cambridge, MA: Harvard Press.

Bryan, J., & Walbek, N. (1970). The impact of words and deeds concerning altruism upon children. *Child Development, 41*, 747–757.

Colby, A., & Damon, W. (1992). *Some do care: Contemporary lives of moral commitment.* New York: Free Press.

Cumyn, A. (1989). *Youth as volunteers.* (Voluntary Action Directorate, Department of Multiculturalism and Citizenship Canada.) Ottawa, Canada: Minister of Supply and Services Canada.

Darling, N., & Steinberg, L. (1993). Parenting style as context: An integrative model. *Psychological Bulletin, 113*, 487–496.

Duchesne, D. (1989). *Giving freely: Volunteers in Canada.* (Statistics Canada, Labour and Household Surveys Analysis Division, Catalogue 71–535, No. 4). Ottawa, Canada: Minister of Supply and Services Canada.

Eisenberg, N. (1995). Parenting and children's moral development. In M. Bornstein (Ed.), *Handbook of parenting.* (Vol. 4, 227–257). Mahwah, NJ: Lawrence Erlbaum.

Eisenberg, N., Cialdini, R., McCreath, H., & Shell, R. (1987). Consistency-based compliance: When and why do children become vulnerable? *Journal of Personality and Social Psychology, 52*, 1174–1181.

Gilligan, C. (1982). *In a different voice: Psychological theory and women's development.* Cambridge, MA: Harvard Press.

Hamilton, S., & Fenzel, M. (1988). The impact of volunteer experience on adolescent social development. *Journal of Adolescent Research, 3*, 65–80.

Hart, D., & Fegley, S. (1995). Prosocial behavior and caring in adolescence: Relations to self-understanding and social judgment. *Child Development, 66*, 1346–1359.

Hart, D., Yates, M., Fegley, S., & Wilson, G. (1995). Moral commitment in inner-city adolescents. In M. Killen & D. Hart (Eds.), *Morality in everyday life.* Cambridge: Cambridge University Press.

Havighurst, R. J. (1972). *Developmental tasks and education* (3rd ed.). New York: David McKay.

Lautenschlager, J. (1992). *Volunteering: A traditional Canadian value.* (Voluntary Action Directorate, Department of Multiculturalism and Citizenship Canada). Ottawa, Canada: Minister of Supply and Services Canada.

Miller, J. G., Bersoff, D. M., & Harwood, R. L. (1990). Perceptions of social responsibilities in India and in the United States: Moral imperatives or personal decisions. *Journal of Personality and Social Psychology, 58,* 33–47.

Oliner, S., & Oliner, P. (1988). *The altruistic personality: Rescuers of Jews in Nazi Europe.* New York: Free Press.

Omoto, A. M., & Snyder, M. (1995). Sustained helping without obligation: Motivation, longevity of service, and perceived attitude change among AIDS volunteers. *Journal of Personality and Social Psychology, 68,* 671–686.

Patton, M. Q. (1990). *Qualitative evaluation and research methods.* Newbury Park, CA: Sage.

Pratt, M., & Arnold, M. (1995). Narrative approaches to moral socialization over the lifespan. *Moral Education Forum, 20,* 13–22.

Pratt, M., Arnold, M., & Hilbers, S. (1998). A narrative approach to the study of moral orientation in the family: Tales of kindness and care. In E. Skoe & A. von der Lippe (Eds.), *Personality development in adolescence: A cross-national and lifespan perspective.* London: Routledge.

Rosenhan, D. (1970). The natural socialization of altruistic autonomy. In J. Macaulay & L. Berkowitz (Eds.), *Altruism and helping behavior* (pp. 251–268). New York: Academic Press.

Ross, D. P., & Shillington, E. R. (1989). *A profile of the Canadian volunteer: A guide to the 1987 Survey of Volunteer Activity in Canada.* Ottawa, Canada: National Voluntary Organizations.

Santolupo, S., & Pratt, M. (1994). Age, gender and parenting style variations in mother-adolescent dialogues and adolescent reasoning about political issues. *Journal of Adolescent Research, 9,* 241–261.

Skoe, E. E. (1998). The ethic of care: Issues in moral development. In E. Skoe & A. von der Lippe (Eds.), *Personality development in adolescence: A cross-national and lifespan perspective.* London: Routledge.

Yates, M. & Youniss, J. (1996). Community service and political-moral identity in adolescents. *Journal of Research on Adolescence, 6,* 271–284.

3. Exploring Adolescent Altruism: British Young People's Involvement in Voluntary Work and Campaigning

DEBI ROKER, KATIE PLAYER, AND JOHN COLEMAN

> What is citizenship? A new youth survey finds a surprising range of views about what it means to be a citizen today   (*The Times*, June 12, 1994)
>
> Today's youth are waving goodbye to party politics – but that doesn't mean they don't care about tomorrow
> (*The Independent*, January 25, 1995)
>
> Alert sounds on youth volunteer programmes: Community service schemes are causing unease
> (*Times Educational Supplement*, May 12, 1995)
>
> Young and adrift in the moral maze – Britain's youth are following a new self-regulated moral agenda   (*The Observer*, October 9, 1994)
>
> Fears about work rekindle youth's spirit of rebellion: Today's youth see elders' world as failing them   (*The Independent*, March 24, 1995)
>
> Rights and wrongs: Teenagers disagree about the balance of rights and responsibilities in society   (*The Observer*, June 11, 1993)
>
> The world's in their hands – but will they shape it?
> (*The Independent*, January 25, 1995)

As these newspaper headlines from the last few years demonstrate, much of the debate concerning British young people today involves issues such as participation, morals, community activities, citizenship, caring, politics, and values. This chapter aims to explore some of these issues further, focusing on British young people's involvement in voluntary and campaigning activities.[1]

The chapter will be structured as follows: First, a brief account will be given of the historical and cultural context of young people's community involvement in the United Kingdom. Second, research being undertaken

The research reported in this chapter is funded by a grant from the Johann Jacobs Foundation, Switzerland.

by the authors, which is looking at the involvement of 14- to 16-year-olds (*N*=1,165) in voluntary activities and campaigning, will be described. Third, some general comments will be made about the political, policy, and social implications of youth engagement and participation.

Focusing on the Positive Side of Youth

As a life stage, adolescence is most commonly presented in terms of antisocial and problem behavior. The image of young people in the British media is certainly very clear – they are presented as uninterested, apathetic, uninvolved, and self-centered. This image is, we believe, both inaccurate and simplistic. Rather, we agree with Jeffs (1994) that "no evidence exists that young people are less altruistic, more reluctant to be active citizens, or more indifferent to the suffering of others than the rest of society" (p. 96).

Research into young people's positive behavior is relatively rare in the United Kingdom, as it is in many other countries. Such work can, however, contribute to a better understanding of young people and challenge the negative stereotype that is so often presented.

Theoretically, our work in this area is derived from the literature on adolescent altruism. The term *altruism* has been most widely used by psychologists to refer to behaviors undertaken for the benefit of others and not for the individual's own benefit; other terms used to describe the concept include *caring, kindness,* and *prosocial* behavior (see Eisenberg, 1990; Batson, 1990; Silbereisen, Lamfuss, Boehnke, & Eisenberg, 1991; Hay, 1994; Chase-Lansdale, Wakschlag, & Brooks-Gunn, 1995, for a discussion).

Altruism has historically been a difficult subject for researchers in most disciplines to discuss. Batson (1990) suggests that psychologists in particular find it a difficult topic to deal with, because it relates fundamentally to our view of human nature. Many of the most widely used psychological models, he suggests, are based on seeing human beings as essentially selfish and self-serving. Batson adds that there is in fact much research evidence to show that in many circumstances we do care about others for their own sake, that is, human beings do have a capacity for altruism (see also Krebs, 1970; Hoffman, 1981).

Research into adolescent altruism in the 1960s and 1970s mainly involved experimental studies of childhood and adolescent altruism (Lowe & Richey, 1973; Midlarsky & Bryan, 1967). This early research led to the identification of a number of key prerequisites for altruistic behavior, including empathy, perspective taking, sympathy, and self-efficacy. Distinguishing factors in altruistic attitudes and behaviors were also explored. Females were often identified as more likely to engage in altruistic activities than males, and a number of differences by age and ethnicity were reported (see Lowe & Ritchey, 1973; Batson, Shaw, & Slingsby, 1991; Bar-Tal & Nissim, 1984).

During this time, there were few real-life and applied studies looking at young people's actual involvement in altruistic or prosocial activities. Also, the areas included in much of this work were narrow – rarely, for example, were campaigning and political activities considered under the heading of "altruistic" activities. More recently, and in particular during the 1980s and 1990s, researchers began to look at altruism in practice. The authors' view is that research into adolescent altruism has benefited greatly from focusing on what young people do in real-life situations. This is why we usually discuss altruism alongside politics, in that both areas focus on young people's potential for participation (and actual participation) in society. In our research in this area, we are operationalizing altruism in terms of young people's involvement in voluntary community activities and in campaigning.

In concluding this brief review of research into adolescent altruism, it should be noted that some commentators have identified the 1980s and 1990s in Britain as a time when both political and altruistic activities were discouraged: "This country represents a culture in which people, although often socialised to help others, are exposed to a value system that places its primary emphasis on individual achievement, competition and success, as well as pressures from the social structure (especially in the occupational sphere) that reinforces these values" (Hoffman, 1981, p. 125). The current situation with regard to British young people's community involvement is described in the discussion that follows.

Young People's Community Involvement in the United Kingdom

Much of the debate about young people and community involvement in Britain stems from a broader discussion about the role of young people in society. The backdrop to this debate includes high rates of youth unemployment, rising youth crime, and claims about youth alienation and disaffection (see Jeffs, 1994; Roker, 1994, for a discussion of these points).

In recent years, a number of individuals and organizations in the United Kingdom have suggested that one approach to dealing with these problems is to encourage more young people to become involved in their communities via voluntary work and campaigning. Thus a number of voluntary and youth organizations, as well as the three main political parties, have recently developed proposals on this issue. Some of the programs are aimed at young people who are still at school; others focus on those who have left school. A number of groups are already involved in providing such opportunities for young people: Community Service Volunteers (CSV) is a large London-based charitable organization that organizes and promotes school-based volunteering schemes, as well as organizing full-time volunteer placements for young people aged 16 and over. Another key organization in this respect is The Prince's Trust, which was founded by the Prince of Wales and also organizes full- and part-time voluntary opportunities for young people. Both these groups have promoted the value of volunteering for both young people and society more generally and are currently seeking political and financial support for extending their schemes.

It should be stressed at this point that the history and nature of community service schemes in the United Kingdom are very different from those in countries such as the United States. Community service and service learning programs are widespread in the United States (see, for example, Keith, 1994). The situation in the United Kingdom is quite different. Although organizations such as Community Service Volunteers help groups (and schools in particular) to organize community service schemes, most community service and volunteering opportunities are still organized informally. There are few nationally organized schemes in the United Kingdom, and very few schools make it a compulsory part of the school curriculum (see Roker, 1994, for a discussion).

The debate over young people and community service in the United Kingdom has been prompted by a wider debate about young people's role and engagement in society. Notions of citizenship and education for citizenship began to be discussed in educational and political circles in the 1980s, focusing on how children and young people could be taught the knowledge and skills that would allow active citizenship. In 1990 the government published *Curriculum Guidance 8*, which made citizenship education a cross-curricular theme in the National Curriculum (the compulsory subjects to be studied by all young people). Organizations such as The Citizenship Foundation (based in London) and the Centre for Citizenship Studies in Education (based in Leicester and headed by Professor Ken Fogelman, a keen advocate of citizenship education) now produce a wide range of educational materials for use at all levels of education.

More recently, the debate about citizenship reemerged after the 1994 report of the Commission on Social Justice. The Commission was set up by the opposition Labour party to investigate contemporary social issues and to develop new policies for the party. This report explored a number of ways of getting young people involved in their communities. The commission recommended the introduction of a Citizen's Service for unemployed 16- and 17-year-olds, comprising 3 months of voluntary community work with a government-paid allowance of £50.00 a week. (It should be noted that at present 16- and 17-year-olds in the United Kingdom who are unemployed are not entitled to receive any welfare payments.) At around the same time, the current Conservative government introduced the Make a Difference scheme and set up the Volunteering Partnership to organize and promote volunteering on a national basis. The partnership's ambitious aim was to provide, by the end of 1997, a voluntary placement for any 15- to 25-year-old who wants one. A recent government publication claimed that "it is important to introduce young people to the concept of volunteering while young, in the hope that this leads to lifelong commitment" (HMSO, 1992, p. 29).

Volunteering is promoted in this document as a means of increasing young people's confidence, broadening their horizons, and providing an outlet for energy and enthusiasm. This issue, however, is not a simple or uncontentious one. Some accuse such schemes of being aimed primarily at reducing the unemployment figures and being a mechanism for exploiting and controlling young people (see, for example, Jeffs, 1994).

Much of the reporting of these various schemes and proposals has implied that the current generation of young people in Britain is apathetic and not interested in becoming involved in their communities. This reflects the negative image of young people that many groups in society hold, an image that is strongly reinforced by media portrayals of young people. However, despite this image there is in fact evidence that many young people in Britain are involved in community and campaigning activities. Statistics such as the following demonstrate this well:

• Membership of Amnesty International's youth section grew from 1,300 in 1988 to 15,000 in 1995.

- Of those applying to do full-time voluntary work with Community Service Volunteers, 6 of 10 are aged under 18.
- Membership of the youth wing of Greenpeace increased from 80,000 in 1987 to 420,000 by 1995.
- A 1991 report from the Volunteer Centre U.K. (now the National Centre for Volunteering) demonstrated that 55% of 18- to 24-year-olds had been involved in some kind of voluntary activity in the last year.

There is thus a clear contradiction between evidence and rhetoric and image in relation to young people and community involvement in Britain. The authors' research, described later, aimed to address some of the issues around British young people's involvement in voluntary work and campaigning.

Challenging the Image: British Young People's Involvement in Community Activities

The authors' research is focusing on 14- to 16-year-olds, those in their final 2 years of compulsory schooling. The aims of the research are to address the following questions:

- *How many* young people are involved in voluntary and campaigning activities?
- *What sorts* of activities are they involved in?
- *How much time* do they give to these activities?
- How do they *feel about* their experiences; what psychosocial or academic benefits are involved?
- How do these experiences *vary* by age, gender, ethnicity, and personal and family background?
- What are the *barriers to involvement* in voluntary and campaigning activities?
- What are young people's *understanding of and views about* concepts such as volunteering, citizenship, and service participation?
- What is *the role of the school* in encouraging or enabling young people to become involved in these activities?

The research methodology is based on case studies of young people and staff at three different schools. Each of the schools has a different approach to encouraging community involvement among pupils, as follows: (1) a school with a long history of promoting community involvement, (2) a school with no such historical or current commitment, and (3) a school with a recently developed commitment to encouraging involvement. All three schools are state run and coeducational. School 1 is located in the north of England, School 2 within a large inner city in the Midlands, and School 3 on the south coast.

The selection of the three schools was designed to address a number of important variables. School 1 is in the north of England, where opportunities for young people to engage in voluntary and campaigning activities are limited by its rural location. School 2 is an inner city school with a large ethnic minority population; specifically, 80% of the school population are from Indian and Pakistani families. The selection of the sample in this way means that we are able to address key variables of age, gender, ethnicity, rurality, and socioeconomic status, as well as the influence of these variables on young people's community service activities.

In each school, a questionnaire survey was undertaken in 1995/96, involving all pupils aged 14–16. The questionnaire contained precoded and open-ended questions to explore the aims indicated; also included were standardized measures of self-esteem, personal and political efficacy, and attitudes to politics and the political process. In total 1,165 questionnaires have been completed. In addition, 95 individual interviews were undertaken with a subsample from all three schools – one group of young people who are very involved in voluntary or campaigning activities and another group who have never been involved in such activities. The aim of the interviews was to look in more detail at the motivation, views, attitudes, and experiences of these two groups. In addition, meetings have been held with senior staff at each school. Information collected included their perceptions of the involvement of their pupils in community activities, and influences on this, as well as the role of schools in encouraging or facilitating pupil involvement.

Analysis of the quantitative results is now under way. What follows is a mainly qualitative analysis of the key themes emerging in the research to date. The themes were identified by the researchers involved in analyzing the questionnaires and conducting the individual interviews, and also by staff at the three schools. Eight primary themes are identified, with several overlapping to a high degree. The themes explored include (i) the range of voluntary and campaigning activities the young people were involved in; (ii) the ways that individual and situational characteristics, such as gender, ethnicity, rurality, resources, and disability, affected young people's involvement; (iii) young people's attitudes about undertaking community activities; and (iv) the outcomes and experiences of young people who were engaged in community activities.

Key Themes in the Research

Theme 1: Forms of Participation. The sample were clearly involved in a much broader range of voluntary and community activities than is often suggested in the literature or in debate on this issue. Thus, for example, just under 1 in 10 of the sample were members of a group or organization that was campaigning for something. Similarly, the majority of the sample had, in the last year, signed a petition, given money to charity, boycotted something because of its source or method of production, and campaigned against a school rule that they wanted changed. The results of the study thus show that a significant proportion of the sample reported being involved in activities such as the following:

- Helping younger children at their school with reading and writing
- Donating money and signing petitions in support of a range of causes
- Campaigning for improved local facilities for young people
- Setting up and running Schools Councils
- Being involved in campaigning groups, for example, Amnesty International, Friends of the Earth, and Greenpeace
- Helping out voluntarily in sports and youth clubs
- Campaigning for animal rights, including not buying products tested on animals and supporting antivivisection groups
- Participating in country-specific campaigns, in particular campaigning against the war in Bosnia
- Volunteering in hospitals, special schools, animal shelters, and charity (thrift) shops

The time commitment involved ranged from occasional or weekly involvement to daily involvement in these activities.

Theme 2: Gender. As was mentioned in the introduction to the chapter, much previous research has suggested that males are less likely to get involved in voluntary activities than females. However, in our study we found that the voluntary activities of males and females are less straightforward than often presented. Rather, we found a higher degree of uncertainty among the males in the study regarding what counted as "voluntary," "community," or "campaigning" activities; this affected how they had completed the questionnaire and answered the questions in the interview. More importantly, we also found a range of "hidden" voluntary and campaigning activities being undertaken by the young men in the study, who were participating in activities of which friends and parents were often not aware. The following examples demonstrate this:

- A 15-year-old male who had spent the night at a local airport as part of a protest against live animal exports; he had not told his friends what he had done and had told his parents he was staying overnight with friends.
- A 16-year-old male who had set up and run a lunchtime reading club at his school, but who didn't mention this in the questionnaire because he didn't think it came under the heading of voluntary or campaigning activities.
- A 17-year-old male who had arranged for a group of pupils to run the school's computer center at times when it would otherwise have been closed; he had not mentioned this on the questionnaire as he had a degree of self-interest in wanting it to be open longer hours.
- A 14-year-old boy who was a member of Amnesty International because he thought it was "an important issue" but who hadn't told his friends because they might make fun of him.

A number of similar cases in the study suggest that the issue of gender and community service is not as simple as it is sometimes presented in the literature. Some of the issues for young men involved in community activities are reflected in the following comments:

> Well I'm a member of Amnesty International. I think that sort of thing is really important, protecting human rights. But as I said none of my mates know. Well, they'd just take the mickey [laugh at me]. (15-year-old male).

> I work at the reading club two lunchtimes a week now. A group of my friends do it too. They didn't want to when I asked, they thought you know that it was a bit creepy. But now most of them are there more hours than I am. We all feel like we're doing something to help the younger ones. (16-year-old male)

The quantitative results will eventually demonstrate more clearly whether or not there is a gender difference in the actual level of participation between males and females. However, preliminary analyses suggest that there may instead be a greater difference between males and females in how they perceive voluntary activity. Thus for boys a voluntary activity that involves a degree of self-interest is less likely to be included, and some boys feel that doing voluntary or campaigning activities is in some respects embarrassing and shouldn't be admitted to friends or family – hence our description of "hidden" activities by some of the males in the study. This is an important development from earlier research, which has often only explored altruistic motives or overt helping behavior in experimental studies.

Theme 3: Rurality and Geography. This was a key issue for some of the respondents, but one that is rarely picked up in the literature on young people's involvement in volunteering and campaigning. It was often difficult, for example, for those at School 1 to find anywhere to do voluntary work. Also, those who wished to join a particular group (for example, a branch of Greenpeace or Amnesty International) found the nearest group was 30 miles away. Similarly several of the pupils at School 2, located in a small town some distance from a larger town, expressed the same views.

The following comments from young people at these two schools demonstrate this clearly:

There's nothing around here, nothing to do or get involved in. (14-year-old female)

It's difficult here. I'd like to get involved in more things. But like there's nothing here . . . and what there is you end up doing along with a load of people from round here. (15-year-old female)

I'd like to join one of the animal groups, maybe the League against Cruel Sports. But they meet in the evening in [the city] and that's 30 miles away. It's just not the same doing it by post. (16-year-old male)

It is clear from these comments that issues for young people around geography and physical location affect what many young people can do within their communities.

Theme 4: Resources and Access. Closely linked to the issue of rurality and geography was the issue of the resources often needed to get involved in voluntary or campaigning activities. Access to transport and the costs of transport were frequently mentioned by the sample on the questionnaires and in the interviews. For young people from more advantaged backgrounds, it was clear that parents were driving them to events or organizations that they were involved in, or they were using buses at what for them was an affordable cost. For the young people in the sample from more disadvantaged backgrounds, a relatively small cost for something like a bus fare was often prohibitive. For example, a 15-year-old female said, "I couldn't do anything like that, not if it cost anything. I don't have any money, never do." In another example, a 16-year-old male said, "I'd only do it round here. I couldn't afford to go on the bus or train or anything."

The issue of resources was also linked to that of access and safety. Several pupils at School 2 from ethnic minority backgrounds expressed concern about any volunteering or campaigning activity that would necessitate their traveling around the city at night; this was a particular concern to some of them in light of recent racial attacks in the area. Again, this issue was linked to the different socioeconomic status of the families in the study, and the fact that many families at School 2 in particular did not have access to a car.

Theme 5: Ethnicity. It became clear that some of the cultural and ethnic groups in the study had very different perceptions and experiences of volunteering and campaigning. Some of the following issues were involved:

- The difficulty of separating voluntary work from those activities done informally within the community – for example, organizing religious events or baby-sitting for other families
- The particular issues for Asian girls regarding the places that they are allowed to go, and the key role of family responsibilities for them
- The importance of parental views and attitudes about young people's activities, and for some the importance of parental agreement to their participation in certain activities

These points are illustrated by some of the young people's comments:
> Well I started helping out at a charity shop on Saturday, in Oxfam. But they needed me to be regular to come every week. Then my mum would say that she needed me to have my younger brothers and sisters today, and that was it. Oxfam said they needed someone more dependable. (16-year-old female)

> It's different for Asians, what you're talking about. Like my father doesn't agree with some things I believe in, and it isn't right in my culture . . . it's just not possible . . . to go against him, to disagree

with him. So eventually I stopped doing the letters and campaigning and stuff. (15-year-old male)

It is of note also that many of the Asian girls suggested that, whereas it was difficult (if not impossible) for them to get involved in such activities as volunteering or campaigning while they were living at home, this did not mean that they would not be doing so in the future. Thus, many added that they did intend to get involved in community activities when they left school or after they had moved out of their parents' home.

Theme 6: Disability. An issue raised by the research was that of young people with disabilities, and their involvement in voluntary and community activities. Young people with disabilities are most often viewed as receivers of care, as those for whom able-bodied young people volunteer. This issue was raised by a number of the staff and young people involved in the present study, who felt that it was not being properly addressed in the research design. As a result, the trust secured funding for an additional study, to focus on this group alone. This second research project is looking at the ways in which young people with physical and/or learning disabilities are encouraged or enabled to become involved in community activities.

This project is in two parts. First, we are undertaking a national survey of schemes and projects involving young people with disabilities in voluntary and campaigning activity. Second, we are undertaking two case studies of particular schemes. The project is focusing on issues such as access and opportunities, support needs, models of good practice, and in particular the experiences of young people with disabilities themselves. This project was completed in 1997; further information about it is available from the authors.

Theme 7: Strength of Views about Community Service. It was clear from the questionnaire and interview responses that the majority of the sample *did* support increased opportunities for community involvement, but that they were against compulsory participation. Many had strong views about the structure of voluntary and campaigning work, and issues related to payment, hours, and so on. These views are reflected in the following comments:

School is all subjects and exams. Young people should do things which make us more aware of what's going on in the world. (15-year-old female)

The "have to" term is an immediate turn off . . . we're meant to be developing ourselves and becoming adults and everything, and the "have to" takes away all of that. (16-year-old male)

Most young people would like to do more things I think. I'd like to do what you said, about doing a half a day a week doing something out in the community. To be honest . . . it would wake some people around here up, make them aware of what's going on. (15-year-old female)

I'd like to get more involved in things, maybe even doing something voluntary for a year or more. But you shouldn't have to do it, that would be daft. Something can't be voluntary if you have to do it. (16-year-old female)

These comments confirm the finding that although most of the sample wanted greater opportunities to participate in their communities, the element of choice was important to them (see also Miller, 1994, for a study that probes young people's attitudes to compulsory community service in the United States). This finding is important in light of recent calls in the United Kingdom, described in the introduction to this chapter, to increase youth volunteering opportunities or to make some aspects of community service compulsory. It also adds weight to the belief of the researchers and others (for example, Jeffs, 1994) that there is no real evidence that young people are any less altruistic or interested in the problems and issues of their societies than any other groups of people.

Theme 8: Positive Outcomes from Volunteering. A wide variety of career, practical, and psychosocial outcomes from involvement in volunteering and campaigning were identified by those who were involved in such activities. These outcomes were very diverse; they included the development of practical skills and abilities such as

• learning first aid skills
• using and dealing with money
• typing and word processing
• learning sign language

The sample also reported more personal and social outcomes of their community involvement, including

• feeling more able to mix with disabled people
• feeling increased confidence

- gaining ability to speak in public
- developing child care skills
- exercising leadership and group management
- learning "to accept people for who and what they are"

The benefits of community involvement are further demonstrated by the following comments from the sample:

> I'm a lot more confident now. I find it much easier to meet people I don't know and get talking to them. (15-year-old female)

> For me it just made me feel good. I'm not very, you know, like I'm not very good at school work. But at the Club [teaching sports at a youth club] I'm the expert, I'm the one who knows. The younger kids look up to me, which really makes me feel good. And you know, I have to do things like organizing them, helping them, encouraging them. It's a real skill. (15-year-old male)

> It's helped me a lot [taking part in the Schools Council]. I'm not nervous like I used to be, not when I'm talking to teachers or speaking in front of groups. And like I can argue now, present a good case for something. It's really given me confidence. (16-year-old male)

It is also of note that the majority of young people who were involved in these activities said that this experience meant they were more likely to get involved in the future. These findings of positive outcomes for young people involved in community activities are important. Claims about the positive benefits for young people of voluntary and campaigning activities are often based only on informal and anecdotal evidence. The results from this study add weight to the view of those politicians, voluntary organizations, and young people who wish to make such experiences available to more young people.

Conclusion

This chapter has described research looking at adolescent altruism, which has been operationalized in terms of young people's involvement in voluntary and campaigning activities. Some of the main themes emerging from this research were described. In the introduction, it was suggested that we know very little about the prosocial activities of adolescents in comparison to young children or adults. Further, it was suggested that research in this area has been limited methodologically, with relatively few studies undertaken in real life settings. The current research aims to contribute to a better understanding of some of the structural issues and social–psychological aspects of issues that affect British young people's attitudes to and involvement in voluntary and campaigning activities.

The research has clear implications in a number of areas, including how we understand the concepts of altruism and involvement. Although the research was designed initially to focus on long-term and regular involvement in volunteering and campaigning, it was clear that a number of young people were involved in many single and occasional voluntary or campaigning activities. Thus in the analysis of the data, we are now looking at involvement that is both long-term and occasional.

Another important issue raised by the study concerned the young people's reasons for getting involved in different activities. For example, many said they joined a campaigning group because the cause was important to them; others, however, added that such activities also "looked good" on applications for jobs or university places or that they took part because "a friend asked me to do it with them." Similarly, one young man who was a member of Greenpeace said that he was "one of the sort of middle class pseudo environmentalists, you know one who signs up and pretends to."

Clearly, involvement in voluntary or campaigning activities results from a wide range of motivations, ranging from the largely altruistic to the more self-interested. Thus, involvement clearly serves a variety of functions including personal, social, career, and image functions. Understanding the variety of reasons for participating in voluntary and campaigning activities is an important focus of the current research.

Understanding young people's attitudes toward and experiences of community service is important, particularly in light of proposals described earlier in the chapter to involve more young people in community service activities. These proposals are often being made despite a poor understanding of British young people's attitudes to such activities, or of the experiences of those who are already involved.

Research such as that described here enables young people's views and experiences to be heard. Also, the current debate in Britain needs to address further some of the issues discussed in this chapter – for example, rural youth's access to voluntary and campaigning activities, the experiences of different ethnic and cultural groups in terms of community involvement, and the way that identifying young people with disabilities who volunteer challenges stereotypes of this group. Without understanding the issues described in this chapter, it will be difficult to enable all young people to participate in and to gain from involvement in voluntary and campaigning activities.

Note

1. The term *campaigning* is widely used in the United Kingdom and Europe but may not be well known in other countries; other terms used refer to involvement in *social movements, interest groups,* and *causes.* Here, *campaigning* is used to refer to activities aimed at getting something changed and includes activities such as campaigning for environmental issues and animal rights, political party activities, and involvement in groups concerned about particular people or issues in society.

References

Bar-Tal, D., & Nissim, R. (1984). Helping behaviour and moral judgements among adolescents. *British Journal of Developmental Psychology, 2,* 329–336.

Batson, C. D. (1990). How social an animal? The human capacity for caring. *American Psychologist, 45,* 336–346.

Batson, C. D., Shaw, L., & Slingsby, J. K. (1991). Practical implications of the empathy-altruism hypothesis: Some reflections. *Altruism in Social Systems.* Toronto: Hogrefe and Huber.

Chase-Lansdale, L., Wakschlag, L., & Brooks-Gunn, J. (1995). A psychological perspective on the development of caring in children and youth: The role of the family. *Journal of Adolescence, 18,* 515–556.

Eisenberg, N. (1990). Prosocial development in early and mid adolescence. In R. Montemayor, G. R. Adams, T. P. Gullotta (Eds.), *From Childhood to Adolescence.* London: Sage.

Hay, D. F. (1994). Prosocial development. *Journal of Child Psychology and Psychiatry, 35,* 29–71.

HMSO (1992). *Volunteering.* London: Author.

Hoffman, M. L. (1981). Is altruism part of human nature? *Journal of Personality and Social Psychology, 40,* 121–137.

Jeffs, T. (1994). Citizens' service. *Youth and Policy, 47,* 95–97.

Keith, N. (1994). Introduction to special edition on school-based community service. *Journal of Adolescence, 17,* 311–320.

Krebs, D. L. (1970). Altruism: An examination of the concept and a review of the literature. *Psychological Bulletin, 73,* 258–302.

Lowe, R., & Richey, G. (1973). Relation of altruism to age, social class, and ethnic identity. *Psychological Reports, 33,* 567–572.

Midlarsky, E., & Bryan, J. (1967). Training charity in children. *Journal of Personality and Social Psychology, 5,* 408–415.

Miller, F. (1994). Gender differences in adolescents' attitudes toward mandatory community service. *Journal of Adolescence, 17,* 381–394.

National Curriculum Council (1990). *Curriculum Guidance 8: Education for Citizenship.* London: HMSO.

Roker, D. (1994). School-based community service: A British perspective. *Journal of Adolescence, 17,* 321–326.

Silbereisen, R. K., Lamfuss, A., Boehnke, K., & Eisenberg, N. (1991). Developmental patterns and correlates of pro-social motives in adolescence. In L. Montada and H. Biefhoff (Eds.), *Altruism in Social Systems*. Toronto: Hogrefe and Huber.

4. Youth, Solidarity, and Civic Commitment in Italy: An Analysis of the Personal and Social Characteristics of Volunteers and Their Organizations

ELENA MARTA, GIOVANNA ROSSI, AND
LUCIA BOCCACIN

The essence of voluntary organizations in Italy lies, first of all, in its deeply meaningful *prosocial motivations*; second, in the centrality of an outlook characterized by altruism and reciprocity that emphasizes *gratuitousness* in the volunteer's actions; and, finally, in the profound significance attributed to the value of *solidarity*. These three distinctive characteristics of voluntary action were brought together, ex post facto, at a legislative level (Law n. 266/1991 in Italian statutes) in order to define the social relevance of volunteer action. To be considered such, volunteer action must be offered "in a personal, spontaneous and gratuitous way, through the organization to which the volunteer belongs, without object of gain, even if indirect, and exclusively for the purposes of fostering solidarity" (article 2, paragraph 1.). This legislation formalized the distinction between *traditional* voluntary action performed by individuals and *contemporary* voluntary work performed within the bounds of an organization. These organizations, which expanded in the seventies and eighties, mostly make use of the work of volunteers.[1]

Voluntary action has deep roots in Italy, springing from a long historical and cultural tradition that is still visible in the continuing presence in the country of large organizations that respond to a vast array of social needs. This is not, therefore, a phenomenon of recent origin but rather a long-standing one. It is characterized by internal differences both in cultural orientation such as whether they are Catholic or socialist and in the specific form each organization takes. Whereas in the past voluntary organizations were active mostly in the areas of social assistance and health in an effort to redress, or to "fill in" for, obvious societal short-

73

comings in these sectors (Amerio, Cafasso, & Calligaris, 1996), at present they enjoy greater autonomy and even provide innovative services that emphasize prevention and awareness.

The present chapter focuses on youth volunteers and their voluntary organizations, examining the volunteers' sociodemographic characteristics and motivations as well as the internal functioning of the organizations themselves. Our purpose is to shed light on the relationships between what is inside voluntary organizations and what lies outside them. The analysis of these elements allows us to understand the possible areas of contact and comparison between voluntary action and other expressions of civil society. As an integral part of this study, we assess the prosocial motivations and values that induce young people to become volunteers and the possible connections between a commitment to volunteer action and political involvement.

Recent research on the condition of young people in Italy (Cavalli & De Lillo, 1988; 1993) provides us with an image of disenchanted youth who are increasingly worldly and pragmatic and who lack a code of ethics. These young people construct the present within a plurality of contexts (family, school, associations, friendship networks, etc.) without precise coordinates and hierarchies of goals: This is, in effect, a generation that contents itself with obtaining "just enough" and no more. They are individuals who have lowered their aims in terms of what "everyday life" can offer. A positive note in this research is the resilience and indeed growth of the value of the family that accompanies a tendency for young people to remain in their parents' home for a long time, even after having reached adulthood.

Do these elements also characterize young volunteers? Or, do these young people represent a new and emerging trend characterized by individuals whose most important values include commitment to the social sphere rather than closure within the confines of the home? In recent years, examples of voluntary action in Italy have increased considerably, in part, because of the diffusion of a "new" conception of the person. This conception emphasizes increasingly the centrality of the person, the commonality of shared inner realities among all people, and the role of human relationships in determining the quality of life (Calvi, 1987; Paolicchi, 1995).

This new culture that, on the one hand, emphasizes the centrality of the person and, on the other hand, claims new possibilities for freedom and plurality is connected to events in recent Italy: the crisis of traditional political parties, the crisis of the welfare state, the fall of ideologies and large-scale collective movements. From this point of view, the option of prosocial action can be seen to derive from a desire to overcome the fragmentation and bureaucratization that permeate Italian society and that fail to acknowledge the personal dignity of its citizens.

Research (Cesareo & Rossi, 1989; 1994; Boccacin, 1993a; Paolicchi, 1995; Rossi, Boccacin, & Bramanti, 1996) has revealed a remarkable variety in Italian voluntary organizations. Nevertheless, they can be described in terms of three main characteristics: (a) *organization* such as degree of formalization, variety in decision-making structures, and the articulation of their internal organization; (b) *areas of intervention* such as health, education, and youth; and (c) *services offered* such as assistance in the home and instruction, the use of traditional and innovative methods, the granting of services that address needs in different ways (emergency, promotional, etc.), and the operative contexts (hospital, listening center, etc.). A recent national survey, which constituted a benchmark for present-day discussions of voluntary organizations in Italy,[2] has identified some *indicators* that better delineate the phenomenon. Let us examine them in detail.

a. *Geographical distribution.* Half of the voluntary organizations are located in northern Italy, another third in the South and on the islands, and the remainder, a mere 17%, in central Italy. This distribution is essentially proportional to population densities, which are greatest in metropolitan areas.

b. *Links between organizations.* More than two-thirds of the organizations are linked to others in associations and/or federations.

c. *Founders and recipients.* For the most part, the founders of voluntary organizations are associations and movements (33%) and parishes and Caritas, the Catholic service organization (17%). Political parties and unions are in a minority. In three-fourths of the organizations, recipients do not belong to the organization itself, and in 10%, they are either members or nonmembers.

d. *Size.* Large organizations are not common – 10% have more than 100 members and just as many have between 50 and 100. Instead, small and medium size entities prevail – 25% have up to 10 members, 25% from 11 to 20, and 25% from 21 to 50.

e. *Volunteers' time commitments.* The typical time commitment (65% of organizations) is 5 hours a week. Next come the organizations in which volunteers work from 6 to 10 hours (22%), and finally those in which the commitment is from 10 to 15 hours a week (7%).

f. *Distribution of volunteers according to sex.* There is an overall parity in the numbers of men and women volunteers, but, despite appearances, this is due to the fact that organizations having a mostly male membership and those that are mostly female are represented in equal numbers.

g. *Volunteers' age.* The group of adults between 30 and 65 years of age (with peaks between 30 and 45 years) is the most numerous (66%), followed by younger volunteers (in 25% of organizations they range in age from 18 to 29 years), whereas entities in which mostly elderly volunteers operate are in the minority (3%).

h. *Training of volunteers.* Sixty-three percent of organizations make an effort to train their volunteers. Of these, 77% conduct their own training programs.

i. *Areas of intervention.* The areas of hardship in which Italian service organizations are active are numerous and include "old" problems (i.e., elderly, illness, etc.), which constitute a time-tested tradition in volunteer work, as well as "new" needs. The latter are being addressed by a remarkable mobilization of volunteer efforts and serve to demonstrate the flexibility of this type of social action and its ability to bring its considerable resources en masse to bear on new emergencies. The largest area of intervention concerns illness, followed immediately by that of elderly and by sociocultural needs. Significant efforts are also being made to assist the handicapped, as well as troubled children, youth, and families. The needs created by immigration are now absorbing a lot of service energies, as do drug addiction, the care of the nonautonomous elderly, and the problems caused by social alienation, in general. The conspicuous presence of voluntary organizations dealing with civil defense and environmental concerns is also noteworthy.

j. *Social product of service.* When speaking of the services performed by volunteer organizations, it is helpful to distinguish between, first of all, a phase of first approach to a problem (first aid, emergency assistance, etc.) whose aim is to lessen the immediate gravity of the situation; second, a more continuous phase, in which the service organization characteristically assumes responsibility for the problem and provides various forms of assistance; and, third, services of a "promotional"[3] nature that aim to eliminate the causes of a problem. The organizations surveyed are divided among the following modes of problem intervention: first-impact (80%), continuous assistance (55%), and promotion (59%).[4]

k. *Types of intervention.* The distinctiveness of Italian voluntary work lies in an increasingly widespread rejection of standardized and undifferentiated intervention practices, in favor of a type of intervention that is more and more often a *helping relationship* managed in an efficient and professional way (Rossi, 1990; 1994). Nevertheless, a more rigorous analysis allows us to differentiate types of intervention on the basis of very different parameters. The traditional distinctions have been (i) between expressive volunteering (in which a component of personal gratification prevails) and service volunteering (in which interpersonal relationships are more important); (ii) among social services activities, recreational activities, civil defense, and environmental action (Morris, 1962); and (iii) between organizations in which service providers and recipients are separate, self-help organizations and organizations involved in public interest causes (Murray, 1969). However, all of these distinctions have been superseded by two classifications that are particularly effective in bringing into focus the differences that today seem to be most relevant to an appreciation of a phenomenon as diversified as the contemporary voluntary world. The first distinguishes between organizations that offer *monovalent* services, which concentrate efforts in only one area of need, and organizations that provide *polyvalent* services, which are active in more than one area of need. The second classification distinguishes between *traditional* services whose function is clearly to substitute for shortfalls in publicly administered assistance (including services such as home health care and transportation of the sick) and *innovative* services (networking, cultural and educational programs, etc.) (Cesareo & Rossi, 1986).

Furthermore, a sort of "complementarity between voluntary organizations" is evident. This complementarity works to ensure that all areas of hardship are addressed with the responses to various needs taking a variety of forms. In this, there appears to be an implicit, yet rather clear logic (FIVOL, 1995) by which the least formalized organizations act in sectors characterized by a high degree of precariousness and social alienation (immigrants, nomads, the homeless, etc.) offering less specialized, first-impact assistance, whereas in the case of more stable targets (civil defense, the ill, the environment, etc.), the more established organizations intervene and do so, moreover, with greater continuity in their efforts.

It is also evident that a sort of "selective distribution" of resources occurs in such a way that the volume of services offered by the organizations is commensurate with the volume of requests made by recipients, as if to guarantee a one-on-one relationship between volunteer and user. This selectivity in the distribution of resources can be explained both by the law of supply and demand and by investigation of the motivations underlying voluntary action. Indeed, it becomes clear that an individual's choice of the area in which to become involved is influenced by the type of personal investment required of the volunteer with an increasingly widespread awareness today that it is necessary to acquire ever greater competence in order to establish an effective "helping relationship." There is a noticeable correspondence, in this respect, between the progression of volunteer involvement and the progression in the average levels of competence in the helping relationship that the different areas of need require (FIVOL, 1995).

Youth and Voluntary Organizations in Lombardy: An Empirical Study

We will now present the data from an empirical study of young volunteers and their organizations. This study was part of a larger investigation of voluntary organizations carried out in the region of Lombardy, in northern Italy. The sample was composed of 225 young adult volunteers, aged between 19 and 29 years (average age is 25), and by 73 organizations made up solely or in large part of young people. Organizations were located using various sources of information including the *Annuario del Volontariato Sociale Italiano*, a national directory of voluntary organizations, and the directory of voluntary organizations provided by the region of Lombardy.

The aims of this study were twofold: first, to become more familiar with the world of voluntary organizations from the point of view of its adherents, and, second, to acquire a deeper understanding of the voluntary organizations and their workings. Data were collected using questionnaires sent through the mail. In order to collect complete information, it was decided to use two questionnaires: the first concerning the service organizations and the second the volunteers who are active in them. Each organization was sent one questionnaire on internal structure (to be filled out by a coordinator) and three questionnaires on volunteer characteristics (randomly chosen from among the members of the organization).

The first questionnaire aimed to identify what constitutes the "inside" and the "outside" of a voluntary organization. It included the geographical range covered by the organization, its legal status, internal decision-making processes, and characteristics of the personnel (presence of volunteer members, paid workers, and so on) and of its recipients. The final section of the questionnaire asked about the organization's financial status, with particular emphasis on fund-raising, and links with other organizations.

The volunteer questionnaire asked not only about sociocultural characteristics, but also about motivations for volunteering, procedures for joining service organizations, types of training, and length of time they dedicate to service activities. Furthermore, a section of the questionnaire sought volunteers' opinions on the role played by voluntary organizations, the state, and the marketplace in relation to outstanding social and civic issues.

The following are the most salient results from the study with respect to both volunteers and organizations. To begin, we describe the service participants' sociodemographic characteristics, motivations, perceptions of the social function of voluntary organizations, and political and social outlooks. A typology of the young volunteers from Lombardy will then be presented.

With respect to the organizations, the data collected concern their legal status, history, development, operative functioning, financial situation, links with other organizations, procedures followed in accepting new members, services offered, and function in society. After a description of these characteristics a typology of the service organizations made up of the young volunteers from Lombardy will then be presented.

Profile of the Young Service Participants from Lombardy and Their Relations with the Organizations to Which They Belong

Sociodemographic Characteristics. In the sample of volunteers, there is an overall parity in the numbers of males and females (respectively, 49% and 51%). As for educational levels, the majority of volunteers have obtained a high school degree (69%) and a substantial percentage have a university degree (11%). Fifty-six percent work full-time, 31% are students, and the remaining 13% have occasional or part-time jobs. Among those who work full-time, the majority are office workers (31%) and blue-collar workers (27%). An analysis of the data concerning the volunteers' familial status reveals that the majority are unmarried (88%) and for the most part still live with their parents (83%): Only a small percentage live alone (5%). Five percent of the volunteers are married and have children, 6% are married or live with a partner in a stable relationship but have no children, only 1% are separated or divorced. The volunteers belong to the middle to upper-middle sociocultural levels of society. In 64% of cases, volunteers profess to being practicing Catholics, 31% are nonpracticing Catholics, and 6% are nonbelievers.

Finally, in order to complete our depiction of a typical volunteer, let us look at the data concerning time dedicated to service activities. Thirty-eight percent spend from 2 to 5 hours a week doing volunteer work, 19% spend from 6 to 10 hours a week, 4% spend from 11 to 20 hours, 1% spend from 21 to 25 hours, and 4% over 25 hours a week. On the other end of the spectrum, 13% spend 1 hour a week. Interestingly, a substantial percentage (21%) are unable to approximate the time they dedicate to service activities. The young volunteers' commitment to organizations tends to remain constant over an extended period of time; in fact, 38% stated that they have been active as volunteers for 2 to 3 years, 20% for 4 to 5 years, 19% for 6 to 10 years, and 5% for over 10 years. Nineteen percent have been active for a year or less.

Motivations. Concurring with the findings of Paolicchi (1995), the volunteers indicated a variety of inducements that prompted them *to join an organization*. The most common was personal initiative (51%), followed by the invitation of a friend or relative already in the organization (41%). Response to invitations made by a parish or religious movement accounted for 5% of new memberships, the inducements of advertising account for 3%, and responses to invitations from cultural associations or the motivation of family needs accounts for 0.4% of memberships.

Distinctively altruistic reasons predominated as basic motivations for *choosing to join an organization:* 57% of volunteers stated that they were prompted by the desire to help those in need. Other reasons have secondary importance: personal or spiritual enrichment (14%), the desire to improve society (9%), and civic commitment (6%). Although in the minority, a few volunteers stated that they began their service activity for religious reasons (6%) or from a sense of duty (4%), and others attributed their choice to more "individualistic" motives, such as the desire to find a way to spend free time (6%).

Taken as a whole, the data revealed that politics, narrowly defined, is extraneous to the concerns of the young volunteers. It seems that the ideals of solidarity expressed by the service participants are in essence linked to a sort of "empathetic" involvement in interpersonal relationships or are of a social nature related to the context in which they live more than to political involvement.

The Social Function of Voluntary Organizations. In order to understand fully the phenomenon of volunteerism, it is important to analyze the participants' thoughts and opinions regarding the social function and goals of their organizations. In this regard, 59% of volunteers professed to disapproving of the possibility of organizations assuming a political role, and this confirms an image of voluntary organizations' maintaining a stance of neutrality vis-à-vis political formations. However, 58% of subjects agree only in part or not at all with the channeling of all the group's resources into its activities to the exclusion of other concerns. It is evident that voluntary organizations cannot remain detached from social transformation in that they address an array of ever changing needs.

The organizational goals that the volunteers seem to share are interventions that address serious national problems and stress solidarity (65% of subjects strongly endorse this proposition); projects that combine efficiency, entrepreneurship, and solidarity (57%); and, finally, action in defense of certain rights, although this was the concern of a smaller percentage of the respondents (25%).

It is evident that the volunteers have clear ideas about their most important goals and have faith in the possibility that formal voluntary organizations will become more efficient and able to rely on entrepreneurial skills. The data also reveal a marked degree of awareness among participants of carrying out an activity of public usefulness. As can be seen from the responses made by a majority of participants (80%), volunteers believed that they were acknowledging the full responsibility of their obligations to society.

Volunteers and Political–Social Outlooks. We have chosen to invest the subjects of this study with the status of "privileged witnesses" in an attempt to delineate a set of guidelines relevant to social policy from the point of view of those who operate in this sector. Three sectors were considered: the institutional, the commercial, and the volunteer. Volunteers were asked to describe what the state, the marketplace, and service organizations *should* be doing in comparison to what they actually are doing and what can be expected of them in the future in response to a particular set of issues. The categories used in this evaluation refer to educational needs, economic needs, social services and health care needs; needs related to free time, creativity, and culture, protection of the environment, and the artistic heritage; and, finally, safeguarding the rights of the most vulnerable members of society.

The service participants were unanimous in thinking that the state should be more involved in the areas mentioned. At the same time, their misgivings about the future were evident. They were convinced that the state will do no more than it does at present or little more, at best.

The respondents are more hopeful regarding the future involvement of the private sector, even if limited in scale. The highest percentages concern the capability/possibility of the private sector to be slightly more active in the areas of educational need (57%), environmental protection (54%), economical needs (50%), and the protection of society's most vulnerable members (45%).

The volunteers stated that volunteer organizations should be much more active in all the areas mentioned, even if the respondents expect that they will be able to accomplish little more than what they do already. In particular, volunteers emphasize the necessity of protecting the rights of vulnerable members of society (79%),[5] followed by educational needs (61%), social service and health care needs (60%), and the protection of the environment and the artistic heritage (57%). Volunteers believe that greater efforts by service organizations are required in these areas. Moreover, 43% of volunteers indicated that the organizations to which they belong should be doing more to ensure their service recipients receive adequate economic support.

Volunteers distinguished between the sectors in determining the appropriate amount and areas of intervention. Although there was substantial support for the existing commitment of voluntary organizations to providing services to individuals, the volunteers believed that the public sector should increase services offered. In the case of private sector initiatives, together with a need for involvement in education (most probably connected to the issue of private schools and to the demand for training programs), it is noteworthy that the volunteers supported increased participation of market forces in meeting cultural needs aimed at ensuring a high quality living environment.

A Typology of Young Volunteers from Lombardy

In order to distinguish general types of volunteers, a cluster analysis was carried out. This analysis was constrained by the manner in which the volunteer joined the organization (personal initiative, invitation of a friend or relative, recruitment by a parish or religious movement, others).

Table 4.1. *Typology of Young Volunteers from Lombardy (N = 225)*

Types	Description of types	Frequency (N)	%
Type 1	Young volunteers with a marked sense of solidarity and civic responsibility	114	50.7
Type 2	Young volunteers motivated by the desire to belong	92	40.9
Type 3	Young volunteers motivated by religious convictions	11	4.9

This analysis differentiated four types of volunteers. We will discuss the three that are the most fully characterized (see Table 4.1).[6]

Type 1: Young Volunteers with a Marked Sense of Solidarity and Civic Responsibility. The first type, the most numerous, consists of volunteers who became involved in voluntary work as a result of their own initiative (100%) and who do not consider this activity as a way to spend free time (92%). Volunteers of this type represented the full age range of the sample, from 19 to 29 years old. The majority of these young people claimed that the motivations underlying their volunteerism were not cultural in nature (98%) but, rather, derived from a desire to help others (76%). These are youth who have obtained a junior high school diploma and dedicate from 11 to 20 hours a week to service activities. Thirty-two percent believe that organizations should be subject to checks by a public body. Fifteen percent agree to some extent with the possibility of their own organization's becoming politically involved. We can hypothesize that these are individuals for whom identity formation takes place by means of "a movement toward another person." It is in this way that meaning is conferred upon their daily lives and the actions that constitute their lives.

Type 2: Young Volunteers Motivated by the Desire to Belong. The second group comprises youth who began their volunteer activity after being recruited by a relative or friend. Their age varies between 25 and 29 years (67%), they have a high school diploma (77%), and, in 25% of cases, they state that they dedicate themselves to organizations as a way to pass time. These volunteers do not express an opinion on the involvement of the state in voluntary organizations or on the possibility of the state's exercising control over organizations. Moreover, they consider the enactment of legislation to regulate such an activity to be useless.

This cluster suggests that, rather than being motivated by prosocial sentiments, these young people desire to compensate for feelings of emptiness and seek to belong to a particular community (group, association, etc.). It is possible that this group's voluntary activities are independent of organizational context, the type of service performed, and the type of recipient. Rather, their activities are for the sole purpose of fulfilling a personal need to belong.

Type 3: Young Volunteers Motivated by Religious Convictions. This is the least numerous type, but the most fully characterized. For these young people, not only was their introduction to voluntary organizations determined by a religious group (100%), but also the motivation underlying their dedication to volunteer action is distinctly religious (64%) and is in no way aimed at personal enrichment (not indicated as a motive for 91% of respondents). Most are students (64%) between 19 and 24 years old (82%), are practicing Catholics (91%), and have been involved in voluntary organizations for about 2 to 3 years (64%). A little more than half belong to upper-middle-class families (55%). These volunteers show little interest in politics and do not believe that the state and the private sector can do more in the way of responding to people's needs, nor, for that matter, do they believe that voluntary organizations will be able to do much more than they do presently.

This group of young volunteers is characterized by a marked tendency toward idealism, typical of the late adolescents that they are, and by strong religious convictions. These convictions seem to translate into a sentiment of solidarity joined with a spirit of service to others and also an inability to recognize possible or latent personal motivations in their volunteerism.

It is interesting to note that the data presented here on young volunteers show marked similarities to those of older adult volunteers (cf. Cesareo & Rossi, 1994; Rossi et al., 1996). The "affinity" that this research suggests between youth and adults in the realm of voluntary organizations throws new light on the relationships between generations, which, in the context of volunteer commitment, seem to be "revitalized" and to find a common ground based upon altruistic action.

The Internal Dynamics of Voluntary Organizations

Let us now examine data pertaining to the organization of voluntary groups in Lombardy. We believe that knowing the internal makeup of a voluntary organization is highly relevant to gaining a better understanding of the young volunteers' experiences. Voluntary organizations result from volunteers' combined motivations, aspirations, and desires. These organizations represent an attempt to translate the vision of volunteers into concrete action.

Legal Status. The legal status of a voluntary organization can be seen to represent an important element in contributing to its creation and promoting its stability. The data show that the majority of entities made up by young people operating in Lombardy have opted for the solution of a "de facto" association (63%). They possess a founding deed of partnership or articles of association (78%) and, in almost all cases, a statute (94%).

The History of the Organizations. In the history of a voluntary organization the occasion of its foundation assumes particular importance because it often holds the key to understanding the basic motivations for its existence. As far as the participants in this study are concerned, in the majority of cases the organization was instituted by a group of citizens (68%). Other common modalities include establishment by persons with a religious vocation (19%); by other, already existing co-operatives/associations (13%); and by health care workers or the family members of those in need of assistance (in both cases, 7%). These data confirm the deeper meaning of voluntarism: The altruistic sentiments of normal citizens are converted into action and give rise to the creation of formalized entities that respond to society's most urgent needs.

There may be numerous and varied motivations underlying the establishment of an organization and they are generally interconnected. The data from this study identify one principal motive mentioned by almost all of the organizations and several that are less important. The motivation most often mentioned for an organization's coming into existence is the most distinctively prosocial one (the desire to respond to the needs of others, principal motivation in 82% of cases). This finding confirms the status of prosocial motivation as the prime mover behind the voluntary world. Motivations linked to the protection of human rights, a prerogative of these organizations, are also somewhat important (principal motive in 12% of cases).

The Development of Voluntary Organizations. Over time, voluntary organizations necessarily evolve as they are constantly obliged to adapt to changes in society. Our data support this proposition. The organizations that were studied have undergone numerous transformations over the years, even if the modifications adopted were almost always partial and not comprehensive. Most of the transformations have concerned the area of the services offered (45%), relationships with other service organizations and public institutions (41%), and the entity's internal structure (39%). In all of these instances, the changes adopted seemed to bring about a substantial improvement in the organization's status as well as establishing stable links with public entities and other voluntary organizations.

Transformations in the recipients of an organization also occur over time. The prevalent trend is toward serving increased numbers of people (50%). An analysis of the principal categories that constitute the recipients shows that in the last 3 years people of all ages have sought the services offered by voluntary organizations (60%).

Operative Functioning. Within a voluntary organization there are various basic tasks to be attended to that are essential to its functioning and can be performed by the volunteers themselves or by paid personnel. The data reveal that volunteers are the true driving force within an organization because they carry out almost all of its critical duties and have a near monopoly on such key activities as coordination (90%) and secretarial work (90%). The data also reveal that the number of participants active over time in the organizations is tending to increase. As far as the size of the organizations is concerned, 27% are small to medium with a stable membership of up to 50 volunteers and 25% are large with the regular participation of 101 to 500 members.

Volunteer training seems to be assuming increased importance. In the opinion of 54% of organizations, training programs should address technical/operative as well as motivational aspects. Organizations mostly conduct their own training programs (76%) or conduct them in collaboration with other voluntary organizations (37%). In a minority of cases, other voluntary organizations directly manage training programs (15%).

The Financial Situation of the Voluntary Organizations. The sources of the funds that are indispensable to an organization's survival vary. They include membership dues, self-financing, private contributions, public contributions, dues paid by recipients, and the sale of products. Contributions can be of a monetary nature or can be made in kind, especially those of public entities, which often give breaks on rents and utility bills and discounts on purchases made by the organization.

The annual income of 26% of organizations is constituted, for the most part, by private contributions; 24% rely on public contributions, 18% on self-financing, and 18% on recipients' dues. Income deriving from public contributions is divided between donations of money (accounting for 46%) and the easing of terms of payment, such as providing free office space to the organization (accounting for 58%).[7] This fact confirms that, more and more, the service sector and public institutions are forming partnership alliances in which benefits made in kind play a prominent role.

The organizations' expenses, besides covering the costs of services, are constituted in good part by the organization's operational costs for such expenses as administration, rent, electricity, telephone, and so forth. There are also expenditures directly tied to the voluntary activities such as transportation, fuel, reimbursements, the delivery of goods in kind, clothing, and money for recipients; health-related costs, cultural activities, and entertainment for recipients and members; and, finally, the cost of insuring and training volunteers.

Federations. Among the organizations that participated in this study, 65% belong to some sort of federation. Clearly, the choice not to remain isolated allows the voluntary organizations better to meet outstanding social needs and to take advantage of greater possibilities, whether they be economic, in the area of information, or in the training offered to members.

Joining an Organization and Motivations for Doing So. Individuals who decide to join a voluntary organization and to become volunteers need only declare their willingness to do so, in the majority of organizations (49%). There are also a substantial number of organizations that require new members to take a specific training course before being allowed to take part in their activities (43%). In some cases, volunteers are asked to cover specific duties for which they will need particular expertise or to adopt certain behaviors when interacting with challenging clients. Only a few organizations require participants to become formal members (36%).

In any case, the fundamental aspect of voluntary action remains the motivational impetus that impels a person to commit him/herself directly and without remuneration. This is what counts the most for an organization when a volunteer asks to be accepted into the group, according to 56% of the respondents. Less frequently is consideration given to the volunteer's ability to provide services to the recipients (of interest to 23% of the organizations) and to his/her available time (17%). The volunteer's ability to relate to recipients is only marginally taken into account (4%).

In the opinion of the organization coordinators, volunteers are motivated to remain in an organization, first, by the shared values that pervade the organization's communal life (67%) and, second, by the satisfaction that each volunteer derives from his/her own activity (30%).

Recipients and Services Offered. The majority of organizations do not direct their activities toward individuals with a specific need but assist an undifferentiated group of recipients (44%). This seems to be the case even if there are organizations that devote themselves specifically to the sick (35%), the handicapped (32%), children and adolescents (27%), the elderly (16%), the poor (14%), and drug addicts, alcoholics, and victims of social alienation (11%).

The quality of the relations that the volunteers establish with recipients is monitored in 53% of organizations. The importance given to relations with those who receive their services is represented by the fact that 43% of organizations arrange for periodic evaluations of their work. The difficulties encountered by the organizations are mostly of an institutional nature (68.%) and only in a minority of cases attributable to volunteers (19%) or to recipients (8%). The organization's "perception" is that they adequately meet the needs that they encounter. In fact, 74% believe that their recipients are satisfied with the services provided to them, as opposed to 18% who state that their recipients ask for more than the group is able to offer. On the whole, the relations between the "voluntary system" and the "recipients' system" appear to be good. Thus, the verdict is essentially positive regarding what the organization offers and the impact this has on the consumers of its services.

But what are the activities and services in question? A first, important category of services offered by the organizations pivots on assistance in medical emergencies and, more specifically, include providing first aid (32%), health care assistance (26%), transportation of the sick (25%), and organ and blood donations (20%). A second, innovative category is defined by activities that focus on "taking care of another person" and establishing a personal relationship between volunteer and receiver as the guiding criteria for providing services. This second category includes educational activities (28%), entertainment (28%), social assistance (17%), provision of escorts (21%), and listening to recipients (15%). A third cat-egory concerns preserving "traces of historical memory." To this end, organizations engage in activities of research and study (10%) and doc-umentation (10%). There is a fourth service category that involves a mi-nority of organizations but is significant in that it is an innovation in the context of volunteerism as an organized phenomenon. This concerns the promotion and defense of civil rights (11%) and environmental protec-tion (10%). As a final note, it is also worth mentioning that 22% of the organizations are involved in activities aimed at prevention in the areas of health care and social hardship.

Where Service Activities Take Place. Where do service activities take place? The classification resulting from the survey lists the locations in the fol-lowing order: neighborhoods and streets (32%); natural environments, such as beaches and woods (30%); and hospitals and outpatient depart-ments (28%). A substantial number of organizations operate in disaster areas (26%) and in educational contexts such as schools (26%), and a slightly smaller percentage carry out their activities in spaces provided for children and youth by churches (22%). Finally, 20% operate in the recipients' homes and 16% dispense emergency services from mobile units.

The Social Function of Voluntary Organizations. An examination of the ranking of responses concerning the significance of voluntary action with respect to the needs of local communities reveals that directly meeting these needs is seen as their most important function (41%), followed by the conviction that voluntary organizations provide concrete opportu-nities for expressing the prosocial sentiments in a community (32%) and create a pervasive culture of solidarity (23%).

An assessment, in more specific terms, of the social function of vol-untary work shows that it consists in substituting for welfare services (48%) and supplementing services provided by other bodies (24%). The implementation of innovative programs aimed at meeting local needs distinguishes the activities of 19% of organizations. A minority of organ-izations (9%) indicate "meeting the needs of the sick" as a significant community function. This specific finding is a confirmation of a genuine "spirit of service" toward individuals, untouched by any consideration of the possible social impact of voluntary organizations.

The Network of Relations with the External Environment. In addition to taking into account a service organization's relationship to the outside world in general, a survey of the relational system activated by the various actors in the third sector of a given geographical area (voluntary organizations, social service associations, social service cooperatives, foundations, etc.) is crucial to an understanding of organized voluntary organizations. The tendency exhibited by the various representatives of the third sector to be connected among themselves does not bear exclusively upon their working relationships but can also be seen to have a specific cultural manifestation. The collaboration of third sector organizations helps make explicit that "acting together" is indispensable to creating "relational well-being," a type of good defined specifically by the practice of sharing.

From an empirical point of view, the data reveal a higher frequency of exchanges among organizations operating in the same service sector. Indeed, 41% of organizations maintain stable relationships with analogous entities. Fewer maintain stable relationships with service organizations operating in different areas (14%); it is more common, in this case, for the organizations to have intermittent exchanges among themselves (47%). Exchanges between voluntary organizations and cooperatives providing assistance in the realm of social services are also decidedly in the minority, involving only 7% of organizations.

The relationship among service organizations and public institutions (understood in a broad sense), the private sector, and the organization's own social context varies. There is an established practice of exchanges with public institutions. For example, 36% of organizations have stable relationships with Unità Socio-Sanitaria Locale (USSL),[8] 31% with hospitals, and 19% with schools. In contrast, there is an almost complete absence of contacts with representatives of the private sector. Nine percent of organizations have only intermittent contacts with commercial enterprises, and this percentage drops to 1% in the case of stable relations. Finally, as regards contacts with the organization's social context, there is an attitude that oscillates between indifference and collaboration (49%), even if incidents of concrete collaboration occur (39%).

A Typology of Youth Voluntary Organizations in Lombardy

As in the case of the volunteers, a cluster analysis was carried out in order to differentiate general types of operating youth voluntary organ-

Table 4.2. *Typology of Youth Voluntary Organizations in Lombardy* *(N = 73)*

Types	Description of types	Frequency (N)	%
Type 1	Complex organizations supporting the health care system	48	65.8
Type 2	Health care assistance organizations	11	15.1
Type 3	Organizations involved in environmental action	10	13.7

izations. The analysis distinguished among four types, of which we will discuss the three most fully characterized (see Table 4.2).[9]

Type 1: Complex Organizations Supporting the Health Care System. The organizations that are grouped together in this type number 48, equal to 66% of the total. They are not well characterized and, for the most part, provide services in support of already existing institutions mostly in health care (29%). In 29% of cases they operate in hospitals and, therefore, have stable relations with these institutions (38%). The volunteers belonging to these organizations are primarily students (29%) involved in blood donations (23%), although some engage in other activities such as listening (in 13% of organizations). In 17% of these organizations, volunteers, associates, and paid personnel are all active.

Type 2: Health Care Assistance Organizations. This type groups together 11 organizations, equal to 15% of the total. In 64% of cases, they see their primary role as responding to their recipients' needs. Their activities mostly involve transporting the sick (36%) and providing health care assistance (36%). Ninety percent of these organizations operate in an isolated manner without contacts with other voluntary associations. It is also notable that in 64% of these organizations, members are insured, as stipulated by recent Italian legislation (Law n. 266/91).

Type 3: Organizations Involved in Environmental Action. Even this type groups together a limited number of organizations, that is, 10, equal to 14% of the total. It is, however, the most fully characterized of the three types. These are organizations in which the volunteers take care of internal operations, carrying out secretarial duties (100%) and coordination (100%). Volunteers work for their cause by becoming part of various institutional entities (for example, regional coordinating commissions) that advocate the protection of the natural environment and public awareness (100%). Volunteers also coordinate activities with public institutions operating in the same sector (100%). In all of these cases these organizations possess a statute, and in 70% of cases its operative structure has not changed from the time of its inception to the present. These organizations are involved, above all, in local ecological matters (40%). The volunteers are mostly male (90%), all of whom hold a stable job (100%) and in 60% of cases undergo comprehensive training. Relations with voluntary organizations operating in different sectors are almost nonexistent in this cluster.

Conclusion

The present study reveals how voluntary action carried out by young people in Lombardy is characterized by distinctively altruistic and prosocial motivations and by the desire to help those in need. The young people surveyed show themselves to be aware of the public usefulness of their actions and the importance of their actions in responding to social transformations. At the same time, they exhibit indifference with respect to political involvement.

A more thorough investigation would be required to determine whether these youth possess "extraordinary" characteristics or, instead, are very similar to youth not involved in volunteer work. They certainly exhibit profound motivations toward volunteer commitment and an awareness of the civic significance of voluntary action. However, in contrast to past trends, voluntary participation in present-day Italy does not assume precise political connotations and has even less to do with political parties. Indeed, there seems to be a sort of rejection of and distancing from traditional politics. As Cavalli and De Lillo (1993) point out, "The new generations appear to be less favorably inclined towards past expedients and to be more interested in a life centered on relationships." We believe that the tendency of young volunteers to distance themselves from political involvement, in a strict sense, is determined by the crisis of the political system in Italy. Indeed, in our country, political commitment and volunteer commitment have never been, even in the past, closely related phenomena; rather they are distinct areas of action. The first has been prominently connected to mechanisms of representation and the second to solidarity.

It is not by chance that both volunteers and their organizations pay ample attention to evaluation of the effects of their activities, to the quality of the receiver–volunteer relationship, and to the satisfaction derived from the work itself. This concern about social relationships is founded on personal motivations. Our data, particularly the typologies, indicate that voluntarism, as practiced by young people, is a "movement toward the other person" rooted in prosocial and altruistic sentiments. Volunteer participation seems to promote the construction of the young person's personal and collective identity, thus augmenting his/her sense of belonging to a community (Melucci, 1991). Furthermore, in contrast to the evident differences between the generations in coping with the requirements of the different spheres of life, in the context of voluntary organizations one witnesses a "rapprochement," a sort of dialogue between people of different ages that has its roots in the shared motivations of altruism. Supporting this argument, the data reveal broad similarities between the voluntary organizations composed of youth and those composed of adults or of multiple generations. The only noteworthy difference is the greater representation in the sample of youth-dominated organizations dedicated to protecting the environment.

This study also discloses the aspiration of volunteers and their organizations to become less amateurish, an aspiration in which the *spirit of service* is joined to the cognizance of having to increase *technical and relational competence*. The necessity of undergoing comprehensive training is generally seen by the young people questioned here in a positive light. It is seen as a fundamental resource, not only in polishing technical and operative skills, but also in creating and strengthening the sense of cohesiveness and belonging among an organization's members (Boccacin, 1994).

Another element indicative of a sort of cultural revolution taking place in the third sector is the tendency toward a progressive reversal in voluntary organizations' relations with public bodies. The long-standing practice of requesting a contribution in exchange for services rendered is giving way to increasingly pressing demands to participate in decision-making processes regarding social policy, thus affirming the social identity and full rights to citizenship of voluntary organizations. To this end, it is essential that these organizations make their entrance onto the social stage with a solid "networking capacity, an ability to connect, to enter into relationships" (Bobba, 1995). The organizations actively seek to avoid the appearance of second-rate participants in a dialogue with the public sector. In this regard, the study highlights the existence of a stable network linking the organizations. For the present, these links remain limited because they are essentially confined within the bounds of a single area of service. On the whole, however, the world of voluntary organizations is sending signals of the profound transformations taking place within itself. It is leaving behind the traditional model of assistance provided to the needy by amateurs and moving toward service that combines solidarity, promotion, and professionalism in the helping relationship. The transition is not a traumatic one because the voluntary sector is giving proof of possessing a remarkably flexible constitution. It is adapting to changes in areas of need and in the strategies required to solve new and complex social problems.

The task of future research is to understand more fully the motivations of the young people who operate in voluntary organizations, motivations that are characterized by the fact of rendering a service without expecting anything in return. The desire of the youth in this study to join the spirit of service to that of professionalism allows us to hypothesize that those who commit themselves to volunteer action are individuals who make their own a logic of "giving" (Godbout, 1993; Scabini, 1995) and of competence. They are individuals who feel that they have received much – from their families, from the social context, from life in general – and who want not only to give back a little of what they have been given, but also to do so in an effective, conscious, and adequate manner.

It remains to be demonstrated empirically whether serving in a voluntary organization, like all meaningful life experiences, significantly influences a young person's construction of identity in the process of growth toward adulthood. In this respect, our convictions echo Erikson, who maintained that the truly adult person is one who takes care of him/herself, others, and the environment.

Notes

1. The present work refers specifically to voluntary organized groups, that is, socially and institutionally recognized associations.
2. This is in reference to research conducted by the Italian foundation for voluntary organization, Fondazione Italiana per il Volontariato (FIVOL), between 1992 and 1993 on 8,893 voluntary organizations that represent about 85% of all such entities in Italy.
3. Examples of promotional services given in the FIVOL report include social and cultural presentations, civic protection of individuals or groups, instruction, training, prevention programs, promotion and defense of civil rights, rehabilitation, reeducation.
4. Examples of first-impact intervention are telephone listening services and soup kitchens; examples of continuous intervention are home care and social services assistance. For a more detailed list of examples of promotional intervention, see note 3. Please note that the sum of the percentages given here is

greater than 100 because some organizations are involved simultaneously and with the same commitment in more than one type of activity.

5. These are the percentages of the volunteers who, for each of the sectors indicated, declared themselves to be very much in agreement regarding the need for an increase in the involvement manifested by their own organizations. It is worth mentioning in advance that in the presentation of the data, in many cases, the sums of the percentages referring to a topic surveyed in the questionnaire are not equal to 100: When this occurs, it means that the subjects, whether individuals or organizations, had the possibility of making multiple choices or of expressing opinions for or against each item and were not obliged to choose one only.

6. For a detailed discussion of this technique, see Lebart, Morineau, and Warwick (1984) and Lanzetti (1989).

7. In this case, also, the sum of the two percentages is different from 100 because some organizations make use of both types of financing.

8. Unità Socio-Sanitaria Locale (USSL) is a local public entity that provides services to one or more towns or cities. It is charged with the management, organization, and granting of services essential to safeguarding residents' physical, psychic, and social health.

9. Even if the second and third types group together a very small number of "subjects," we should not forget that these are organizations, that is, "groupings of subjects," and complex entities. In virtue of this consideration, even these types are commented upon.

References

Amerio, P., Cafasso, R., & Calligaris, A. (1996). L'intrigante problema dell'altruismo: ovvero Solidarietà e psicologia social [The intriguing problem of altruism: Solidarity and social psychology]. In P. Amour (Ed.), *Form DI solidarity e language dell politic* (pp. 57–93). Turin: Bollati-Boringhieri.

Bobba, L. (1995). Introduzione [Introduction]. In A. Bassi (Ed.), *Organizzazioni di successo. Studio di caso di organizzazioni third in Italia e in Europa* (pp. 13–18). Milan: Angeli.

Boccacin, L. (1993a). *La sinergia della differenza* [Synergy of difference]. Milan: Angeli.

Boccacin, L. (1993b). Il ruolo del terzo settore nelle politiche sociali [The role of the third sector in social politics]. In P. Donati (Ed.), *La cittadinanza societaria* (pp. 155–170). Rome-Bari: Laterza.

Boccacin, L. (1994). Il volontariato in Lombardia: Un monitoraggio del fenomeno dopo la legge 266/91 [The voluntary organizations in Lombardy: Monitoring the phenomenon after Law 266/91]. In V. Cesareo, & G. Rossi (Eds.), *Il volontariato in Lombardia* (pp. 139–21). Milan: Vita e Pensiero.

Calvi, G. (Ed.). (1987). *Eurisko, indagine italiana: Rapporto 1986* [Eurisko, Italian survey: Report of 1986]. Milan: Angeli.

Cavalli, A., & De Lillo, A. (Eds.). (1988). *Giovani anni '80* [Youth in the eighties]. Bologna: Il Mulino.

Cavalli, A., & De Lillo, A. (Eds.). (1993). *Giovani anni '90* [Youth in the nineties]. Bologna: Il Mulino.

Cesareo, V., & Rossi, G. (Eds.). (1986). *Volontariato e Mezzogiorno: Aspetti e problemi* [Voluntary organizations and Southern Italy: Aspects and Problems]. Bologna: Dehoniane.

96   E. Marta, G. Rossi, and L. Boccacin

Cesareo, V., & Rossi, G. (Eds.). (1989). *L'azione volontaria nel Mezzogiorno tra tradizione e innovazione* [Voluntary action in Southern Italy between tradition and innovation]. Bologna: Dehoniane.
Cesareo, V., & Rossi, G. (Eds.). (1994). *Il volontariato in Lombardia* [Voluntary organizations in Lombardy]. Milan: Vita e Pensiero.
Fondazione Italiana per il Volontariato (FIVOL) (1995). *Il volontariato sociale italiano: Rapporto di ricerca* [Italian social voluntary organizations: Research project]. Rome: Author.
Godbout, J. T. (1993). *Lo spirito del dono* [The spirit of giving]. Turin: Bollati-Boringhieri. (Original work published in 1992).
Lanzetti, C. (1989). Appendice metodologica [Methodological appendix]. In V. Cesareo & G. Rossi (Eds.), *L'azione volontaria nel Mezzogiorno tra tradizione e innovazione* (pp. 279–295). Bologna: Dehoniane.
Lebart, L., Morineau, A., & Warwick, K. M. (1984). *Multivariate descriptive statistical analysis*. New York: Wiley.
Melucci, A. (1991). *Il gioco dell'Io* [The play of Ego]. Milan: Feltrinelli.
Morris, M. (1962). *Social enterprise*. London: National Council of Social Service.
Murray, G. J. (1969). *Voluntary organizations and social welfare*. Edinburgh: Oliver & Boyd.
Paolicchi, P. (1995). Narratives of volunteering. *Journal of Moral Education, 24,* 159–173.
Rossi, G. (1993). Politiche sociali e volontariato [Social politics and voluntary service]. In R. De Vita, P. Donati, & G. B. Sgritta (a cura di). *La politica sociale oltre la crisi del Welfare State* (pp. 181–200). Milan: Angeli.
Rossi, G., Boccacin, L., & Bramanti, D. (1996). *Pubblico e privato in Lombardia: eterogeneità dei settori di intervento e nuove possibilità di collaborazione* [Public and private in Lombardy: Heterogeneity of intervention sectors and new possibilities of collaboration]. Milan: Region Lombardy.
Rossi, G., & Colozzi, I. (1985). *I gruppi di volontariato in Italia* [Groups of voluntary service in Italy]. Rome: Ministry of Work and Social Security and Department of State.
Scabini, E. (1995). *Psicologia sociale della famiglia* [Social psychology of the family]. Turin: Bollati-Boringhieri.

5. Political Socialization in the New States of Germany

HANS OSWALD

The study of political socialization in the former Communist part of Germany, the Eastern "new states," is of great practical and theoretical interest. It is of practical interest because it directly bears on questions regarding the future development of democracy in unified Germany. Will it be possible to integrate the younger generations in the East into the liberal and democratic tradition of the Federal Republic of Germany (FRG)? Will these youth be able to adapt to the institutional rules of democracy? The study of political socialization in the new states of Germany is of theoretical interest because it allows the investigation of the influence of contextual conditions in an extraordinary historical situation. This situation in Germany presents the opportunity to examine which contextual conditions adolescents identify with democratic procedures and which conditions encourage a drift toward antidemocratic attitudes and behaviors including right-wing or left-wing party identifications. The breakdown of the political system of the German Democratic Republic (GDR) in 1989 (*Wende*) and the subsequent entry into the FRG in 1990 (*Beitritt*) were accompanied and followed by rapid social changes in the economy, the labor market, and societal institutions. All these changes influenced everyday life, including consumer habits, mobility, and politically relevant attitudes and behaviors. Adolescents may react differently to these events, depending on family traditions and experiences, on school and work experiences, and on interactions in peer groups and friendships as well as in neighborhoods and communities. The study of such influences should enlarge our empirical and theoretical knowledge of socialization and development in general.

The aim of this chapter is to compare adolescents' political attitudes and behaviors in the new states (the former GDR) and the old states (the former FRG) and to relate the current situation to conditions before 1989. Most of the data used to analyze the current situation have been published very recently in German books and articles. Some data have been collected by the author and his team in a longitudinal study of adolescents in one of the new states. The first wave of these data was collected in 1996; it included 2,663 10th graders.

Political Socialization in the GDR

In the GDR, educational indoctrination and repression were paramount (Hille, 1991). A paternalistic–authoritarian system inside and outside schools was established in order to form the universally educated socialist personality (*allseitig gebildete sozialistische Persönlichkeit*), who is loyal to the party and to the government and eager to construct the genuine socialist society in everyday solidarity (Lemke, 1991). This education started very early in life through a day-care system that involved nearly all children. To the degree that indoctrination was successful, the task lying before the democratic FRG is to reeducate adolescents in a way similar to that used by the Western Allies after World War II with the Nazi-educated youth of the Third Reich.

It is now apparent that the indoctrination machine was only partly successful and some indications suggest that it was rather ineffective. The Youth Research Institute in Leipzig (Zentralinstitut für Jugendforschung [ZIJ]), financed by the GDR government, conducted youth surveys every year. These researchers found that the acceptance and, therefore, the legitimacy of the Communist party and government were decreasing during the 1980s. At the same time, the popularity of the FRG population was increasing (Müller, 1991). Such findings could not be published in the GDR and were widely ignored by officials of the party youth organization (FDJ) and by the federal secretary of people's education, Mrs. Margot Honnecker.

One explanation of adolescents' views is that their criticism of the government was fed by heavy consumption of Western television and radio programs. In 1988, up to 78% of working youth and 96% of school students watched television channels from the FRG several times a week, according to recently published studies of the ZIJ (Stiehler 1991). "Growing up with the TV world 'West' in the everyday world 'East' " (Schmeling, 1995, p. 70) led to a critical attitude toward the promises of the party and the government with respect to consumption possibilities; civil rights, especially freedom of travel; and the reality of socialist habits in work and life-styles among ordinary people.

It is highly questionable whether membership in the party youth organization (FDJ – Freie Deutsche Jugend) or school-based civic education was effective in promoting loyalty to the GDR government. Over two-thirds of adolescents were members of the party youth organization (see Zilch, 1992); however, for at least half of the youth, membership was a ritual obligation, necessary to avoid disadvantages in school and in vocational careers. The socializing effect of belonging to the youth organization seemed restricted mainly to the officers, who were afforded opportunities to gain organizational and leadership competence and, at the same time, to develop affinity to the communist ideology, the party, and the government. About 80% of the FDJ officers at the level of schools were female. "Civic" education in schools and universities was based on Marxism–Leninism and was ridiculed as merely a formal requirement. The ritualistic character of indoctrination at all levels led to a decreasing interest in politics and to withdrawal into the private sphere. The development of individualism among adolescents was clearly shown in the unpublished surveys of the ZIJ mentioned (see also Stock, 1995). This change in attitudes may be interpreted as modernization in a Western sense that already had begun before the *Wende* in 1989.

There were also educationally related differences in youth's attitude toward government and politics. Access to the highest track of secondary school (EOS) was very restricted. Approximately 14% of any age group studied in universities during the final years of the GDR. The access to EOS and universities was completely controlled by the authorities. Therefore, the percentage of loyal socialists at grades 11 and 12 (EOS) and at universities might have been higher than that of working youth and adolescents in early vocational training because of the selection process and the students' gratitude and career prospects.

At the end of the Communist regime, we can differentiate at least four groups of adolescents with respect to their political orientation (see Schmeling, 1995, for a similar classification): (1) loyal socialists who benefited from the GDR system in party and governmental organizations, in universities, and at the upper levels of the labor force; (2) politically interested, well educated critics of the system who wanted a better socialist system after the Soviet Perestroika, a socialist system with a "human face," many of whom participated in protest rallies organized in church buildings; (3) politically interested opponents of the system who wanted to change it into a Western-style democracy and capitalist economy, many of whom were among the embassy refugees in Prague and Budapest in 1989; (4) a large group of politically disinterested and withdrawn adolescents, especially among working youth.

The adolescents in these groups have differentially experienced the *Wende* and the transformation process caused by the complete incorporation of Western institutional systems into the new states. As a function of their experiences in the GDR and after unification in the new states, these adolescents have developed different political attitudes and behaviors.

Identification with Democracy in the New States

After World War II, identification of the West German population with the new democratic system was facilitated by the economic success of the 1950s (Almond & Verba, 1963). In addition, the reeducation program implemented by the Western Allies – the United States, United Kingdom, and France – influenced the gradual integration of the young generation into a civil, liberal culture during the first two decades after the war. It is assumed that the future economic success and functioning of the welfare system in the new states will be crucial for the development of liberal-democratic attitudes and behaviors. Despite its poor economy and rundown infrastructure, the GDR had a very secure welfare and public health system, and social security and stability were highly valued. There was no unemployment; all adolescents leaving school got work or vocational training. Almost 90% of women joined the labor force. The housing supply was sufficient and inexpensive, and homelessness was unknown. Criminality and juvenile delinquency were low and not of public concern.

After the *Wende*, there was a rapid increase in unemployment combined with career disruption, especially for women. Youth who leave school now have difficulty finding work or vocational training, and youth unemployment is of great concern in the new and old states. Rates of criminality have increased rapidly in the new states and juvenile delinquency is now more prevalent in the East than in the West. Furthermore, the free market for housing, formerly nonexistent, has led to increases in rents and feelings of insecurity.

According to one of the most representative surveys since unification, "Youth and Democracy in Germany" (Hoffmann-Lange, 1995), the advantages and disadvantages of unification were balanced for two-thirds of the adolescents in the East in 1992 (Bütow, 1995). Among the advantages were freedom of travel (Bütow, 1995) and a better supply of goods (Förster, Friedrich, Müller, & Schubarth, 1993). Among the disadvantages, the unemployment rate in combination with insecure vocational future prospects ranked highest (Bütow, 1995). Criminality and public security also were of great concern. In-depth interviews have offered insight into Eastern adolescents' dissatisfaction with the political and economic development after unification (Vollbrecht, 1993). Satisfaction with the situation was closely related to attitudes toward democracy: The less satisfied the adolescents were in several domains of everyday life (social and vocational security, financial and other aspects of the life situation, civil rights, and freedoms), the less they accepted the democratic system of the FRG (Hoffmann-Lange, 1995).

Recent surveys have shown a gap between youth's support for general ideas about government and the specific implementation of these ideas in Germany. In 1992, 80% of adolescents in the new states found the idea of democracy "good," but less than a third had the same attitude toward the realization of democracy in today's Germany. This gap was found to be larger in the new states than in the old states. With respect to the idea of socialism, two-thirds of youth evaluated it as "quite good" or "very good." However, an overwhelming majority (94%) were critical with respect to the realization of socialism in the GDR. The acceptance of the idea of socialism was highest in the highest track of school, the gymnasium, which gives access to university studies. With respect to the idea of socialism, the data show the same tendencies among adolescents in the new and old states (Hoffmann-Lange, 1995). These figures were almost identical in youth surveys of 1993 and 1995 (IPOS, 1996). (See Easton, 1965, for a theoretical discussion of this gap in youth's political attitudes.)

The results of another 1992 study in Saxon, one of the new states, are similar in revealing that a majority of the 14- to 25-year-olds was dissatisfied with the political system of the unified Germany (Förster et al., 1993). Almost all adolescents were happy with the ending of the GDR's socialist regime, but one-quarter wanted a reformed humanistic socialism, and the percentage of adolescents having this idea increased up to half among those who were dissatisfied with the new unified Germany. Satisfaction with German politics and politicians decreased after the general elections of 1990. For example, adolescents' trust in the largest democratic parties of the FRG – the conservative CDU of Chancellor Kohl and its opponent, the liberal SPD – decreased continuously between 1990 and 1993 (Förster, 1994).

If we compare the attitudes of adolescents and adults toward democracy, toward the realization of democracy in today's Germany, and toward the idea of socialism, we can speak of an effective socializing milieu. According to surveys, the majority of adults also accepted basic democratic rights and principles (Meulemann 1996). There was no difference in this respect between the East and West. But the adult population of the East, compared to that of the West, was, and still is, much more skeptical about the realization of democracy in the new Germany. More people in the East than in the West think that a renewed socialism would be better than the free-market economy. Meulemann concluded that in the East, the idea of socialism works as a measure for the evaluation of democracy and, according to this measure, democracy looks bad. Almost unchanged over the years, surveys in the new states have shown that social welfare ranks much higher in value than freedom, with many people in the East believing the GDR was superior to the FRG in this respect.

An important aspect of the acceptance of democracy in a given country is the acceptance of its constitutional institutions and the balance of power between the federal and state governmental institutions, including parliaments, the court system, police, and military forces, on the one hand, and societal organizations like the mass media, the churches, the unions, and the parties, on the other. Data from the adult population of the FRG from 1984 until 1992 show two secular trends (Krüger, 1995). First, trust in institutions was decreasing continually in all age cohorts, although a majority trusted the institutions. Second, the cohort of the 18- to 29-year-olds felt less trust than older cohorts.

According to a 1992 survey, adolescents' trust in institutions was higher in the old states than in the new (Krüger, 1995). On a scale of political alienation, one-quarter of the Western adolescents compared to one-third of the Eastern adolescents scored high on political alienation. With respect to education, there was a difference between the West and East that is difficult to explain without additional information. In the West, trust in institutions decreased in the higher tracks of school, but in the East, trust increased in the higher tracks in 1992. Further research is needed to verify these tendencies for later years and to explain such differences if they hold over time.

Political Participation

Participation begins with interest and information. During the dramatic processes of the fall of the wall in 1989, interest in politics, information seeking through the mass media, and discussions about politics increased rapidly in the GDR and later in the new states (Förster et al.,

1993; Starke, 1995). Until 1991, interest in politics of adolescents (Oester-reich, 1993) as well as adults (Meulemann 1996) was much higher in the East than in the West. But interest was short lived and the educational system in the new states was unable to keep students interested for long (Vollbrecht, 1993). Between 1989 and 1992, political interest of 14- to 18-year-olds in Saxon declined from 70% to 11%, indicating that they were "very interested" (Förster et al., 1993). Already in 1992, interest in politics was very similar in the East and West; 22% versus 21% of 14- to 29-year-olds were strongly interested (Schneider, 1995). In East and West Berlin, a cohort of 10th graders in 1995 was less interested in politics than a cohort of 10th graders in 1993 (Jülisch, 1996). Representative survey data show a similar decrease in political interest between 1993 and 1995, with East German adolescents being less interested than West German ado-lescents (IPOS, 1996). School track is one of the best predictors of political interest over time; students in higher tracks were more interested in pol-itics than were students in lower tracks in 1991 (Oesterreich, 1993), 1993 and 1995 (IPOS, 1996), and 1996 (Oswald & Weiss, 1996).

In response to a general question about political interest, more boys than girls said that they were "very interested." This gender difference was uniformly found in several studies in East and West Germany as well as the Netherlands and France (Barnes & Kaase, 1979; Jennings & van Deth, 1990). However, if specific questions were asked about interest in different political issues such as social policy, ecology, and peace, the sex difference disappeared in the Western part of Germany and the fe-males rated even higher than the boys in the Eastern part in 1991 (Mel-zer, 1992) and in 1996 (Oswald & Weiss, 1996). It seems as if girls are less interested in the official political agenda of political parties and gov-ernmental institutions than in specific political topics connected with car-ing and humanistic ideals.

Interest in politics is closely connected to seeking information in the mass media and to discussing political issues in the family, in school, and with peers. The preferred political information sources are news broadcasts on television followed by radio news, with newspapers being of minor significance. The more interested adolescents were in politics in 1996, the more they sought information in the mass media, including newspapers, and the more they discussed political matters with parents and peers (Oswald & Weiss, 1996). Political interest, political information seeking, and discussions with parents and peers seem to increase the readiness for political participation. The influence of teachers in school, especially the influence of the Communist trained teachers in the new states, is unknown. It can be assumed that formal political instruction by these teachers is confined to the description of political institutions and the general principles of democracy. However, teachers' attitudes toward the reality of democracy in the unified Germany may be just as skeptical as those of the majority of the Eastern adult population, and it can be suspected that many teachers communicate their skepticism to their students.

In the tradition of previous studies of political action (e.g., Barnes & Kaase, 1979; Jennings & van Deth, 1990), German researchers usually differentiate between legal and illegal actions. In terms of illegal actions, they have differentiated between civil disobedience and power assertive behavior against property and persons.

Voting in general elections is the most accepted form of political behavior for adolescents. The readiness to vote in general elections increases with age. According to a representative survey in 1992 (Schneider, 1995), 80% of the 18- to 29-year-olds in the East and 87% in the West had already voted at least once. According to our own study, almost two-thirds of 10th grade students in one of the new states in 1996 said they would vote next Sunday if they had the right. As in other countries like Great Britain (Bynner & Ashford, 1994), the readiness to participate in general elections was higher in the upper track of the school system than in the lower tracks and was higher for males than for females in 1995 and 1996 (Jülisch, 1996; Oswald & Weiss, 1996).

For other forms of legal participation, an overwhelming majority of adolescents in the East and West, in both sexes and age groups, valued petitions and legal demonstrations as reasonable ways to express their own political opinions. As with voting, these other legal forms of participation were more favored in the higher tracks of the school system than in the lower tracks in 1995 (Jülisch, 1996).

In contrast to legal protest behavior, forms of civil disobedience were less accepted. In 1992, only 37% in the East and 27% in the West approved of illegal demonstrations, with males showing more readiness to use this form than females (Schneider, 1995). In our own 1996 study, one-fifth of the 10th graders were ready to participate in illegal demonstrations. The objections toward participating in acts of civil disobedience were more prevalent in the lower tracks of the school system than in the highest track.

Forms of illegal participation like graffiti, vandalism, and aggression against persons were less accepted than acts of civil disobedience. In a 1992 study, only 12% in the East and 7% in the West, predominantly males, accepted such power assertive behaviors as possibilities for themselves (Schneider, 1995). In our own study, graffiti were accepted by 13%, fights by 12%, and vandalism by 7%. Fights and vandalism as forms of political demonstration were most accepted by male adolescents in the lower tracks of the school system (Klein-Allermann, Kracke, Noack, & Hofer, 1995). In the literature on right-wing extremism, we find some indications that, in addition to school track, failure at school and family processes like power assertive educational styles or neglect may influence the acceptance of illegal political participation forms (Hagan, Merkens, & Boehnke, 1995; Klein-Allermann et al., 1995). It is our view that the political nature of such behaviors seems questionable and that they may simply be seen as ordinary forms of deviant or delinquent behavior.

The Antiliberal Syndrome

In the official language of the party and government, the GDR was an antifascist country in which right-wing extremism was nonexistent and the roots of fascism had been extinguished.

In contrast to this public image, recently published survey data showed that already in 1988, 2% of adolescents were skinheads, another 4% were sympathizers, and 10% to 15% of adolescents minimized the crimes of the Nazi dictatorship (Melzer, 1992). These figures are quite similar to those of several studies of adolescents in the FRG before 1989, and we have some indications that rightist and fascist stereotypes including anti-Semitism were, and still are, communicated in the family in both the new and old states (Melzer & Schubarth, 1995). Many of the skinheads and other rightists had been criminalized and imprisoned without publicity by the GDR authorities. It now seems that lasting networks of hard-core rightists were formed in institutions like the ill-famed prison of Bautzen.

Very soon after the *Wende* and the unification, the rightist scene of the East became publicly known. Aggression against foreigners and asylum seekers made headlines worldwide. However, the problem of rightist aggression is as prevalent in the West as in the East. A small minority of adolescents in both parts of Germany, most of them from lower socioeconomic backgrounds, used and will probably continue to use power in combination with fascist ideas, language, songs, and symbols. That does not mean that all skinheads, hooligans, and wearers of Nazi symbols are politically committed rightists. Studies have shown, for example,

106   Hans Oswald

that some hooligans waving war flags or singing Nazi songs do this by imitation and for fun on weekends without deep involvement in rightist ideologies during the week (Bohnsack, Loos, Schäfer, Städtler, & Wild, 1995). Another study showed that deviant groups including skinheads were quite heterogeneous; their members were – depending on family ties and sustaining networks – to some extent integrated and functioning in the adult world (Kühnel & Matuscheck, 1995). Most skinheads may be rightists but not all of them are political extremists.

Despite these reservations, the problem of rightist antidemocratic and antiliberal attitudes of adolescents is of public and educational concern because of their latent potential for right-wing parties and antidemocratic movements. This potential may be of similar size in the East and West. It is fed by growing youth unemployment and an insecure future for adolescents not doing well in school and, consequently, in the labor market.

Some authors argue that a right-wing extremism syndrome exists that combines (1) anti-Semitism and ethnocentrism, (2) nationalism and glorification of the German past including the Third Reich, (3) authoritarian personality traits, and (4) manifest hostility against foreigners (Melzer & Schubarth, 1995). Indeed, Melzer and Schubarth found that all these constructs were interrelated and that the constellation of the first three features explained 42% of the variance in foreigner hostility in the old states and 45% in the old states. Other authors do not deny the correlations between antiforeigner attitudes and the different aspects of rightist attitudes and authoritarian personality traits, but they add qualifications (Oesterreich, 1993). For example, several studies have reported differences between the new states and old states in the right-wing extremism syndrome as it relates to antiforeigner attitudes. This finding may be partly due to the greater difficulties encountered in finding a job in the new states. In places where foreigners are seen as direct competitors in the labor market, attitudes against them may follow, notwithstanding an authoritarian syndrome (Oesterreich, 1993).

This interpretation is sustained by the fact that East–West differences in other aspects of the rightist syndrome are less clear or nonexistent. Lederer and Kindervater (1995) compared GDR adolescents of 1990 with West German adolescents of 1991. They found some statistically significant, but small, differences in the proportion of authoritarian personalities. Using the same data and including a comparison with U.S. adolescents, Rippl and Boehnke (1995) found few differences between the GDR adolescents and the adolescents from the two Western democratic countries. The authors conclude that the authoritarian system of the GDR did not produce noticeably more authoritarian personalities than the liberal systems of democratic societies. The differences between boys and girls were significant and high in East and West alike, with boys being more often authoritarian than girls. In both parts of Germany, authoritarianism decreased with age, with a turning point at the age of seventeen.

After World War II, the proportion of authoritarians among Nazi-raised German adolescents in the Western parts of Germany had been much higher than among adolescents of the same age in the United States (McGranahan, 1946). In subsequent decades, the proportion of authoritarians in the FRG decreased continuously, and it reached the U.S. level in 1979 (Rippl, Seipel, & Lederer, 1995). A certain number of "enemies of freedom," as Altemeyer (1988) called them in the case of Canada, seem to exist in many democratic societies.

A popular hypothesis states that authoritarian personality is closely related to an authoritarian educational style and family structure (Adorno, Frenkel-Brunswik, Levinson, & Sanford, 1966). In the old states, the educational style in families became more and more permissive during the 1950s and 1960s. Despite the antidemocratic and dogmatic ideology and the authoritarian structure of organizations in the GDR, the increase in the practice of permissive education in families was apparently similar to the increase in the FRG. Studies after the *Wende* showed only slight differences between East and West in parents' educational styles as well as in the percentage of authoritarian personalities among youth. On average, parents in East Berlin were more strict and protective than in West Berlin, but the majority of parents in both parts answered very similarly (Uhlendorff, Krappmann, & Oswald, 1997). The relationship between authoritarian educational style in the family and authoritarianism of adolescents found in several studies in the old states (Hopf, Rieker, Sanden-Marcus, & Schmidt, 1995; Rippl et al., 1995) was true also for the new states. Hagan et al. (1995) found that power assertive education and failure at school, in combination with anomic tendencies (hanging around in large peer groups), explained right-wing orientation in the East as well as in the West. Kracke, Oepke, Wild, and Noack (in press) found a strong influence of parents in the socialization of antiforeigner and antidemocratic attitudes in both parts of Germany.

Conclusion

Most studies comparing East and West German adolescents during and after the *Wende* showed only small differences. Over a wide array of attitudes and behaviors, the similarities between adolescents from the East and West seem to be of greater importance than the differences. This may partly be due to a process of modernization during the 1970s and 1980s in the GDR that was similar to changes in the FRG. Over the years, youth surveys of the ZIJ found increasing individualization and growing orientation toward Western ideas and values (Förster et al., 1993; Müller, 1991; Schmeling, 1995). Supposedly, these tendencies were in part a result of the extensive consumption of Western television programs by Eastern adolescents during the last decade of the GDR.[1]

Differences between Eastern and Western adolescents after the unification can be interpreted with respect to conditions prevalent in the GDR and with respect to peculiarities of the transformation process. Adolescents in the East were more interested in politics than were adolescents in the West during the first phases of the unification and transformation process because of their immediate involvement in the ongoing changes. After 1990, the interest of Eastern adolescents decreased; it gradually reached the level of their Western age mates in 1992. Today, the extent of political interest among adolescents in the East is even less than in the West. This difference may be the result of Eastern youth's disillusionment after the excitements at the beginning of the unification process.

Although most adolescents as well as most adults in both parts of Germany identify with basic democratic values, more people in the East than in the West are skeptical about the functioning of the German democratic system. A majority of citizens in East and West trust in the main institutions of the political system, but this trust seems to have decreased during recent years and is less often expressed by members of the younger age cohorts than by members of the older cohorts. These tendencies are more pronounced in the East than in the West, and a kind of GDR nostalgia can be noticed in many parts of the Eastern society.

Satisfaction with the economic situation in general as well as the specific experiences of personal gains and losses as a result of the *Wende* affect attitudes toward the German democratic system and trust in governmental institutions by adolescents and adults alike. Therefore, economic development will be just as crucial to increasing the legitimacy of the democratic system as it was after World War II in West Germany (Almond & Verba, 1963). However, in addition to the problems faced after the war, the matching of economic conditions in East and West Germany (e.g., same living standard) is and will be of great importance. For as long as many people in the East are paid less for the same kind of work, consider themselves to be viewed as second-class citizens, and have lower chances in life than the population of the old states, their identification with the existing democratic system will remain biased. This biased identification may be transmitted to the next cohorts of children and adolescents by disappointed and dissatisfied parents, teachers, and neighbors. It is reinforced by strong feelings of insecurity with respect to increasing rates of delinquency, rising rents for housing, and a rapidly changing labor market. For a majority of citizens in the new states, social welfare, social security, and a caring government are much more important than civil rights.

The challenge for the future development of democracy in Germany is to promote political interest in the young generations in a way that leads to democratic political participation. The readiness to participate in legal democratic processes is more prevalent in the higher tracks than in the lower tracks of the school system. This is supported by the finding that adolescents in the lower tracks of the school system are more ready to use vandalism and aggression against persons to demonstrate their own political aims. Because such behavioral tendencies are related to a lack of interest in politics and a lack of information, teachers face the task of heightening political interest as well as raising the level of information.

It is an open question whether right-wing extremism can be counteracted by school education. The decreasing proportion of authoritarians after the age of 17 may be the result of school instruction. However, the fact that the percentage of authoritarians among adolescents is very similar in different countries may indicate the rather low success of schools in dealing with hard-core extremists. As postulated by Adorno et al. (1966), the syndrome of the authoritarian personality may still be transmitted through family processes today (Hopf et al., 1995; Hagan et al., 1995; Klein-Allermann et al., 1995) and is rather resistant to the educational efforts by schools. In normal times, the existence of a small number of authoritarians and right-wing extremists might pose little danger to a healthy democracy. Public opinion in Germany and political authorities take the stance that right-wing extremism can be controlled by the existing legal system, on the one hand, and by a policy of economic growth and social security, on the other.

But the potential danger lies in the possibility that a hard core of rightists and authoritarians will be able to attract more people in times of economic hardship and, thus, be able to initiate a broad antidemocratic social movement. To a certain extent, this danger is given in all former

Communist countries including East Germany, as long as economic growth and social security are not guaranteed and as long as large sections of the respective populations do not develop strong ties to the democratic institutions. Economic development and acceptance of the legitimacy of the democratic system are interrelated. Therefore, adolescents in the new states of Germany need secure future prospects as well as possibilities to practice democratic attitudes and behaviors inside and outside school.

Note

1. An alternative explanation of the striking similarities of Eastern and Western adolescents may lie in the pitfalls of cross-cultural research. In the literature the question was raised if the similarities were overestimated for statistical reasons (Boehnke & Merkens, 1995).

References

Adorno, T. W., Frenkel-Brunswik, E., Levinson, D. J. & Sanford, R. N. (1966). *The authoritarian personality*. New York: Plenum.

Almond, G. A., & Verba, S. (1963). *The civic culture: Political attitudes and democracy in five nations*. Princeton; NJ: Princeton University Press.

Altemeyer, B. (1988). *Enemies of freedom – understanding right-wing authoritarianism*. San Francisco: Jossey-Bass.

Barnes, S. H. & Kaase, M. (1979). *Political action: Mass participation in five Western democracies*. Beverly Hills, CA, London: Sage.

Boehnke, K., & Merkens, H. (1995). Sozialer Wandel als Methodenproblem [Social change as a methodological problem]. *Zeitschrift für Pädagogik, 41*, 731–744.

Bohnsack, R., Loos, P., Schäffer, B., Städler, K. & Wild, B. (1995). *Die Suche nach Gemeinsamkeit und die Gewalt der Gruppe* [Search for unity and the violence of the group]. Opladen: Leske & Budrich.

Bütow, B. (1995). Jugend im politischen Umbruch (Youth in time of political change). In U. Hoffmann-Lange (Ed.), *Jugend und Demokratie in Deutschland* [Youth and democracy in Germany] (pp. 85–107). Opladen: Leske & Budrich.

Bynner, J., & Ashford, S. (1994). Politics and participation: Some antecedents of young people's attitudes to the political system and political activity. *European Journal of Social Psychology, 24*, 223–236.

Easton, D. (1965). A re-assessment of the concept of political support. *British Journal of Political Science, 5*, 435–457.

Förster, P. (1994). Jungwähler Ost – Das unbekannte Wesen? [Youth voters from East Germany: The unknown citizen] *Media Spectrum, 1/1994*, 45–50.

Förster, P., Friedrich, W., Müller, H., & Schubarth, W. (1993). *Jugend Ost: Zwischen Hoffnung und Gewalt.* [Youth in East Germany: Between hope and violence] Opladen: Leske & Budrich.

Hagan, J., Merkens, H., & Boehnke, K., (1995). Delinquency and disdain: Social capital and the control of right-wing extremism among East and West Berlin youth. *American Journal of Sociology, 100,* 1028–1052.

Hille, B. (1991). Nicht nur Blauhemden. Die Situation der Jugendlichen in der ehemaligen DDR [Not only "Blue Shirts"! The situation of young people in the former GDR]. Reihe: *Deutschland – Report No. 13.* Melle: Ernst Knoth.

Hoffmann-Lange, U. (Ed.) (1995). *Jugend und Demokratie in Deutschland* [Youth and democracy in Germany]. Opladen: Leske & Budrich.

Hopf, C., Rieker, P., Sanden-Marcus, M., & Schmidt, C. (1995). *Familie und Rechtsextremismus* [Family and right-wing extremism]. Weinheim, Munich: Juventa.

IPOS (1996). *Youth survey* (unpublished, data communicated by U. Hoffmann-Lange to the author).

Jennings, M. K., & van Deth, J. W. (1990). *Continuities in political action.* New York: de Gruyter.

Jülisch, B.-R. (1996). Zwischen Engagement, Apathie und Resignation. Politische Orientierungen Jugendlicher in Ost-und West-Berlin [Between commitment, apathy, and resignation: Political orientations of adolescents in East and West Berlin]. In J. Mansel & A. Klocke (Eds.), *Die Jugend von Heute* [Adolescents of today] (pp. 69–87). Weinheim, Munich: Juventa.

Klein-Allermann, E., Kracke, B., Noack, P., & Hofer, M. (1995) Micro-and macrosocial conditions of adolescents' aggressiveness and antiforeigner attitudes. In J. Youniss (Ed.), After the wall: Family adaptions in East and West Germany (pp. 57–70). *New Directions for Child Development, 70,* San Francisco: Jossey-Bass.

Kracke, B., Oepke, M., Wild, E., & Noack, P. (in press). Adolescents, families, and German unification: The impact of social change on anti-foreigner and anti-democratic attitudes. In J. E. Nurmi (Ed.), *Adolescents, Cultures, and Conflicts: Growing up in Contemporary Europe.* New York: Garland.

Krüger, W. (1995) Vertrauen in Institutionen [Trust in institutions]. In U. Hoffmann-Lange (Ed.), *Jugend und Demokratie in Deutschland* [Youth and democracy in Germany] (pp. 245–274). Opladen: Leske & Budrich.

Kühnel, W., & Matuschek, I. (1995). *Gruppenprozesse und Devianz* [Group processes and deviance]. Weinheim, Munich: Juventa.

Lederer, G., & Kindervater, A. (1995). Internationale Vergleiche [International comparisons]. In G. Lederer & P. Schmidt (Eds.), *Autoritarismus und Gesellschaft* [Authoritarianism and society] (pp. 167–188). Opladen: Leske & Budrich.

Lemke, C. (1991). *Die Ursachen des Umbruchs 1989. Politische Sozialisation in der ehemaligen DDR* [Reasons for the breakdown of 1989: Political socialization in the former GDR]. Opladen: Westdeutscher Verlag.

McGranahan, D. V. (1946). A comparison of social attitudes among American and German youth. *Journal of Abnormal and Social Psychology, 41,* 245–257.

Melzer, W. (1992). *Jugend und Politik in Deutschland. Gesellschaftliche Einstellungen, Zukunftsorientierungen und Rechtsextremismus-Potential Jugendlicher in Ost-und Westdeutschland* [Youth and politics in Germany: Social attitudes, future orientations, and potential for right-wing extremism of young people in East and West Germany]. Opladen: Leske & Budrich.

Melzer, W., & Schubarth, W. (1995). Das Rechtsextremismussyndrom bei Schülerinnen und Schülern in Ost-und Westdeutschland [The right-wing extremism syndrome among female and male students in East and West Germany]. In W. Schubarth & W. Melzer (Eds.), *Schule, Gewalt und Re-*

chtsextremismus [School, violence, and right-wing extremism] (2nd ed., pp. 51–71). Opladen: Leske & Budrich.

Meulemann, H. (1996). *Werte und Wertewandel. Zur Identität einer geteilten und wieder vereinten Nation* [Values and value change: The identity of a divided and reunited nation]. Weinheim, Munich: Juventa.

Müller, H. (1991). Lebenswerte und nationale Identität [Human values and national identity]. In W. Friedrich & H. Griese (Eds.), *Jugend und Jugendforschung in der DDR* [Youth and research on youth in the GDR] (pp. 124–135). Opladen: Leske & Budrich.

Oesterreich, D. (1993). *Autoritäre Persönlichkeit und Gesellschaftsordnung. Der Stellenwert psychischer Faktoren für politische Einstellungen* [Authoritarian personality and social order: The significance of psychological factors for political attitudes]. Weinheim, Munich: Juventa.

Oswald, H., & Weiss, K. (1996, May). *Political socialization among youth in the Eastern part of Germany*. Paper presented at the 5th Biennial Conference of the European Association for Research on Adolescence, Liège, Belgium.

Rippl, S., & Boehnke, K. (1995). Authoritarianism: Adolescents from East and West Germany and the United States compared. In J. Youniss (Ed.), *After the wall: Family adaptions in East and West Germany* (pp. 57–70). *New Directions for Child Development, 70*. San Francisco: Jossey-Bass.

Rippl, S., Seipel, C., & Lederer, G. (1995). Wandel des Autoritarismus bei Jugendlichen in Westdeutschland: 1945–1991 [Change of authoritarianism among young people in West Germany]. In G. Lederer & P. Schmidt (Eds.), *Autoritarismus und Gesellschaft* [Authoritarianism and society] (pp. 102–135). Opladen: Leske & Budrich.

Schmeling, D. (1995). Jugend, Politik und politische Sozialisation in der DDR. Überlegungen zu einem widersprüchlichen Verhältnis und seinen problematischen Interpretationen. [Youth, politics, and political socialization in the GDR: Reflections upon a dialectical relationship and its problematic Interpretations]. In A. Bolz, C. Fischer & R. Herrmann (Eds.), *Deutschdeutsche Jugendforschung* [German-German research on youth]. (pp. 67–98). Weinheim, Munich: Juventa.

Schneider, H. (1995). Politische Partizipation – zwischen Krise und Wandel [Political participation – between crisis and change]. In U. Hoffmann-Lange (Ed.), *Jugend und Demokratie in Deutschland* [Youth and democracy in Germany]. (pp. 275–335). Opladen: Leske & Budrich.

Starke, U. (1995). Young people: Lifestyles, expectations and value orientations since the Wende. In E. Kolinsky (Ed.), *Between hope and fear: Everyday life in post-unification Germany* (pp. 155–175). Keele, England: Keele University Press.

Stiehler, H.-J. (1991). Blicke in den Medienalltag Jugendlicher [Views of young people's media use in everyday life]. In W. Hennig & W. Friedrich (Eds.), *Jugend in der DDR* [Youth in the GDR] (pp. 67–78). Weinheim, Munich: Juventa.

Stock, M. (1995). Jugendliche Subkulturen und gesellschaftlicher Wandel im Osten Deutschlands [Youth subcultures and social change in East Germany]. In H. Sydow, U. Schlegel & A. Helmke (Eds.), *Chancen und Risiken im Lebensverlauf: Beiträge zum gesellschaftlichen Wandel in Ostdeutschland* [Changes and risks during the life span: Contributions on social change in East Germany]. Berlin: Akademie Verlag.

Uhlendorff, H., Krappmann, L., & Oswald, H. (1997). Familien in Ost- und West-Berlin – Erziehungseinstellungen und Kinderfreundschaften [Families in

East and West Berlin – Educational attitudes and children's friendships]. *Zeitschrift für Pädagogik* 35–53.

Vollbrecht, R. (1993). Ost-west-deutsche Widersprüche. [East–West German contradictions]. Opladen: Leske & Budrich.

Zilch, D. (1992). Die FDJ-Mitgliederzahlen und Strukturen [FDJ membership numbers and FDJ structures]. In Jugendwerk der Deutschen Shell (Ed.), *Jugend '92* (vol. 3, pp. 61–79). Opladen: Leske & Budrich.

6. Community Service and Social Cognitive Development in German Adolescents

MANFRED HOFER

This chapter addresses German youth's participation in community service in four steps. First, it relates the German system of market economy to some of the special characteristics of community service in this country after unification. Second, it discusses possible effects of community service on adolescents' development. Third, it presents an empirical study that is based on the idea that community service may have positive effects on adolescent identity formation and improve adolescents' understanding of societal structures. The chapter closes with some reflections about the context of community service for adolescent development in German society.

Community Service in Germany

The concepts of "community service" and "volunteering" used interchangeably in this chapter do not have exact equivalents in the German language. The expressions *gemeinnuetzige Taetigkeit* and *soziales Ehrenamt* come closest. They traditionally describe voluntary and continuous unpaid work within an organization that is performed in the interest of others during one's spare time, the *soziales Ehrenamt* having a higher degree of organization and obligation (Gaskin, Smith & Paulwitz, 1996; Olk, 1992). In the last years, structural changes in the meaning of the two concepts weakened the foregoing criteria. Financial rewards are diverse and include expenses and pocket money. Community service activities in Germany also have a strong leisure component and only some are designed for direct promotion of public interests. And the voluntary criterion applies to most but not all cases meant by the two terms. For

Thanks are extended to Brigitte Hick, Sabine Hofer, and Mary Jo Pugh for their help in preparing this chapter.

instance, "civil service" in 1998 is a 13-month engagement in social work as an alternative to 10-months obligatory military service for young males. Thus, the traditional meaning of an engagement as a nonreciprocal charitable activity is fading. Instead, there is a rising interest in activities that allow creativity, adventure, and personal initiative, and that may enhance social reputation as well as individual gratification.

Role of Community Service in the German Social Welfare State

Community service in Germany has to be understood within the German "conservative" type of state-run welfare system in contrast to a neoliberal model that rests fully on the market economy and individual responsibility. The keystone of the German model is the state contribution to welfare. It is based on a philosophy that attributes causes of social friction to societal organization rather than to individual defects in morality. The state then takes care of those who are in need. Also, in the 1960s and 1970s, the state's duties were legally extended and social work was increasingly professionalized in order to satisfy legal entitlements. Between 1974 and 1990, the number of professionals in the juvenile aid institutions (e.g., kindergarten, homes for children and adolescents) rose by 50% (Rauschenbach, 1994).

At the same time, the need and readiness for voluntary social work declined markedly. The percentage of persons who viewed themselves as potential participants in community service declined from 49% in 1962 to 37% in 1979 (Olk, 1992). A 1994 survey of youth volunteering in Europe (Eurovol study) found that only 5% of nonvolunteers indicated they would volunteer if requested. This was the lowest percentage of all countries included in the study. Even among volunteers, only 37% agreed with the statement "It is a moral obligation of everyone to do unpaid work some time in his life" (Gaskin et al., 1996).

In German speaking countries, the concept of *Muendigkeit* as a major aim of education emphasizes the development of an autonomous personality more than civic identity and participation. Even though Germany matches other countries in having 90% of charitable organizations include volunteers, juvenile and welfare aid legislation regulating volunteer activities is nearly absent. Community service in Germany is not a natural part of the social system. The system of charitable organizations does not penetrate the different sectors of society. National, or even state, programs of the sort mentioned in Yates and Youniss's (1996b) review of community service activities in the United States do not exist. In the

Eurovol study (Gaskin et al., 1996), the institutions in which volunteers were engaged had problems integrating volunteers into their organizational structure, separating professional from nonprofessional work, and training and supervising the volunteers. Obviously, for German charitable institutions the cost–profit ratio with volunteers is uneven. They expressed a much higher degree of uncertainty than institutions in other European countries that volunteers offer special competencies useful for their work.

Uncertainty is also expressed by the volunteers, who felt that their engagement is not recognized sufficiently and their work could be organized much better. Furthermore, within families and schools, adolescents are not systematically encouraged, rewarded, supported, or trained in activities of this kind and community service is not part of school requirements. In fact, adolescents who want to volunteer have limited access to the relevant institutions, such as hospitals and homes for the elderly.

Some welfare institutions deplore the decline in readiness to engage in community service. At the same time, youth are increasingly interested in engaging in social professions. For example, since the 1970s, 350,000 to 450,000 young persons sought social work as a profession. Those who don't find a regular job engage in unpaid work. They regard volunteer activities as a means to gain professional experience and eventually attain a paid position. The government supports this engagement because it saves federal funds. Thus, the borders between community service and the job market overlap.

Despite the conditions just described, community service does play an increasing role in the social welfare system. Since the economic crisis in the 1980s, there have been a reduction in public assistance programs and a call for increased self-help and volunteerism. The leading welfare organizations estimate the value of volunteer work performed at approximately 180,000 full-time jobs (about 5.5 billion German marks) per year (Bendele, 1992).

In sum, attitudes in Germany are mixed. On the one hand, community service and volunteering are seen as forces important for society. On the other hand, they play a minor objective and subjective role. During his 1993 visit to Germany, Amitai Etzioni discussed his thesis of communitarism in which the idea of volunteering plays a central role. Although he received the approval of some political leaders, others feared communitarism might serve as a justification for continuing reduction of the social network. Volunteering in their view is a kind of charity of the rich to ease their bad conscience (Etzioni, 1994).

Prevalence of Community Service

Although community service is gaining importance in German society, very few empirical studies have been conducted. In the Eurovol study (Gaskin et al., 1996), 23% of 14- to 24-year-olds volunteered; two-thirds of them belonged to established organizations. Other European countries with welfare systems had higher rates of volunteering: Belgium, 37%; Great Britain, 37%; Ireland, 42%; Netherlands, 34%; and Sweden, 32%. Our own results, based on a longitudinal study addressing family processes under conditions of social change in East and West Germany (Noack, Hofer, Kracke, & Klein-Allermann, 1995), were similar. In 1992, when the first assessments took place, 13% of 15-year-olds from Mannheim (West Germany) and Leipzig (East Germany) indicated they were actively engaged at least once a week in a political group (such as a youth group run by the town council or a political party) or a church organization. One year later, the percentage of those who gave a positive answer dropped to 10%. At the third wave of measurement, in 1994, when participants were 17 years old, the percentage answering affirmatively again rose, up to 14%. These data are quite different from those in the U.S. literature. Yates and Youniss (1996a) reported that 22% of U.S. high school seniors said that they volunteered daily, weekly, or monthly, and 58% of 14- to 17-year-olds reported volunteering in the past 12 months.

Obviously, a major reason that community service in Germany plays a minor role is related to the features of the welfare system. This interpretation is strengthened by data from adults. Approximately 12% of the Mannheim and Leipzig parents indicated that they participated in some kind of social work, and that proportion resembles the amount of monthly involvement of their adolescent sons and daughters. In the Eurovol study, the population of adults showed a lower participation rate than young people (Gaskin et al., 1996). On the other hand, even if the degree of participation in Germany is low compared to that in other countries, an investment of 10% to 18% of the population amounts to a considerable contribution to the welfare system.

Type of Activities

Volunteers are involved in a wide range of organizations. Three main types of *gemeinnuetziger Arbeit* or *soziales Ehrenamt* can be distinguished. The first type of service is related to *sports*. Sport clubs are independent institutions that are subsidized by communities, but to a low degree.

Adolescent volunteers with advanced abilities train and supervise youth participants and organize tournaments. Thus, in Germany, sport activities can be regarded as community service because they meet the criteria of being voluntary, unpaid, and in the public interest. The second type is work aimed at helping people who have *special needs* such as the sick, poor, or elderly and children. For example, adolescents organized in the youth divisions of the Red Cross meet their groups regularly to give training in first aid and in "handling accidents." They are actively engaged as helpers with blood donations, as first-aid attendants at organized public events (e.g., sports meetings), and in spare time activities such as biking tours and Christmas celebrations. The abilities that they acquire can be used later in paid activities (e.g., work as emergency medical technicians). The third type of service is related to the *political process.* As in other democratic societies, public life in Germany is dependent on the voluntary participation of its citizens in societal, legal, and political matters at the community level. Adolescents can be involved in school organizations and also be members of various auxiliary political organizations for youth.

In our own study, adolescents were asked about their involvement in organizations. The answers were categorized as follows: church (e.g., administration of religious services for children or youth work), sports (e.g., training of children in a specific kind of sport or representation of adolescents in a sport organization), social welfare (e.g., ambulance workers or fire fighters), politics (e.g., member of political youth organization or member of peace movement), school (e.g., editorial staff of student journal or newspaper or school or class representative), and other. Church-based activities were most frequent (48% with 16-year-olds), followed by engagement in school (18%), sports (15%), and social service (15%). In the Eurovol study, sport and leisure organizations were most frequently mentioned (29%), followed by charity institutions (26%) and participation in the community (24%), education (24%), and religion (21%). A wide variety of other institutions such as animal protection, culture, health, and international development were mentioned (Gaskin, et al., 1996).

Stability and Intensity of Community Service

There is evidence from the U.S. literature that community service is a rather stable variable for adults and that relatively long-term commitments are possible in both adolescence and adulthood (e.g., Hart, Yates,

Fegley, & Wilson, 1995). In our study, we found stability of engagement over a 1-year period, $r(\phi) = .56$, $p < .01$ (for adolescents), $r(\phi) = .72$, $p < .01$ (for fathers), and $r(\phi) = .68$, $p < .01$ (for mothers). The continuity hypothesis is also strengthened when tested within activity categories. Contingency coefficients indicated high stability in type of activity (.80 for adolescents, .85 for fathers, and .80 for mothers). Once individuals become engaged in a specific area, they are likely to continue in that area.

With regard to intensity of engagement, in both the Eurovol study and our own study, German youth who were engaged in volunteering activities showed a higher degree of regular commitment than in other European countries: 85% were involved at least once a month in 1994. For this subgroup, the mean investment was 10 hours per month. These results are interesting considering that during adolescence many psychological changes occur. Because adolescents tend to be in an exploration phase, there is good reason to expect that many will abandon the activities they engage in at this time. Nevertheless, it seems that community service can play a central part in their development.

Family Background

In Germany, individuals engaged in service traditionally come from higher social classes and stable financial conditions. The Eurovol study and our own study indicated a correlation with education, but not with family income. We also found a strong within-family agglomeration of community service with correlations for father–adolescent (ϕ) = .30, $p < .01$) and mother–adolescent ($\phi = .32$, $p < .01$) engagement for 16-year-old adolescents. Adolescents tend also to be engaged in activities similar to their mothers' (contingency coefficient = .74) and fathers' (.82). These findings correspond to the literature showing that youth whose parents volunteer are more likely to volunteer themselves (Pugh & Condon, 1995).

Parents may shape their children's initiatives through their styles of interacting and the actions they model. In our longitudinal analysis, we had the opportunity to look at cross-lagged panel correlations. They revealed a relationship between fathers' engagement when adolescents were 16 years old and adolescents' engagement 1 year later ($\phi = .37$, $p < .01$). This correlation was significantly higher than the correlation between adolescents' engagement at age 16 and fathers' engagement 1 year later ($\phi = .19$, $p < .05$). A similar pattern occurred for kind of activity (contingency coefficient = .80, $p > .05$, vs. = .69, $p > .05$). Possibly, the intensity of relevant discussion inside the family is a mediating factor. Grundmann (1994) demonstrated that the issues discussed with parents and friends are correlated with the readiness of adolescents to participate in actions. For example, the more adolescents discussed environmental and pollution issues with families and friends, the more the adolescents endorsed actions in this field, such as spending money and working in groups to protect the environment. This corresponds to our finding that a scale of communication intensity in the family, as rated by adolescents at age 16, was significantly associated with their engagement at age 17 ($t = 4.2$, $p < .05$). The higher the communication score the more probable that the adolescents engaged in some kind of community service.

Motives to Participate in Community Service

There is little information about the motives of German youth involved in community service. One notion is that volunteers just stumble into activities, mostly by chance. In the Eurovol study, the primary means of initiating volunteering was being asked to participate (53%); the next was actively searching and offering help (34%). Accepting the idea of individualization and pluralization of the society (e.g., Beck, 1984) and their consequences for adolescents (Heitmeyer & Olk, 1990), adolescents see the need to deliberate about their decisions and to choose those activities that make most "sense" to them (Bartjes, 1996). What kind of sense do adolescents make out of their volunteering activities? One position is that adolescents are driven mainly by self-serving motives. Fend's (1991) study with 14- and 15-year-olds found that altruistic motivation was not significantly correlated with participation in school matters, whereas awareness of one's own competency was related. According to Fend, "egoistic motivations are widely distributed" (p. 183). In a study of German rural youth organizations from 1970 to 1990, the role of social-, activity-, and leisure-related reasons for participation rose over time from 4% to 30% (Bund der Deutschen Landjugend, 1995).

Yet, results from other studies show that this view is only part of the story. In the Eurovol study (Gaskin et al., 1996), even when volunteers began through personal contacts of family and friends, and 49% (more than in most other European nations) indicated as reasons for engagement their "own needs," 42% of them indicated "moral, social, and political convictions" and 24% "needs of the community" as reasons for volunteering. Obviously, egoistic and altruistic motives can be present simultaneously.

Bierhoff, Burkart, and Woersdoerfer (1995) classified motives of volunteers in the fire fighters, Red Cross, and Amnesty International using factor analysis. They found one altruistic factor, "feeling of responsibility," which had the highest mean, and three "egoistic" factors, "seeking leisure contacts," "seeking approval," and "needing knowledge about oneself." A similar mix of motives showed up in the "civil service" study (Bartje, 1996). Many young male adults viewed their civil service (alternative to the military service) as taking social responsibility by contributing to the well-being of others as well as benefiting in their own personality development. Thus, the young adults can experience personal agency, exercise methods of self-assertion, and learn about aspects of society that were hidden to them during school, and they begin an acceptable transition to the world of labor. In this view, it is not surprising to learn from the Eurovol study that German volunteers saw as the main advantages of their engagement the opportunities to act according to their moral, religious, and political principles; to meet other people and friends; to be active and healthy; to see results of their activity; to gain life experiences; and to learn new skills. For two-thirds of the youth, having fun was an additional advantage (Gaskin et al. 1996).

Community Service and Gender

The tension between paid and unpaid work, in part, results from a historical tradition in which women have to strive for professional work. Since the late nineteenth century, charity for the poor in Germany has been mainly in the hands of middle-class women who volunteered for community and welfare organizations. The history of female social work is partially complementary to the history of female gainful employment. Whenever females were excluded from gainful employment, they became involved in the "social front," with the result that females constitute the majority of employees in the service area (Rabe-Kleberg, 1992).

Data about gender, however, are mixed. According to Bendele (1992), 66% to 75% of community service participants are female. In our study and in the Eurovol study, however, no overall differences in the amount of community service and in the time spent serving were found. But there were substantial differences in the types of involvement. Male volunteers showed higher engagement in sport areas, whereas females' activities centered around the categories of education, church, and social service (Gaskin et al. 1996). Hence, traditional gender roles are still apparent in the service activities in which males and females engage.

Community Service in Unified Germany

Before unification in 1989, the population of East Germany lived in a Communist system that allegedly eliminated social problems. By definition, unemployment, poverty, criminal behavior, and substance abuse were absent in a Communist society. Community service, therefore, had to be of a different kind. Members of the Communist society were expected to engage in activities related to the Communist party and their workplace. At the same time, community ties were important for daily life in the East. Involvement in private networks was necessary to guarantee the provision of material goods needed to make life comfortable.

Since 1989, East German society has undergone radical change and has begun to adopt the structures of the Western social market economy, with its more individualistic and competitive features. In our study, in 1993 and 1994, adolescents, fathers, and mothers from East Germany were less likely to participate in community service than their peers in West Germany. Moreover, the type of activities in which individuals engaged differed substantially. East Germans rarely engaged in church-related activities but participated more frequently in political and school matters. Similarly, in the Eurovol study, religion-based activities were less evident in the East than in the West. Collecting money and participating in training activities played more of a role in the West than in the East (Gaskin et al. 1996).

These findings reflect both the former and the current societal structure. Political activities had been demanded in the former German Democratic Republic, whereas churches had been strongly suppressed. Since it is well known that in a market economy, education influences achievement in society, adolescents and their parents invest considerable energy in school-related activities. Hence, the opportunity structure a society provides for its members channels their service activities.

Theory of Individualization

In an attempt to interpret the low degree of volunteering by German youth and their stated motives, we draw on a theory that in the last decade has attracted intense attention. Beck (1986) called "individualization" a new mode of socialization in Germany. It rests on the notion that within the last 30 years, German society has become more complex. Production systems, families, economy, policy, and religion have differentiated themselves as separate systems. Members of society face many different roles and have to decide about their life course individually. One consequence is pluralism of possible life patterns. Individualization is not only seen as increase of individual freedom, but also as loss of traditional bounds, controls, and values as society has lost its orienting function for the individual. Youth no longer conveys a uniform status for everyone (Heitmeyer & Olk, 1990). Adolescents are facing a dilemma: As the process of making decisions about life has become more complex, decision supports and standards have declined. Increased alternatives are accompanied by increased insecurity. "Anything goes" is a fine thing as long as you know which of the alternatives are good for you. On the basis of this line of thinking, it seems plausible that adolescents display the tendency to assert themselves *(Selbstbehauptung)*. In maximizing the probability of making the right decision, adolescents look at their own needs and try to strengthen their individual position. As a consequence, they hesitate to invest in activities with low visible value. Given this context, volunteering is seen as an altruistic endeavor that may be too costly in investment of time and energy.

Community Service and Adolescent Development

In Germany, it is also commonly accepted that community service has advantages not only for those who receive help, but also for the individual who provides it. Acceptance, satisfaction, social contacts, self-awareness, and increased prestige are some of the symbolic values that allegedly result from the activity. In the Anglo-American literature, different kinds of effects have been studied more thoroughly. In a recent review, Yates and Youniss (1996a) specify three general types of outcomes: *agency, social relatedness,* and *moral–political awareness.* Overall effects appear positive, even though they are not large. The point, however, is that the range of activities covered by the term *community service* entails a wide variety of opportunities for experiences in the areas of self, social relations, and moral–political awareness.

Transcendent Experiences and Identity Development

Yates and Youniss (1996b) argue that community service by high school students offers opportunities for stimulating that aspect of the identity process that involves situating oneself within a social–historical context. They propose a theoretical framework based on the ideas of Erikson, who stressed the social–historical aspect of identity. Youth need to identify with values that supersede family and self and have historical continuity. Community activities facilitate interactions with people representing distant, but significant parts of societal structures. Experiences with them may play an important role in fostering reflections concerning the relationship between adolescents and general structural features of society like inequality, justice, and responsibility.

Transcendence is described as a process through which concrete experiences are transformed into abstract concepts. The use of language is an important means to construct knowledge that transcends and integrates the concrete "here and now." Daily interactions provide experiences based on perception and action. The accumulation of experiences of a similar kind and the reflection about them give rise to a process of abstraction, in which the concrete object becomes representative of an abstract category. Idiosyncratic variables are overcome and general and common attributes are seen.

Yates and Youniss (1996b) describe this process using a three-level scheme. At the first level, adolescents reflect on their stereotypes about formerly distant groups; they become able to see others as individuals with specific biographies, rather than in global and simple categories. At the second level, adolescents compare the situation of the people with whom they interact with their own situation. This frequently results in awareness of their own good fortune compared with that of those they serve. At the third level, they are searching for the causes of the social problems they experience in their work. They think about solutions and how they can help in changing the situation at hand. The end of the transcendence process is the ability to think about societal principles in abstract terms and to relate themselves to principles of the society in general.

This scheme was developed with a group of U.S. high school juniors who worked regularly at a soup kitchen as part of their required school curriculum. In a pilot study, we tried to apply the scheme to 54 German adolescents ages 15–19 (Hick & Kern, 1994). One group worked with children in church contexts. The second group consisted of Boy Scouts. Data about transcendence came from two sources, group interviews and individually administered questionnaires. The questions assessed reflections about service experiences on each of the three transcendence levels: "Which concrete experiences with other people do you have?" (Level 1:

experiences with other people); "What can you learn in this job?" "Has this work changed your personality in any way?" "Why did you choose to get involved here and not somewhere else?" (Level 2: changes they observed in themselves); and "What do you think is the 'social' aspect of this work?" "Do you believe that your commitment is doing any good?" "What do you think about the statement 'The Germans are on their way to an Ego-Society'?" (Level 3: the social value of their work).

The statements were categorized with high interrater reliability using a scheme for transcendence adapted from Yates and Youniss (1996b). Table 6.1 illustrates the three levels (and six sublevels) for the two samples of youth. The results show that as a tool to investigate the reflections of adolescents about their service, the transcendence concept can be applied to study the thinking of German adolescent volunteers as well. Of course, it had to be adapted to the specific contexts of church, work with children, and Boy Scouts.

A Study of Volunteering

Building on this pilot study, in another investigation we tried to find out whether adolescents involved in community service differed from non-involved agemates in transcendence, identity development, and political knowledge (Schnepf, 1995). Three associations were expected: (1) The experiences made in interactions with persons from remote parts of the society may stimulate thinking about one's relation to them. (2) In the course of transcendent reflections, adolescents may explore their own identity. They think about their position within interpersonal relations and within society. They gain clarity about their choices and values, political standpoint, and religious thoughts. (3) In the course of experiences in community service and transcendent reflections, adolescents may acquire general knowledge about aspects of society as their knowledge grows in both quantity and differentiation.

Sample. The volunteer group consisted of 38 male and female members of Youth Fire Police and Youth Red Cross, age 12 to 17 (mean age 14.7). The participants were recruited from a small city in southern Germany. Thirty-eight adolescents formed a matched comparison group and were recruited from three tracks of the German school system. The matching procedure was done according to sex, age (in years), school track, grade point average, and occupational status of at least one parent. Sixty-six percent of the participants were in the lowest school track (*Hauptschule*),

Table 6.1. Examples of the Three Levels of Transcendence for the Two Volunteer Groups

	Church group	Examples	Boy Scout group	Examples
Level 1: Little transcendence				
1.1	To observe children and adolescents more closely in their contacts	Well, the younger ones are far more spontaneous. It happens that a ... child interrupts the service. One cannot plan the children as one writes software for a computer. They have their own ... head.	To view oneself as a special kind of group	...Boy Scouts, what are they doing. It roughly means how can one lead a responsible life.
1.2	To check the initial opinions of children and adolescents	Well, often one changes one's opinion about people. Some time ago, for example, a few people came to the coffee room which were known to be Right-extremists or Nazis. But one talks and changes one's opinion. Yes, sometimes one needs to change one's opinion. One gets more open minded toward people that way.	To learn to recognize positive influences on one's own personality	It simply is a certain way of education. I didn't get this education from my parents but treated myself with this group.
Level 2: Intermediate transcendence				
2.1	To compare oneself with the children/ adolescents	Well, I had problems with this matter because it made me furious. I mean, to me it doesn't matter what brand name I am wearing. In former times we dressed up a little in the twelfth grade but today in the seventh or eighth grade they dress up.... I don't even go dancing that way. And they attend school like that.	Comparison between Boy Scouts and other societal groups	It is different from being in a sports club. There one is together as well, but somehow everybody is there depending on his own performance. But here this doesn't count.

2.2	To address general problems of children/adolescents. To examine causes and possible solutions	To take actions as a Boy Scout outside the group	Usually the whole background is the problem. We do all this in order to get kids away from TV and sometimes one realized that too much has already happened in their background, in the families . . . those are often the problematic children.	. . . [project] animal testing: We want to find out which companies are involved in animal testing and we asked around in pharmacies what their opinion is of that matter.

Level 3: Bigger transcendence

3.1	To reason about societal aspects that are not functioning well	To reflect on society, politics, morality, and religion	I believe this has much to do with our society. At the moment it is simply a matter of fact that we are very selfish and materialistic . . . Materialistic matters play a too important role nowadays.	Today in our competitive society it is simply like that that from all sides you are being told: You have to be the best. If your grades aren't good you'll be unemployed, have no place to stay, and depend on the welfare system.
3.2	To reflect about possible changes and their own activities	To reason about changes of existing problems, to develop a sense for taking action	We try to hand on values so that the world may change when this generation is parenting. A value destines the respect for the next, which comes too short, today, in my opinion. This respect is not there with the children today; they use the fist immediately. There are . . . lots of them in this group meeting, here. One has to explain to them that this is impossible.	Maybe awake others as well with this – the whole population, maybe.

32% in the middle (*Realschule*), and 13% in the highest (*Gymnasium*). Thirty-four percent of the participants were female.

Measures. To measure transcendence independently of the concrete experiences of their community service, two fictitious situations concerning social issues were presented. Participants were asked seven questions about homelessness and five questions about large families with more than three children. Questions were open-ended and directed toward the levels of transcendence. For example, the adolescents were asked to report their experiences with homeless people (Level 1), to compare themselves to people experiencing homelessness (Level 2), and to reflect on the causes and solutions of these social problems (Level 3). Again, a category system assessing transcendence based on Yates and Youniss (1996b) was constructed. All answers were rated according to transcendence level. An utterance was included in a category only when it was obvious to the raters that the subject had really understood the respective concept. Interrater agreement was 92%. Each participant was given an overall transcendence score calculated from average scores across the two situations.

To assess identity status, four subscales from Adams, Bennion, and Huh (1989) were translated into German. The friendship and recreation subscales were used to measure interpersonal identity, and the politics and religion subscales were used to measure ideological identity. The instrument consisted of 32 statements (e.g., "I have only friends with which my parents agree," "I am not really interested in politics; it isn't fun"). Response options ranged from "1 = totally correct" to "6 = totally incorrect." According to the cut-off provided by Adams et al., the scores were grouped into the following categories: diffusion, foreclosure, moratorium, and achievement. The authors report internal consistencies of .58 and .80 for the interpersonal subscales and .62 and .75 for the ideological subscales (Adams et al., 1989).

Knowledge of the functioning of the social welfare system in Germany was assessed by six multiple choice questions addressing the concepts of "welfare aid allowance," "earnings-related benefits," "income tax," "welfare state," "payments of health insurance," and "child allowances." For example, one question was "What does 'welfare state' mean?" The following response options were provided:

(a) The state gives to anybody as much as he or she needs,
(b) the state guarantees a minimum income,

(c) the state does not provide support for the unemployed,
(d) I don't really know.

For this measure, internal consistency (Cronbach's alpha) was .56.

Results. The Wilcoxon test indicated that transcendence scores were significantly higher for service volunteers (M = 1.45) than for the matched comparison group (M = 1.02, p < .05). Male and female adolescents did not differ in their level of transcendence. Grade point average correlated significantly with transcendence, r = .24, p < .05; better grades were associated with higher transcendence scores. The t test indicated that older adolescents (15–17 years, M = 1.43) achieved significantly higher transcendence scores than younger adolescents (12–14 years, M = 1.00), p < .05.

The scores for the two identity measures were ranked in the following order: Diffusion, Foreclosure, Moratorium, Achievement. In interpersonal identity, most of the adolescents were in the Moratorium status. Participants in the volunteer group, however, had higher status scores than those in the comparison group (Wilcoxon test, p < .05, one-tailed). In the volunteer group, more participants had reached the Achievement group (33% vs. 24%), whereas in the comparison group more participants had remained in the Diffusion group (18% vs. 5%). With regard to ideological identity, most of the participants had remained in the Diffusion group and no significant difference between the two groups were found.

Volunteer participants scored higher in knowledge about the nation's welfare system (M = 2.68) than the comparison group (M = 2.14). The Wilcoxon one-tailed test indicated that this difference was of marginal significance (p < .10). Knowledge also correlated with age (r = .36, p < .01) and with duration of community service (r = .24, p < .05).

The scenario technique seems to be an efficient means of generating transcendent reflection. The transcendence scheme thus can be used to investigate the process as well as the effect of community service. There were hints of the impact of community service on transcendent reflection, interpersonal identity status, and abstract knowledge about society. The use of a matched comparison group strengthens our conclusions regarding the effect of service. Moreover, participants in the volunteer group were not favored by the use of the two scenarios because their service activities were not directly related to homelessness or large families. Answers to the questions about the social system cannot be inferred readily from experiences volunteers had in their community service. The volunteers in the study were not participating in activities that provided direct and intense interactions with members of distant groups in the society. They were not regularly confronted with real emergency situations like acute health problems or fire alarms. Still, differences emerged.

Developmental Contexts for Adolescents in German Society

The last part of the chapter addresses the question of desirability of community service in terms of society and its individual members. Unpaid work is in the public interest because it saves the costs of the service provided and is essential for the functioning of the democratic political system. In Germany, as a consequence of the global economic crisis of industrialized countries and of the immense costs related to political unification, discussions about cost savings are quite serious. Difficult times have engendered the spirit of communitarianism, which stresses the responsibility of the individual citizen within the community (see Etzioni, 1994), and voluntarism has entered into political discussions at the state and local levels. Very slowly, a climate of cooperation and mutual help may evolve within the coming decades.

Berger and Luckmann's (1995) recent reflections make another relevant aspect of community service visible. They state that personal identity consists in subjective control over consistent actions for which objective responsibility is taken. Children gradually learn to understand their own behavior as meaningful within a historical pattern of experiences when they learn to understand the meaning of their partner's behavior, which is determined by the collective meaning in the society. Collective meanings are produced and distributed by primary institutions created by the society. The authors parallel Beck's (1986) thinking in diagnosing modern societies as split systems that do not act according to a uniform value system. Modern pluralism requires individuals to reconcile different and sometimes opposing value systems. For example, children must contend with splits in values between the home and institutions outside the home. This condition can produce "subjective crises of meaning." A crisis of meaning consists in a loss of *Selbstverstaendlichkeit*, of obviousness, of the taken-for-granted and normality in life.

Berger and Luckmann diagnose only a rankling, latent crisis of meaning. They see "intermediary institutions" as forces in society that can mitigate or even neutralize the crisis. Berger and Luckmann designate intermediary institutions as mediating effectively between individuals and established action patterns. On the one hand, they produce and distribute meaning; on the other, they provide individuals with the opportunity to express their personal values and to contribute to the value system of the society. For example, psychotherapy, counseling, adult education, and mass media can mediate between collective and individual experience. Intermediary institutions do not stay in the center of society as primary institutions but serve specialized functions and offer interpretations for typical problems. Berger and Luckmann point out that mediating structures are most likely to be successful when institutions address small life sectors, when they act at the local level, and when they offer opportunities to construct meaning within interactions. The authors do not address volunteering, but it could function readily as an intermediate institution. Volunteerism operates at a local level and addresses small sectors of life.

Erikson assumes a general need in adolescents to transcend concrete experiences to build a mature identity that links past, present, and future. Yates and Youniss (1996b) assert that community service is an effective way to provide these experiences, which may help deal with a society that has wide variations in education, income, and wealth and in which individuals face quite high risks in their lives. It is unclear whether in a different society these assumptions would still hold. For instance, does community service in a welfare society affect individual development? (See also Flanagan, Jonsson, Botcheva, et al., chapter 7 this volume.) Germany is a welfare society, but, according to Berger and Luckmann's analysis, it is also a society with high risk for crises of meaning. Our preliminary results suggest that volunteering has positive effects. The following reflections on how to promote individual development are based on this assumption.

Which psychological processes should be promoted? In terms of the framework chosen in this chapter, advancement in the level of transcendent thinking seems a worthwhile goal to be fostered by educational means. Adolescents need to reflect about the here and now and to find connections among the self, the family, and the structures of society. They need to relate present experience to the past and the future. This process can be useful for the individual and perhaps for the society in which the individual lives.

Which types of conditions or contexts help to reach the goal? Probably, different aspects of volunteering have different effects on adolescents. Research on the question of differential work characteristics should be done along the line of Pugh and Condon (1996), who looked at the relationship between specific characteristics of service activities and adolescents' developmental outcomes. The authors classified activities as "assisting" if students performed organizational or desk work in their service projects; as "teaching" if they tutored, coached, or taught classes; and "attending" if they were involved in interactive types of service in which they attended to the visible needs of individuals or a group such as the poor and the homeless. They found that youth who performed "attending" service activities perceived more opportunities for *agency* and *cognitive challenge* than did youth who performed "assisting" and "teaching" activities.

Data on benefits from different kinds of volunteering have also been collected in the Eurovol study. The most frequent types of volunteer activities were care for other persons (32%), training and educating (28%), collecting money (25%), and working on committees (25%). Most fun was experienced in training activities. Work in committees provided the most frequent social opportunities. Counseling was rated as adding the most to life experience, whereas personal care generally was rated low, especially in social recognition (Gaskin et al., 1996). Studies like these are needed to design volunteer activities and to work out appropriate programs and recommendations. On the basis of Berger and Luckmann's (1995) analysis, research should center on the question of how volunteers can participate actively in the construction of meaning.

Which actions or experiences may create the conditions necessary to enhance adolescents' development? In their discussion of moral commitment in youth, Hart et al. (1995) described context characteristics that may have influence on the development of transcendence. These include warm relationships with persons who themselves have a sense of historical continuity and social responsibility, opportunities to participate in activities that provide experiences with individuals or groups outside the microworlds of family and peers, and active involvement in discussions about social issues that link individual lives to societal structures. In our view, a focus should be placed on the creation of opportunity structures, incentives, and discursive and participatory educational structures.

Opportunities for volunteering can be provided in different, but carefully selected, fields. For instance, volunteer positions at homes for the elderly, libraries, hospitals, and even theaters could be promoted for youth. This is not an easy task. Integrating outsiders with no professional qualification in routinized professional systems requires special organizational structures that may also have legal implications. Practices in U.S. institutions, however, may provide useful models to pursue in Germany.

Second, educational programs should be offered in schools to encourage young children to volunteer, to train them, and to give them incentives for participation. New organizational forms of social work may begin to develop, such as community service as an alternative to military service and respective possibilities for females. Such programs are attractive because they provide some forms of nonmonetary incentive such as an easy transition to university studies and work life, constructive work to perform during a jobless period, and relevant participation in the local public life.

Third, a culture of participatory discussion in families and schools could enhance reflections of adolescents about issues of morality and justice and help them to link the self with society. Argumentative discussions in the family, even if they are controversial and restricted to personal issues, may enhance intellectual and moral development and facilitate the transformation of the parent–child relationship. Moreover, such discussions may have a positive impact on readiness to be involved in societal matters. Connected to this and in the tradition of Kohlberg's conception of the "just community school," Oser and Althof (1992) propose the vision of a school in which learning rests on experience rather than on acquisition of abstract knowledge and in which students and teachers work jointly in building democratic structures. Community service surely fits this scheme, especially because it seems to promote transcendent thinking.

References

Adams, G., Bennion, L., & Huh, K. (1989). *Objective measure of ego identity status: A reference manual.* Department of Family Relations and Applied Nutrition, University of Guelph, Guelph, Ontario, Canada.

Bartjes, H. (1996). *Der Zivildienst als Sozialisationsinstanz* [The "civil service" as socialization agent]. Weinheim/Munich: Juventa

Beck, U. (1986). *Risikogesellschaft* [Risk society]. Frankfurt/M.: Suhrkamp.

Bendele, U. (1992). Soziale Hilfen zu Discountpreisen [Social help at discount prices.]. In S. Mueller & T. Rauschenbach (Eds.), *Das soziale Ehrenamt. Nuetzliche Arbeit zum Nulltarif* (2nd ed., pp. 71–86). Weinheim /Munich: Juventa.

Berger, P. L., & Luckmann, T. (1995). *Modernitaet, Pluralismus und Sinnkrise* [Modernity, plurality, and crisis of meaning]. Guetersloh: Bertelsmann.

Bierhoff, H. W., Burkart, T., & Woernsdoerfer, C. (1995). Einstellungen und Motive ehrenamtlicher Helfer [Attitudes and motives of volunteers]. *Gruppendynamik, 26,* 373–386.

Bund der Deutschen Landjugend (Ed.) (1995). *Landjugenportrait '90. Kurzfassung* [Portrait of rural youth] (2nd ed.). Muenster: Landwirtschaftsverband.

Etzioni, A. (1994). Die Entdeckung des "Dritten Sektors" [The discovery of the "Third Sector"]. *Psychologie Heute, 21(8)* 22–25.

Fend, H. (1991). *Identitaetsentwicklung in der Adoleszenz* [Identity development in adolescence] (Vol. 2). Bern: Huber.

Gaskin, K., Smith, J. D., & Paulwitz, I. (Eds.). (1996). *Ein neues buergerliches Europa. Eine Untersuchung zur Verbreitung und Rolle von Volunteering in zehn Laendern.* Freiburg: Lambertus. (English Original: Gaskin, K., & Davis, J. (1995). A new civic Europe? A study of the extent and role of volunteering. London: Volunteer Centre UK.)

Grundmann, M. (1994). *Diskussionsthemen im Freundes-und Familienkreis: Ihr Einfluss auf soziales Engagement bei Ost-und Westberliner Jugendlichen* [Discussion themes with friends and in the family]. Poster presented at the 39th Biennial Meeting of the German Psychological Association, Hamburg

Hart, D., Yates, M., Fegley, S., & Wilson, G. (1995). Moral commitment in innercity adolescents. In M. Killen & D. Hart (Eds.). *Morality in everyday life.* (pp. 317–341). New York: Cambridge University Press.

Heitmeyer, W., & Olk, T. (Eds.) (1990). Individualisierung von Jugend [Individualization of youth]. Weinheim/Munich: Juventa.

Hick, B., & Kern, S. (1994). *Auswirkungen freiwilliger sozialer Taetigkeit auf die Entwicklung von Jugendlichen* [Effects of community service on the development of adolescents]. Unpublished master's thesis; University of Mannheim.

Noack, P., Hofer, M., Kracke, B., & Klein-Allermann, E. (1995). Adolescents and their parents facing social change: Families in East and West Germany after unification. In P. Noack, M. Hofer, & J. Youniss (Eds.), *Psychological responses to social change: Human development in changing environments* (pp. 129–148). Berlin/New York: de Gruyter.

Olk, T. (1992). Zwischen Hausarbeit und Beruf. Ehrenamtliches Engagement in der aktuellen sozialpolitischen Diskussion [Community service in the actual discussion of socal policy]. In S. Mueller & T. Rauschenbach (Eds.). *Das soziale Ehrenamt* (2nd ed., pp. 19–36). Weinheim/Munich: Juventa.

Oser, F., & Althoff W. (1992). *Moralische Selbstbestimmung* [Moral self-determination]. Stuttgart: Klett-Cotta.

Pugh, M. J., & Condon, G. (1996, March). *Community service and developmental opportunities: All service is not created equal.* Poster presented at the Biennial Meeting of the Society for Research on Adolescence, Boston, MA.

Rabe-Kleberg, U. (1992). Wenn der Beruf zum Ehrenamt wird [When the job becomes volunteering]. In S. Mueller & T. Rauschenbach (Eds.), *Das soziale Ehrenamt. Nuetzliche Arbeit zum Nulltarif* (2nd ed., pp. 87–101). Weinheim/Munich: Juventa.

Rauschenbach, T. (1994). Wo gehts hin mit dem Ehrenamt? [What direction goes the volunteering?]. *Sozialpaedagogik, 36,* 5–17.

Schnepf, H. (1995). *Erfahrungstranszendenz bei ehrenamtlich taetigen Jugendlichen im Vergleich mit nicht ehrenamtlich taetigen Jugendlichen.* [Transcendence of volunteering adolescents compared with a control group]. Unpublished master's thesis, University of Mannheim.

Yates, M., & Youniss, J. (1996a). A developmental perspective on community service in adolescence. *Social Development, 5,* 85–111.

Yates, M., & Youniss, J. (1996b). Community service and identity development in adolescents. *Journal of Research on Adolescence, 6,* 271–284.

7. Adolescents and the "Social Contract": Developmental Roots of Citizenship in Seven Countries

CONNIE FLANAGAN, BRITTA JONSSON, LUBA BOTCHEVA, BENO CSAPO, JENNIFER BOWES, PETER MACEK, IRINA AVERINA, AND ELENA SHEBLANOVA

> Genuine politics – politics worthy of the name, and the only politics I am willing to devote myself to – is simply a matter of serving those around us: serving the community, and serving those who will come after us. Its deepest roots are moral because it is a responsibility, expressed through action, to and for the whole.   (V. Havel, 1992)

According to Walzer (1989), "a citizen is, most simply, a member of a political community, entitled to whatever prerogatives and encumbered with whatever responsibilities are attached to membership. The word comes to us from the Latin *civis*; the Greek equivalent is *polites*, member of the polis, from which comes our political" (p. 211). Becoming a citizen, assuming the rights and responsibilities of membership in a social group, is a marker of attaining adult status in many societies. But what prepares people to assume those responsibilities? How do they come to understand and exercise their civic rights? What motivates them to become engaged in civil society?

The project discussed in this chapter, Adolescents' Interpretation of the "Social Contract," addresses such issues. We focus on the roots of citizenship and ways that young people develop a commitment to the commonwealth. By the *social contract* we refer to the set of mutual rights and obligations binding citizens with their polity. We contend that there is an intergenerational bargain implied in the process of social integration, that is, a promise that one will enjoy the rights and reap the benefits of the social order if s/he lives by its rules and fulfills the responsibilities of membership. Of course, social change upsets the conditions of the bargain. Thus, it is not surprising that attention to questions of citizen-

Adolescents' Interpretation of the "Social Contract" is a collaborative project directed by Connie Flanagan. This project was supported in part by grants from the William T. Grant Foundation and the Johann Jacobs Foundation to Connie Flanagan.

ship – what it means and how it is fostered – tends to increase when concerns about the stability of political regimes are on the rise. Such anxieties may arise when new, untested democracies are born, the situation, for example, in contemporary Central and Eastern Europe. Concerns are also voiced when massive social movements challenge the status quo, as was the case in the youth movements of the 1960s in Europe, Australia, and the United States.

In recent years, the themes of political stability and civic trust have again become prominent in public discourse. Several factors may be contributing to these apprehensions. First, trends of rising self-interest among adults and adolescents in Western democracies have motivated discussions about whether the values of the market have extinguished commitments to the commonwealth. Engaging youth in service to their communities has been recommended as an antidote to these trends. Second, political stability is jeopardized when the economic security of large segments of a population erodes. Under the pressures of globalization, opportunities for secure employment and a good standard of living, especially for people with little formal education, are diminishing. Relatedly, the stage of adolescence, the time before the age of majority, has become a protracted period in postindustrial societies, leaving many youth with no clear social niche. If large numbers of young people feel disaffected from the political system, its stability may be undermined.

The lack of a social niche is a problem shared by youth across industrialized societies, but it is exacerbated by the pace and unpredictability of social change in Central and Eastern Europe. During the era of state socialism, partnerships between industries and schools ensured a relatively smooth school-to-work transition with students guaranteed a job after completing their education. In the 1990s there have been profound changes in the social contracts of these countries. As many state-run enterprises closed, unemployment soared, and youth, especially those with few skills and little experience, were disproportionately affected.

The terms of the new contract imply more individual initiative and less reliance on the state. However, it seems that many members of the current generation as well as their parents would prefer aspects of the old bargain. About half of the several hundred Bulgarian teens in a recent study felt that the state should take care of most needs in society (Botcheva & Kitanov, 1996). In Hungary, Csapo (1995) found that adolescents' initial euphoria about political and economic changes in 1989 had declined by 1993 as the hard realities of the transition set in. The most pessimistic youth felt that the problems associated with the transition were inherent in the new social order, whereas the optimists (who were in the majority) felt such problems were a temporary phenomenon. Education may account for some of these differences in outlook since the better educated are more likely to reap benefits in the new social order. In fact, Macek, Tyrlik, and Kostron (1996) have shown that better educated youth in the Czech Republic tend to assess the social changes there more positively than their less educated peers.

Scholars seeking answers to the question of how polities are stabilized point to the importance of diffuse support in the population for the principles of the social order (Easton & Dennis, 1969). Our project focuses on the developmental roots of that diffuse support by examining ways that young people in different countries and from different social backgrounds within a country construct an understanding of the contract that binds members of society together. Drawing from Vygotsky (1978), we contend that an individual's thinking about and relationship to the polity are the product of social activity. In this chapter, we argue that engagement in the voluntary sector connects young people to the broader polity, and, in that process, they develop an understanding of themselves as civic actors, engaged in the issues and capable of addressing the problems of their polity.

Our findings are based on a survey of more than 5,600 12- to 19-year-olds from seven countries. The decision to survey a broad age range was based on our interest in uncovering developmental change in young people's perceptions of the social contract as well as in their civic values and commitments. The choice of countries for the study (Australia, Bulgaria, the Czech Republic, Hungary, Russia, Sweden, and the United States) was based on two criteria: (a) the length of their experience as democracies and (b) the role of the state in the provision of social services.

Four countries in the study (Russia, Bulgaria, the Czech Republic, and Hungary) could be considered fledgling democracies. Because these nations have had only a short period when democratic institutions or infrastructure could develop, we have labeled them "transitional societies." The current generation of young people and several that preceded it grew up with relatively little experience of a political community in the sense of opportunities to practice open public debate (Karpati, 1996). Prior to 1990, one of the major tasks of schools, media, and youth organizations was to achieve political homogenization by minimizing differences between individuals (Karpati, 1996; Pastuovic, 1993). The political activity of youth in that era was restricted to officially sanctioned groups such as the Young Pioneer and Comsomol organizations. Membership, although quite high among secondary school students, was expected, if not required (Csapo, 1994).

Since 1990 building democratic societies has been a high priority of these nations, and changes in curricular content and instructional styles in schools have been recommended as primary means for achieving that goal (Rust, Knost, & Wichmann, 1994). Gradually, membership in youth organizations including the Boy and Girl Scouts, 4-H, and church-related groups is growing, replacing the void left by the disintegration of groups like the Young Pioneers. There is consensus in these countries about the need to prepare young people to participate in democratic societies but less agreement about how to accomplish that objective. Much of the focus has been on curricular reform. However, since teachers who trained and worked under the old system would assume primary responsibility, there is some concern about their reverting to past practices.

During the Soviet era, the situation in schools mirrored that in society, where low levels of civic trust and political efficacy constrained public discourse and political action. There were, however, significant differences between countries in the amount of constraint and the freedom to voice dissenting opinions. For example, in the 1980s, political satire was openly broadcast on Hungarian television, and signs of youth's disaffection from the official ideology were apparent as early as the seventies and eighties. Not only were there subgroups of youth who were clearly disaffected from the system, but it was young people who organized demonstrations to commemorate the 1848 struggle of Hungary for independence from Austria (Csapo, 1994). These actions reflected a growing national spirit that contradicted the politics of international socialism.

In contrast to the relative freedom in Hungary, in Czechoslovakia a so-called double morality was obvious in the caution with which people monitored their interactions in public (Macek & Rabusic, 1994; Scheye, 1991). Only in private interactions did many feel free to speak their mind. In such a context where political parties were banned, voluntary associations played a critical role as an outlet for dissent and a means of organizing political opposition. According to Havel (1990), the roots of citizen movements such as KOR, Solidarity, Neues Forum, Charter 77, and Civic Forum can be traced to the opportunities people had in nongovernment and nonpublic contexts to be authentic and to feel free to disagree. Eventually these movements were successful in achieving the political reforms of the early 1990s. And, as in most historical movements, youth played a prominent role.

In Bulgaria youth were active in the strikes and demonstrations of 1990–1991, movements that later led to changes in the government. Representatives of the student movement participated in the work of parliament in the early days of political change there. In Hungary the first new political party was a youth party with membership restricted to those under the age of 35. FIDESZ, the Alliance of Young Democrats, which was already organized in 1988 when the Communist party was still in power, gained 21 seats in the first free parliamentary election of 1990. However, in the years since free elections in the Central and East European nations, many students and young people have withdrawn from the political fray. Despite early euphoria about the pace at which political change was expected to occur, scholars now believe the work of building the new democracies will take generations (Keri, 1996).

In these four transitional societies, the state has played a major role in providing entitlements. However, the standard of living for the average family is quite low. Since the introduction of fiscal shock therapy and rapid privatization in the early 1990s, the results of free elections have swung back and forth on the political spectrum as the citizens of these nations seek a balance between the efficiencies of private enterprise and the assurances of state entitlement and welfare programs.

All of the remaining three countries in the study (Australia, Sweden, and the United States) have enjoyed longer histories as democratic polities with practices of electoral politics in place and partisan allegiances that reflect group interests relatively stable. Practices in schools, families, and youth organizations that are meant to prepare young people for civic participation have evolved. In each of these countries children, especially those from middle-class backgrounds, are encouraged to form their own opinions and to voice them, even if that means disagreeing with adult authorities (Flanagan et al. 1996). Underlying such practices is the belief that the foundation of a democratic system is a citizenry that can think independently and disagree in a civil fashion.

Youth groups such as Scouts and 4-H serve a similar function in stabilizing the polity. Although typically thought of as apolitical organizations, these groups teach young people life skills that integrate them into the extant social order. For example, the principles of a market economy are learned via projects that emphasize entrepreneurship, individual initiative, and competition for awards. Democratic principles of tolerance are learned in workshops and clubs; cooperation and interdependence are fostered via leadership training and group projects. By contributing to the norms, ethics, and values of youth, these voluntary organizations strengthen support for the polity as well as commitments to the principles of the market in the next generation.

As the primary educational institutions of democratic societies, schools have a special charge to foster the civic competencies of the next generation, and research has shown that certain practices have proved effective in accomplishing that goal. For example, in classrooms where students are free to dissent and are also expected to listen to different perspectives, students are more aware of and able to think critically about civic issues (Newmann, 1990), are more tolerant of dissenting opinions (Ehman, 1980), and know more about international affairs (Torney-Purta & Lansdale, 1986).

The three stable democracies in our study can be contrasted on a second dimension of interest to the project, that is, the role of the state in providing social welfare. With its ardent commitment to equality in social distribution and broad entitlements for residents, Sweden epitomizes the modern social welfare state (Jonsson, 1996). In a society with such an interpretation of the social contract, the civic responsibility of a good citizen is to contribute to the equalizing of outcomes by paying a significant portion of personal income toward the public welfare.

By contrast, the principles of an "opportunity" society prevail in the United States (Verba & Orren, 1985). The rules of the social contract emphasize an even playing field where each individual is supposed to have an equal chance to prove him/herself. But there is an expectation of uneven outcomes. Thus, many Americans tolerate large disparities in income believing that such disparities are due to individual differences in effort or merit. In fact, the United States has the dubious distinction among the countries in our study of having the largest differences in income and the fewest entitlements for its members. Even in the political arena, a supposedly level playing field, inequalities in participation are more pronounced in the United States than in other democratic countries (Verba, Nie, & Kim, 1978). However, a high proportion of the political participation that does take place is motivated by concerns for the broader community (Jennings, 1991). Individuals are encouraged to compensate for what the system fails to provide. Charity and philanthropy are considered acts of goodwill to the needy, and young people are introduced to these norms via volunteer projects in schools and youth organizations.

Like the United States, Australia is committed to an individualist ethic but one that is tempered by strong social welfare assurances. Not only does government assistance subsidize the welfare of a broad range of groups, but the health care of the entire population is insured by a system of socialized medicine. These entitlements are supported by a progressive tax system. However, the fact that every large city has a homeless population suggests that individuals do fall through the cracks, and there are voluntary efforts by charitable groups to respond to such needs. Approximately 19% of the population 16 years of age and older does some type of volunteer work, but there is not a strong emphasis on getting adolescents involved.

In this chapter we highlight some of the results of our collaborative project, which indicate that voluntary work in the community may enable young people across these different types of polities to identify with the commonwealth and the contributions they can make to it. The advantage of such a cross-national study is that it allows us to look both for commonalities across countries as well as for differences between them in the definition of civic responsibility and the practices that promote it. By comparing volunteers within each country with their compatriots who have not been volunteers we believe claims can be made that voluntary work is associated with adolescents' commitment to the commonwealth across different types of polities. At the same time, the content of that voluntary work is likely to differ between countries.

We present differences between countries in terms of the percentage of youth engaged in voluntary work and the hierarchy of civic values they endorse and interpret these differences in light of the contrasting social contracts and concepts of citizenship espoused in the countries. Because societies differ in the way they have defined social goals and in what they consider just policies (Dworkin, 1978), we expect that youth growing up in different systems would have distinct ideas about the role of the state and the rights and obligations of citizens. Finally, we elaborate on the distinct forms of voluntary work across countries and discuss the special functions or meanings of engaging in such activity in different political contexts (Goodnow, 1996).

Connecting Community Service to Citizenship

As part of the survey for our study, we asked youth in each country, "Do you ever do volunteer work in the community?" The response to this question alone provides interesting information (see Table 7.1) and

Table 7.1. *Patterns of Youth Volunteering Across Seven Countries*

Do you ever do volunteer work in the community?

	Australia	U.S.	Sweden	Hungary	Cz. Rep.	Bulgaria	Russia
Yes (%)[a]	149 (28.1)	366 (51.5)	152 (19.9)	605 (60.4)	515 (46.3)	390 (42.2)	143 (23.4)
No	381	345	610	397	597	535	469

[a]Percentage of youth in each country who indicate they do volunteer work is shown in parentheses.

we focus on two findings. First, according to the youth's reports, volunteering in the community is a practice in all of these countries – from a "low" of nearly 20% of the Swedish sample to a high of 60% in Hungary. In fact, in four countries (Bulgaria, the Czech Republic, Hungary, and the United States) nearly half or more of the adolescents reported that they had engaged in some type of voluntary effort. Second, we can infer that the differences between countries in terms of the percentage of youth who do such work reflect, in part, the social contracts and norms in each country. For example, it is not surprising that Swedish youth are the least likely to volunteer. In a country with a high standard of living and a strong social welfare system, the need for volunteers is minimal. One of the rights of citizenship is an assurance from the state that people's needs and the health of the whole community will be met. The social contract also provides many guarantees in Australia, and there is not a strong emphasis on youth involvement in community service. The main responsibility of a young person is to do well in school and qualify for higher education. Finally, the large number of American youth who have volunteered points to the emphasis on such activity in general and in schools in particular. The United States prides itself on a tradition of community volunteering, and there has been a trend in recent years of school districts' mandating the practice as a prerequisite for high school graduation.

The percentage of youth who report they have done volunteer work is high in three of the four transitional societies with Russia an exception to this pattern. The relatively low percentage of Russian youth reflects the fact that this is not a common practice for any age group in the country. By comparison, youth from Hungary, Bulgaria, and the Czech Republic report very high rates of participation, a result that should be understood within a historical context. In the socialist era, volunteering was an activity expected of good citizens, a way to express one's loyalty and patriotism. Not only was it normative, but there were some social pressures to volunteer. In such a milieu, one could question the extent to which youth were genuinely motivated to volunteer. However, this question is not substantively different from ongoing debates in the United States about mandating community service as a prerequisite for high-school graduation. The data reported in this chapter were collected 5 years after the political transitions in the Central and East European nations. Perhaps the mandate of the socialist era was effective in making volunteer work a normative aspect of young people's lives. We can only speculate. There has, however, been considerable discussion about the need for youth organizations and school curricula that prepare the next generation to assume an active civic role.

Forms of Voluntary Work

In most of the countries in our study, schools and youth organizations seem to be the main route to involvement, followed by churches or temples and local community projects. By far the most common activities in the Central and East European countries are ecological ones – from recycling and cleaning up of parks, rivers, and public lands to reforestation in response to natural and man-made disasters. Reforestation projects are critical in the former Czechoslovakia (now the autonomous Czech and Slovak Republics), where reliance on burning high sulfur coal for energy production has effectively destroyed half of the forests, a trend that is expected to continue for several years (Adamova, 1993). "Clean the World" day is an annual event in Hungary, when adults and youth in communities come together to clean up their neighborhoods. In the Czech Republic youth engage in collecting herbs and fruits that may be used as pharmaceuticals, and on summer holidays they help reconstruct and restore historical ruins, castles, and fortresses. Some Czech youth also help to monitor the disposal of waste in their local communities.

Cleanup days are also a popular activity in Australia, where an environmental consciousness is promulgated in schools and communities. Individual initiative is often the impetus for such activities as the origins of "Clean Up Australia" day attest (i.e., a local yachtsman, appalled by the rubbish around Sydney Harbor, promoted the concept). Now, volunteers of all ages come together yearly to clean up parks, beaches, rivers, and Sydney Harbor. The American youth in our study reported a high rate of involvement in one-time efforts such as walkathons or bikathons to raise money for a wide range of causes such as combating hunger or cancer. Those who engaged in volunteer work on a regular basis primarily worked with younger children, either reading to them, tutoring, coaching, or directing plays. Nationally, about 36% of Swedish youth are members of some government-supported youth organization. The overriding goal of these groups is to keep youth occupied and out of trouble. Raising money to support these organizations is a common form of the youth's voluntary effort. As we have already noted, there is little need for social aid within Sweden. However, relief efforts for nations ravaged by wars or by natural disasters and fund-raising for medical research are outlets for those who seek out such involvement.

Although it accounts for a smaller percentage of youth activity in most of the countries, assistance for the disabled, elderly, poor, and homeless and relief work for refugees are typical activities organized by religious groups. To return for a moment to the "social contract" metaphor, it is worth noting that, compared to the ecological activities listed, this form of voluntary work affords a qualitatively different opportunity for youth development. Whereas most of the ecological activities are group oriented and focus on "our" water, forests, and air – resources and quality of life indicators that are common to everyone – efforts to assist the needy or displaced members of society tend to be individual acts of charity directed at others. These contrasts may be important distinctions in terms of the civic lessons learned in each type of activity and the function or meaning of the activity within the culture (Goodnow, 1996). The target or content of the activity, that is, protecting the environment or tutoring children, may be less important than whether it is organized as a group or individual effort. Political goals are rarely accomplished by the efforts of a single individual, and youth may be more likely to learn political skills in activities that emphasize collective action.

Finally, in some communities, local organizations offer opportunities for youth involvement. Examples are provided from two countries. In the Czech Republic volunteer fire fighters, foresters, or amateur theater groups operate in some communities and youth can usually get involved. In Australia, outlets for youth engagement can vary by the ecology of the region. Youth may participate in the Bush Fire Brigades, common in rural areas during the summer. In coastal areas surf lifesaving is a voluntary effort in which primarily teens are involved.

Importance of Civic Goals

Is volunteering in the community a developmental precursor of civic engagement? Our study was correlational so we cannot answer this question definitively. Yet ample evidence from other studies shows that involvement in voluntary youth groups is related to civic engagement in adulthood. Furthermore, adolescence is a time for exploring interests, forming personal commitments, and making preliminary decisions about the direction of one's life. With this in mind, we thought it important to explore the relationship between adolescents' engagement in voluntary work and the concepts they were forming of themselves and their future. Therefore, as part of our survey, adolescents were asked, when they thought about their life and their future, how important it was for them to achieve various goals. Among the choice of goals were a set of civic commitments such as contributing to their communities; contributing to their society and country; helping the less fortunate; preserving the earth and protecting the environment for future generations; doing something to protect animals; combating pollution; and being active in politics. Table 7.2 shows the results for these questions for volunteers and nonvolunteers in each country.

In terms of the hierarchy adolescents assigned to these goals, environmental objectives were at the top of the list – far more important to the average adolescent than any other civic commitments. Next in overall importance ratings was the adolescents' intentions to do something for their society and country, and to help the less fortunate, in that order. Lower overall ratings were given to doing something to improve their communities. Being active in politics was rated least important, far below the other goals. The low importance attached to political activism is consistent with other work, which shows that youth, especially from working-class families, are generally uninterested in politics (Bhavnani, 1991; Bynner & Ashford, 1994; Torney-Purta, 1990). Although we were not asking adolescents about being active in electoral politics, perhaps the word *political* is just too narrowly construed in this way. Unfortunately, because political activity is often conceived within a partisan framework, voluntary work and other types of community involvement tend to be ignored as opportunities for political activity and learning (Flanagan & Gallay, 1995; Sigel & Hoskin, 1981). Furthermore, political action implies a belief in one's ability to be an effective member of the polity, a belief that social change is possible and that one's actions can impact the political process (Campbell, Gurin, & Miller, 1954). The relative inexperience of adolescents in connecting political activity with group goals may be implicated in their cynicism about politics. In another study, comparing how late adolescents and young adults in Hungary perceived the domain of politics, Josza et al. (cited in Keri, 1996) found that, whereas young adults thought of it as something malleable, adolescents felt that people could have little impact.

In contrast to the goal of political activism, the importance ratings for the other civic commitments were all above the midpoint, indicating that overall young people endorsed goals that went beyond a narrow notion of self-interest. However, there was a general decline in such commitments between early and late adolescence, a trend that was consistent across countries. This result converges with the trends in political cynicism we have reported in other work (Bowes, Chalmers, & Flanagan,

Table 7.2. *Comparisons of the Civic Commitments of Volunteers with Nonvolunteers in Seven Countries*

	Helping the less fortunate M (SD)	Being active in politics M (SD)	Helping my society/country M (SD)	Improving my community M (SD)	Protecting the natural environment M (SD)
Australia					
Volunteer	3.89 (.80)***	2.46 (1.12)	3.65 (.72)**	3.57 (.75)***	3.95 (.78)
Nonvolunteer	3.47 (.88)	2.34 (1.10)	3.41 (.83)	3.15 (.77)	3.85 (.84)
Sweden					
Volunteer	3.50 (.84)***	2.66 (1.04)*	3.48 (.77)**	3.09 (.87)*	3.97 (.79)
Nonvolunteer	3.10 (.89)	2.36 (1.06)	3.22 (.82)	2.84 (.85)	3.83 (.79)
U.S.A.					
Volunteer	3.81 (.90)*	2.89 (1.14)**	3.65 (.83)***	3.65 (.85)***	3.64 (.86)
Nonvolunteer	3.58 (1.01)	2.58 (1.14)	3.38 (.92)	3.23 (.92)	3.57 (.85)
Bulgaria					
Volunteer	3.81 (.75)***	2.50 (.97)	3.81 (.76)***	3.64 (.76)***	4.21 (.62)***
Nonvolunteer	3.53 (.84)	2.42 (1.07)	3.58 (.82)	3.40 (.78)	3.97 (.68)
Czech Republic					
Volunteer	3.65 (.69)***	2.19 (.87)	3.74 (.67)***	3.79 (.61)***	4.21 (.61)***
Nonvolunteer	3.28 (.77)	2.11 (.83)	3.42 (.74)	3.44 (.70)	3.97 (.67)
Hungary					
Volunteer	3.58 (.81)***	2.06 (.92)	3.41 (.78)***	3.33 (.68)***	4.05 (.66)*
Nonvolunteer	3.22 (.90)	1.97 (.95)	3.23 (.84)	3.09 (.80)	3.92 (.74)
Russia					
Volunteer	3.75 (.94)***	2.34 (1.19)	3.98 (.86)***	3.88 (.84)***	4.38 (.73)***
Nonvolunteer	3.11 (1.07)	2.32 (1.20)	3.44 (1.02)	3.29 (1.01)	3.93 (.90)

Note: Results of ANOVAs. Means and standard deviations are presented for each country. All scales ranged from 1 = not at all important to 5 = very important.
*$p < .01$, **$p < .001$, ***$p < .0001$.

1996; Flanagan et al., 1996), and we suggest several interpretations of this age-related decline in civic commitments and parallel increase in cynicism. First, whereas younger adolescents may find it easier to think altruistically, older youth, approaching the end of their formal school years, may focus on issues of self-sufficiency, such as how they are going to earn money and support themselves. Alternatively, the decline in civic commitments may be part of a larger developmental trend. Between early and late adolescence, there is an increase in sociocentric awareness – of the social order, of institutions, of the economy (Adelson, 1972). We believe that one of the costs of this expanded sociocentric awareness is a growth in cynicism as youth become aware that the world is not a perfect place and leaders are not uniformly benevolent. Sigel and Hoskins (1981) contend that, after the massive dose of indoctrination about the virtues of the polity and its leaders students get in civics and social studies classes, late adolescents may become cynical when faced with dissonant information.

Youth's Civic Commitments across Countries

We turn next to a comparison between countries in the hierarchies of adolescents' civic commitments. As the results in Table 7.2 show, whereas environmental goals were, overall, the highest priority of youth, Americans, on average, rated them significantly lower than their peers in other countries. Adolescents in the four transitional polities (Bulgaria, the Czech Republic, Hungary, and Russia) seemed to have a particularly strong commitment to environmentalism. Compared to youth in the stable democracies, they gave higher ratings to stopping pollution, protecting animals, and preserving the earth for future generations. The role of environmental movements in the political changes of Central and Eastern Europe and the salience of these activities as outlets for youth will be discussed in a subsequent section.

Commitments to do something for the less fortunate were lower among Swedish and Russian youth compared to all others. The low ratings of the Russians are hard to explain but may reflect the lack of emphasis on charity in the society. They may also reflect the impact of the devastating economic decline of Russia during transition. In effect, Russian youth may be too busy surviving to help their neighbors. The low ratings of the Swedes are less surprising, given the relative absence of less fortunate people in a society with a strong commitment to equality and a high average standard of living. Compared to their peers in the other countries, the Swedes rated doing something for their society and making a contribution to their local communities as less important goals as well. Perhaps our indicators of civic commitments were too internally focused in the sense of asking youth about their own societies. In a society where the state ensures the general welfare, the civic commitments of youth may be better tapped with measures of global rather than local concerns. Finally, although being politically active was low overall, American youth were more likely than any other group of adolescents to endorse this goal.

Comparisons of Volunteers with Nonvolunteers

Turning next to comparisons between those youth who volunteered and their compatriots who did not, the results in Table 7.2 show that community volunteer work was consistently and significantly associated with three measures of civic commitment. The pattern was the same in each country: That is, compared to their compatriots who did not volunteer, those who did attached a greater personal importance to (1) working to improve their communities, (2) helping the less fortunate, and (3) doing something to help their country and society.

As noted earlier, the environmental goals were more important overall in the transitional societies. Within those societies it was the volunteers who were most committed to such goals; that finding is not surprising in light of the ecological emphasis of their voluntary work, for example, cleaning up rivers, reforesting, and monitoring the disposal of waste. Apparently, environmental consciousness was associated with such activity since these youth, more than any others in the study, tended to think of themselves as stewards of the earth.

The environmental awareness and activities of youth may be an offshoot of the prominent role that ecological movements in these countries played in fostering political change and in developing constructive, democratic methods of protest (Fisher, 1993; Jancar-Webster, 1993; Persanyi, 1993). The environment provided a perfect symbol to garner public support for overthrowing the old regimes. Not only was its deterioration symbolic of the myopic planning behind much of the Soviet press for industrialization, but the polluted air and water were a cost that everyone bore equally. Furthermore, in a context where political parties were banned, these causes were attractive because political issues could be raised in what was arguably an apolitical framework, a context that others have referred to as a safe public talking-space (Jancar-Webster, 1993).

One can point to environmental actions prior to 1990 in each of the Central and Eastern European countries that ultimately led to the demise of the old regimes. In 1989 public demonstrations protesting the low quality of air and water engaged whole families in Czechoslovakia. In October 1988, 40,000 demonstrated in Budapest against plans to dam the Danube River. Pollution of the Danube from chemical plants in Romania was a focus of protest movements in Bulgaria, and some scholars contend that imprisonment of some leaders of those movements ultimately led to the fall of the Zhivkov regime (Jancar-Webster, 1993). Since the early 1990s, when the political objectives of overthrowing the old regimes were met, much of the vitality and membership in these movements has waned (Jancar-Webster, 1993) and some of the environmental goals of these movements may be sacrificed to market pressures.

Conclusion

The social contract study focuses on the fact that, in the course of growing up, children develop an understanding about the bargain that inheres between people and the polity that make their society "work." One important way that democratic polities "work" is that people become engaged in defining them and in creating the social glue that holds them together. The stability of political regimes depends on such commitments to the commonwealth, and in the twenty-first century the voluntary sector is expected to play an increasingly prominent role in building civil societies and stabilizing polities. As part of the third sector, what Rifkin (1995) refers to as the "social economy," it is likely to compensate for the private (market) and public (government) sectors' failures and will also provide an arena where, collectively, people can bring political pressures to bear on those sectors.

In this chapter we have argued that voluntary work is an opportunity through which the next generation can develop a sense of membership in the polity. At a time when they are considering who they are and where they are headed, exposure to others' perspectives, to social conditions and social groups with which they may not be familiar, can be a means for enlarging an adolescent's community of relationships and concerns. Aristotle defined the *polis* as, above all, a network of friends pursuing a common good. The voluntary sector provides an opportunity for young people to step beyond the boundaries of their familiar surroundings and see the common good in broadened perspective.

Cross-cultural studies provide a unique window for understanding an

activity such as volunteer work. According to Goodnow (1996), by looking at the form and the function of activities across cultures, we gain a
better understanding of the role those activities play in human development. The results of this study suggest that the activity of voluntary
service assumes somewhat different forms across countries, in some
cases focusing on environmental concerns and in others emphasizing
service to the needy. There seems to be a universal function of service
in fostering a civic ethic and integrating youth into the broader polity.
At the same time, service may have specific functions or meanings within
cultural or historical contexts. For example, in the United States, it con-
notes charitable work that compensates for the shortfalls of the private
and public sectors. In contrast, during the Soviet era in the Central and
East European countries, the voluntary sector functioned as one of the
few "free spaces" (Evans & Boyte, 1992) for expressing political opposition.

Across countries, voluntary youth organizations are one of the primary
avenues through which young people engage in service. Because these
groups play a unique role in stabilizing polities by developing diffuse
support among the younger generation, we turn to a brief discussion of
these organizations. Historically, youth organizations from the Scouts to
4-H to Young Pioneers have shared a common mission in fostering the
character of the next generation of citizens. By providing structured outlets for leisure time under the guidance of adults, such groups integrate
young people into the norms and mores of the broader society. Although
these organizations tend to attract conformists rather than rebels, longitudinal studies of American youth suggest that, because they provide a
reference group with prosocial values, voluntary youth groups other
than sports teams may inculcate a resistance to delinquency (Larson,
1992).

Besides encouraging constructive prosocial norms, youth organizations stabilize political and social systems either overtly by emphasizing
specific ideological commitments or more subtly by communicating an
affinity with the nation (Harber, 1991; Yogev & Shapira, 1990). In this
chapter we have alluded to the political agendas of the Young Pioneer
and Comsomol organizations. But even supposedly apolitical groups
serve social and political agendas by communicating the ethos underlying the society's social contract or, conversely, by providing a context
where alternative perspectives can be aired. For example, in the early
twentieth century, the Boy Scouts provided a counterbalance to what
some perceived as the softening effects that urbanization and white-

collar work were having on traditional male roles (Hantover, 1978; Macleod, 1983). In a similar vein, debates in some contemporary 4-H groups in the United States point to a clash between those who want youth to appreciate the principles of free enterprise and those who would rather the organization promote democratic principles and social tolerance as values for youth (Meredith, 1996).

Politics, according to Easton (1990), is the authoritative distribution of values. But politics is also contested ground. The voluntary sector provides a context in which youth can explore the competing principles that are the foundation of their social order and decide for themselves which they stand for or against. We have discussed voluntary work as an opportunity for the social integration of youth – enabling them to be contributors to and feel like an integral part of their communities, and to "buy into" the norms and values of those communities. To the extent that voluntary work gives youth a voice, encourages them to discuss and even question the conditions of the "social contract," it can be a force not only for social stability but also for social change.

References

Adamova, E. (1993). Environmental management in Czecho-Slovakia. In B. Jancar-Webster, (Ed.). *Environmental action in Eastern Europe: Responses to crisis* (pp. 42–57). New York: M. E. Sharpe.

Adelson, J. (1972). The political imagination of the young adolescent. In J. Kagan & R. Coles (Eds.), *Twelve to sixteen: Early adolescence* (pp. 106–143). New York: Norton.

Bhavnani, K. K. (1991). *Talking politics: A psychological framing for views from youth in Britain.* Cambridge: Cambridge University Press.

Botcheva, L., & Kitanov, K. (1996). Changes in the "social contract" in Bulgaria and Eastern Europe. Poster presented at the XIVth Biennial Meetings of the ISSBD, Quebec City, Canada.

Bowes, J. (1996). Children's ideas about their responsibility for household work. In C. Flanagan & B. Csapo (Convenors), Social change and social development across cultures. Symposium presented at the XIVth Biennial Meetings of the ISSBD, Quebec City, Canada.

Bowes, J., Chalmers, D., & Flanagan, C. (1996). Adolescents' ideas about social and civic responsibility. Paper presented at the Ninth Australasian Human Development Conference, Perth, April, 1996.

Bynner, J., & Ashford, S. (1994). Politics and participation: Some antecedents of young people's attitudes to the political system and political activity. *European Journal of Social Psychology, 24*, 223–236.

Campbell, A., Gurin, G., & Miller, W. (1954). *The voter decides.* Evanston, IL: Row & Peterson.

Csapo, B. (1994). Adolescents in Hungary. In K. Hurrelmann (Ed.), *International Handbook of Adolescence.* Westport, CT: Greenwood.

Csapo, B. (1995). Students' perceptions of the effects of social transition. In C. Wulf (Ed.), *Education in Europe: An intercultural task*. Munster, Germany: Warmann.

Dworkin, R. (1978). *Taking rights seriously*. Cambridge, MA: Harvard University Press.

Easton, D. (1990). *The analysis of political structure*. New York: Routledge.

Easton, D., & Dennis, J. (1969). *Children in the political system*. New York: McGraw-Hill.

Ehman, L. (1980). The American school in the political socialization process. *Review of Educational Research, 50*, 99–119.

Evans, S. M. & Boyte, H. C. (1992). *Free spaces: The sources of democratic change in America*. Chicago: University of Chicago Press.

Fisher, D. (1993). The emergence of the environmental movement in Eastern Europe and its role in the revolutions of 1989. In B. Jancar-Webster (Ed.), *Environmental action in Eastern Europe: Responses to crisis* (pp. 89–113). New York: M. E. Sharpe.

Flanagan, C., Averina, I., Botcheva, L., Bowes, J., Csapo, B., Jonsson, B., Macek, P., & Sheblanova, E. (1996). Adolescents' interpretation of the "social contract": National and developmental differences. In C. Flanagan & B. Csapo, (Convenors), Social change and social development across cultures. Symposium presented at the XIVth Biennial Meetings of the ISSBD, Quebec City, Canada.

Flanagan, C., & Gallay, L. (1995). Reframing the meaning of "political" in research with adolescents. *Perspectives on Political Science, 24*, 34–41.

Goodnow, J. (1996). Discussion and commentary. In C. Flanagan & B. Csapo (Convenors), Social change and social development across cultures. Symposium presented at the XIVth Biennial Meetings of the ISSBD, Quebec City, Canada.

Hantover, J. P. (1978). The Boy Scouts and the validation of masculinity. *Journal of Social Issues, 34*, 184–195.

Harber, C. (1991). International contexts for political education. *Educational Review, 43*, 245–255.

Havel, V. (1990). *Disturbing the peace: A conversation with Karel Hvizdala*. New York: Alfred Knopf.

Havel, V. (1992). Politics, morality, and civility. In *Summer Meditations* (p. 6), P. Wilson (trans.). New York: Knopf.

Jancar-Webster, B. (1993). The East European environmental movement and the transformation of East European society. In B. Jancar-Webster (Ed.), *Environmental action in Eastern Europe: Responses to crisis* (pp. 192–219). New York: M. E. Sharpe.

Jennings, M. K. (1991). Thinking about social injustice. *Political Psychology, 12*, 187–204.

Jonsson, B. (1996). Youth, schooling, and societal change in Sweden. In C. Flanagan & B. Csapo (Convenors), Social change and social development across cultures. Symposium presented at the XIVth Biennial Meetings of the ISSBD, Quebec City, Canada.

Karpati, A. (1996). Hungarian adolescents of the 1990's: Ideals, beliefs and expectations. In D. Benner & D. Lenzen (Eds.), *Education for the new Europe* (pp. 29–42). Providence, RI: Berghahn Books.

Keri, L. (1996). Hungarian political culture in the 1990's—antecedents and timely issues. Paper presented at the International Political Science Association/

RCPSE Round Table Conference on "Changes in political education and political culture in East/Central Europe," July 5–10, 1996, Appalachian State University, Boone, NC.

Larson, R. (1992). Youth organizations, hobbies, and sports as developmental contexts. In R. K. Silbereisen & E. Todt (Eds.), *Adolescence in context: The interplay of family, school, peers, and work in adjustment* (pp. 46–65). New York: Springer-Verlag.

Macek, P., & Rabusic, L. (1994). Adolescence in Czechoslovakia. In K. Hurrelmann (Ed.), *International handbook of adolescence.* Westport, CT: Greenwood Press.

Macek, P., Tyrlik, M., & Kostron, L. (1996). Adolescents' opinions about society: The case of Czech Republic. In C. Flanagan & B. Csapo (Convenors), Social change and social development across cultures. Symposium presented at the XIVth Biennial Meetings of the ISSBD, Quebec City, Canada.

Macleod, D. I. (1983). *Building character in the American boy: The Boy Scouts, YMCA, and their forerunners, 1870–1920.* Madison: University of Wisconsin Press.

Meredith, R. (1996, Nov. 7). What's 4-H without competition for blue ribbons? Extremely stormy. *The New York Times*, p. A-16.

Newmann, F. (1990). A test of higher-order thinking in social studies: Persuasive writing on constitutional issues using the NAEP approach. *Social Education, 54,* 369–373.

Pastuovic, N. (1993). Problems of reforming educational systems in post-communist countries. *International Review of Education, 39,* 405–418.

Persanyi, M. (1993). Red pollution, green evolution, revolution in Hungary. In B. Jancar-Webster (Ed.), *Environmental action in Eastern Europe: Responses to crisis* (pp. 134–157). New York: M. E. Sharpe.

Rifkin, J. (1995). *The end of work: The decline of the global labor force and the dawn of the post-market era.* New York: G. P. Putnam's Sons.

Rust, V. D., Knost, P., & Wichmann, J. (1994). Education and youth in Central and Eastern Europe: A comparative assessment. In V. D. Rust, P. Knost, & J. Wichmann (Eds.), *Education and the value crisis in Central and Eastern Europe* (pp. 281–308). Frankfurt am Main: Peter Lang.

Scheye, E. (1991). Psychological notes on Central Europe 1989 and beyond. *Political Psychology, 12,* (2), 331–344.

Sigel, R., & Hoskin, M. (1981). *The political involvement of adolescents.* New Brunswick, NJ: Rutgers University Press.

Torney-Purta, J. (1990). Youth in relation to social institutions. In S. S. Feldman, &. G. R. Elliott (Eds.), *At the Threshold: The developing adolescent* (pp. 457–478). Cambridge, MA: Harvard University Press.

Torney-Purta, J. & Lansdale, D. (1986, April). *Classroom climate and process in international studies: Data from the American Schools and the World Project.* Paper presented at the American Educational Research Association.

Verba, S., Nie, N. H., & Kim J. (1978). *Participation and political equality: A seven nation comparison.* Cambridge: Cambridge University Press.

Verba, S. & Orren, G. R. (1985). *Equality in America: The view from the top.* Cambridge, MA: Harvard University Press.

Vygotsky, L. S. (1978). *Mind in society: The development of higher psychological processes.* Cambridge, MA: Harvard University Press.

Walzer, M. (1989). Citizenship. In T. Ball, J. Farr, & R. L. Hanson (Eds.), *Political innovation and conceptual change* (pp. 211–219). Cambridge: Cambridge University Press.

Yogev, A., & Shapira, R. (1990). Citizenship socialization in national voluntary youth organizations. In O. Ichilov (Ed.), *Political socialization, citizenship education, and democracy,* (pp. 205–220). New York: Columbia University Teacher's College Press.

8. Political Socialization in a Divided Society: The Case of Northern Ireland

JEAN WHYTE

Political socialization may be defined as the process through which young people become aware of how power is distributed in society and acquire their orientations and patterns of behavior as citizens. The outcome of the process, which takes place in both formal and informal ways, will vary according to a number of factors and may lead, on one end of the scale, to an individual who is highly active in community matters or, on the other end, to an individual who is apathetic. Within those groups, individuals will differ in degrees of participation or apathy, in motivations underlying their stances, and also in degrees of allegiance or hostility toward the structures and ideals of the society in which they live.

A narrow interpretation of the process and the outcome might define political socialization within the parameters of knowledge of party politics and support of particular political ideologies within a given community. A broader interpretation, as is adopted in the present volume (see the Introduction, this volume), views political socialization as a process dependent not only on an awareness of matters political, but also on an awareness of how one's particular society deals with issues of power as related to gender, ethnicity, and religious affiliation. The process and outcome for young people will also be dependent on the views of significant individuals in their lives.

One factor that may be hypothesized to influence the process of political socialization and, of course, the outcome is the extent to which there is consensus among the members of a state or society about the form of government in which they currently live, the principles according to which it functions, and how they see themselves as relating to it. There will inevitably be differing degrees of consensus within any society, but in some societies it is possible to identify clearly distinguishable communities whose views are at variance on at least some of the issues relating to government and politics. In the majority of cases, these communities coexist peacefully in spite of their differences; for instance, anglophones and francophones in Canada, Walloons and Flemings in Belgium, and ethnic minorities and majorities in very many other countries. Nevertheless, there are exceptions. In Northern Ireland, there was peaceful coexistence until 1968, when civil violence erupted between the mostly Protestant supporters of the form of government then in place and the mostly Catholic nonsupporters, who did not feel allegiance to the government.

Civil violence or physical conflict between communities within the same society might be expected to influence the outcome of the political socialization process for young people and their notions of what constitutes a good citizen. Violence of itself ought to affect the minority of people who have direct contact with it and the larger majority whose contact is at best indirect. For example, under conditions of violence, there could be less supervision and attention from adults and the authorities as well as limited opportunities for prosocial development that could contribute to political socialization. But in either case, violence is a restricted outward expression of a much deeper malaise that constitutes the basis of the divisions within that society.

In Northern Ireland, the malaise has its roots in problems of constitutional identity, and it is commonly manifested in the sectarian modes of experience that have penetrated the routinized practices of everyday life. In a society such as Northern Ireland, we must take into account, therefore, not just the violence per se but also young people's relationship to it, including what is known about their participation in it and its effects on their political socialization. In addition, according to Bronfenbrenner's (1986) socioecological model of development, we must also look at the totality of the sociopolitical environment, including the contextual factors that affect the process of political socialization. The present chapter attempts to identify the factors specific to Northern Ireland that affect the political socialization of its young people, particularly with regard to their sense of efficacy in promoting change.

The presumption is that Catholic and Protestant youth are affected differently by a host of factors that include socioeconomic conditions. As a consequence, one might expect different outcomes on such measures as social and political identity, perceptions of democratic values, feelings of political efficacy, and political trust. One might also expect dissimilar attitudes toward the legitimacy of state authority and its agents such as the police, army, and local militias. The process of political socialization in Northern Ireland is mediated formally and informally through the subcultures of the different ethnic–religious traditions, the educational system, recreational provision for young people, cross-cultural community relationships fostered by state funding, and family practices and opportunities for prosocial activities. Associations between the level of political interest and knowledge and differing socialization experiences within the two main communities are explored in the concluding section.

Historical Background

There are historical reasons for the existence of communities with differing loyalties in Northern Ireland. Since 1921, the island of Ireland has been divided into two states, the Republic of Ireland, an independent state with about 3.5 million people, and Northern Ireland, which is a part of the United Kingdom and has about 1.5 million citizens. Many people in Northern Ireland are descended from Protestant English and Scottish settlers or planters who arrived when the English colonized the island in the seventeenth century, displacing Catholics from their land. In 1921, the Irish Free State was established in the southern part of the island, and a devolved parliament, known as *Stormont*, from its location in Belfast, was set up to govern that part of the island now known as "Northern Ireland." The majority there were Protestant and "unionist," with most feeling they were British. But a minority of about 40% of the population were Catholic and nationalist and did not consider themselves British. They were reluctant to accept the legitimacy of Northern Ireland. Their attitude toward the Stormont government was basically one of noncooperation and this contributed to their "out-group" status in the eyes of the unionists.

Between 1921 and 1973, the parliament in Stormont, Belfast, governed Northern Ireland, and although it was subject in theory to the parliament at Westminster, in practice it functioned with a significant degree of autonomy. This was not a situation of normal democracy because the demographic situation was such that it was impossible to envisage a time when the unionists would not be in a majority and the nationalists not in opposition. The unionist party's control tended to exclude those who were loyal to Ireland and especially those whose politics were nationalist. Hence, Catholics were excluded from public office and little if any effort was made to draw them into fuller participation in the public affairs of the region.

In the 1960s, initiatives were attempted by some members of parliament (MPs) at Westminster to draw attention to abuses of power in Northern Ireland, and at the same time some Catholics became more proactive through campaigns that were organized to draw attention to issues of social justice and its underlying structures. By the early 1970s, most of the grievances had been addressed, at least on paper, but a legacy of bitterness remained. Many Protestants identified civil rights with republican and nationalist politics, and this belief renewed their fear of being swallowed by a united Ireland. Intimidation and street violence led to mass movements and to the emergence of paramilitary groups, including the Irish Republican Army (IRA), to protect their communities. In response, between 30,000 and 60,000 people were forced to leave their homes between August 1969 and February 1973, leading to a neighborhood segregation of Catholics and Protestants that has continued to the present. It is estimated that the majority of urban working class people now live in neighborhoods that are predominantly of their own tradition. This inevitably limits encounters with and knowledge of the "other side" and promotes the exaggeration of differences.

Research on the Continuing Conflict in Northern Ireland

In view of these historical events, what kinds of differences in attitudes have developed and how might they influence political socialization? Since the outbreak of the current "Troubles" in 1968, researchers have investigated reasons for the continuing conflict. Here, we offer a brief overview of the state of research on differences between Catholics and Protestants and then focus on findings with relation to constitutional arrangements, democratic values, national identity, and attitudes toward the police. This overview is important because it describes the general context of political attitudes that youth encounter in their day-to-day lives.

Researchers have examined differences from a variety of perspectives. Fraser (1973), for example, proposed a biological hypothesis, contending that community inbreeding in Northern Ireland has exaggerated unique characteristics that resulted in physically, emotionally, and ideologically contrasting races. Burton (1978) found himself becoming aware of cues used for social categorization: name, face, dress, demeanor, residence, education, language, and iconography that those in the know use to distinguish one community from the other. Other researchers have proposed that specific personality differences can be discerned between Catholics and Protestants and have presented findings in support of this.

But research evidence (see John Whyte, 1990) on differences between the groups has not been consistent and there have been problems replicating a number of studies on this issue (Trew, 1989).

Recent data from the Northern Ireland Social Attitudes surveys have shown general differences between the two communities on issues such as their views on the expression of antigovernment feelings. Catholic opinion in favor of political protest corresponds more closely, almost paradoxically, with opinion in Britain than does Protestant opinion. There was more heterogeneity among Catholics of different generations than among Protestants. In relation to the transmission of attitudes toward authority, more Protestants were in favor of schools teaching children to obey authority, but among Catholics fewer younger than older supported this view (NISA, 1992). On the other hand, there was similarity between the communities in their attitudes toward sexual morality, illustrating the underlying stability of religious influence for both communities. And there were more liberal views on sexual morality among those aged 18 to 34 in both groups (NISA, 1992). But on the fundamental issue of how the country should be governed there are clear-cut differences between the communities.

Constitutional Arrangements

Agreement on how one's country should be governed should, one might think, be basic to citizenship. But dissension about constitutional arrangements is probably the central problem underlying the conflict in Northern Ireland. The outcome of the election for a Consultative Forum in May 1996 illustrates how the population as a whole is split and runs close to the religious divide, in particular for the Protestants. In that election the results showed that Unionists, who wished to remain part of the United Kingdom, won 56% of the votes overall. Nationalists of all hues, who were not happy with being part of the United Kingdom, won 38% of the vote. The middle ground, composed of Alliance, Women's Coalition, and others, who sought a compromise position, won 10% of the vote. These divisions appear to be deep-rooted and relatively impervious to modification even as other conditions change.

Opinion polls over the years inviting respondents to choose between seven possible constitutional arrangements for Northern Ireland consistently showed no clear majority for any of the options, even within the different communities. The most popular option tends to be power sharing, in which political power is distributed among the representatives of the communities by some method other than that of a simple majority. This option excluded links with the Republic of Ireland and was chosen by 22% of the people questioned in September, 1996. But the most consistent finding was that what Catholics wanted, Protestants did not want, and vice versa. Almost 39% of Catholics – not a majority in that community – favored a united Ireland, as did 0.5% of the Protestants, who constitute 56% of the population. About 30% of Protestants – not a majority – believed that Northern Ireland should be more deeply integrated within the United Kingdom. This view was shared by 3% of the Catholics. Close to two-thirds of Protestants said that the Republic's constitutional claim to Northern Ireland should be dropped now. Almost half of the Catholics said that it should never be dropped.

Similar findings were reported by the Northern Ireland Social Attitudes Survey carried out in 1994 (NISA, 1996). There are also differences between the groups with regard to their openness to change. When these results were compared with the NISA surveys going back to 1989, little change was found in the Protestant position over the 5 years. But there was an increase in Catholics favoring union with the United Kingdom in the years up to the most recent survey. Two significant points should be emphasized. First, there is not unanimity in either group, and, second, there appear to be more heterogeneity and openness to change within the Catholic community.

Democratic Values

Even though the two communities hold opposing views on how the province should be governed they might still agree on the underlying values that would support the successful operation of the democratic process. This is a complex issue since their experiences have been different from those of typical democracies. Northern Ireland was never a competitive democracy in the conventional sense because there was no possibility that the Protestant and unionist majority would ever lose an election, nor that the Catholic and nationalist minority would ever win one. It was a hegemonic state in which one community enjoyed permanent government while the other was in permanent opposition.

The Northern Ireland Social Attitudes Survey, 1994 (reported in 1996), investigated citizens' views on political efficacy, trust, and authority. *Political efficacy* was defined as the belief that a citizen can influence the political process and that public officials and political leaders are both responsible and responsive to the electorate, the belief that governments will act in their best interests and remain responsive to the demands they make upon them. *Political trust* assesses more broadly based values about how government and its representatives act within the society as a whole. The results showed that popular support for political efficacy in Northern Ireland is low with little difference between Protestants and Catholics. Only 14% disagreed with the statement "People like me have no say in what the government does," with no difference between Catholics and Protestants. There was some difference on the question of whether the party in power could change things; 26% of Protestants thought change was possible, only 17% of Catholics that change was possible. This finding might be interpreted as indicating a sense of alienation and powerlessness with regard to the political system. The 1996 youth survey reported by Democratic Dialogue provides further evidence to support this interpretation. A similar conclusion was reached by Jean Whyte (1995) as an explanation of the low levels of knowledge about current political affairs shown by 12-year-olds and in particular those from the Protestant community in a study carried out in 1981 and 1992.

Consistent differences were found between Catholics and Protestants on questions of political trust. Protestants were more trusting by a substantial degree, especially in relation to the trustworthiness of government and the practices of civil servants. Religious affiliation was found to be a stronger predictor of trust than any other sociodemographic characteristic. The differing experiences of the two communities in interaction with the political system over the past century and more specifically since the start of the Troubles have obviously had a major impact. People's beliefs about how government operates and whom it benefits probably account for the major differences in political trust observed. The degree of political efficacy and political trust felt by each community will obviously have an influence on the process and outcomes of political socialization of the upcoming generations. The low level of efficacy felt by both communities militates against proactive political socialization.

National Identity

Trew (1996) observed that in Northern Ireland choice of a national identity label was associated with a range of attitudinal and belief variables, defying any simplistic linking of Irish with Catholic nationalism or British with Protestant unionism. Around four-fifths of Protestants consider themselves to be "British" or "Ulster," with a majority of the remainder picking either the label "Northern Irish" or "sometimes British, sometimes Irish"; 3% or less chose the description "Irish." Among Catholics, just over 60% regarded themselves as "Irish," just under 30% as "Northern Irish" or "sometimes British, sometimes Irish," and 12% as "British" or "Ulster." When the question was put another way – Do you think of yourself as a nationalist, a unionist, or neither? – about 75% of Protestants said "unionist," and the rest said "neither." In distinction, Catholics were almost equally split between "neither" and "nationalist." The balance has been changing over time and Catholics appear to be more heterogeneous in this regard than Protestants.

Trew concludes that although Protestants tend to see themselves as British and Catholics to see themselves as Irish, these identifications are not necessarily political or automatically associated with either nationalism or unionism. She proposed that cultural identity, more than political identity, may be at stake. The formation of an individual's cultural identity has been explored in Northern Ireland through Identity Structure Analysis (ISA) by Weinreich (1992). Taking a broader perspective than Social Identity Theory, which tends to separate the individual from the social, ISA gives a central place to actual value and belief systems that are informed by interdisciplinary conceptualizations. The initial findings for research using this paradigm, however, suggest a large overlap between religious and national identities. This result is contrary to what researchers using alternative paradigms have found.

Attitudes toward Authority

Because consensus about the acceptance of state authority underlies stable democracies, it is reasonable to ask whether the two main communities in Northern Ireland express similar messages about authority to the younger generation. A crucial area of concern is attitudes toward police and army in their treatment of Catholics and Protestants. It should be remembered that in Northern Ireland, parts of the population define the very existence of the police as illegitimate insofar as the police are considered an arm of the illegitimate state of Northern Ireland. Therefore, these people regard everything the police do as illegitimate. Some portion of the population defines antipolice violence as legitimate and, by implication, suggests that such violence is the most appropriate way of dealing with police harassment. Leaving aside this extreme group, there remain significant differences between the Catholic and Protestant communities in their perceptions of how the police do their job.

A majority of Protestants believe that the security forces treat Protestants and Catholics equally, and a minority believe that they treat Protestants better. A slight majority of Catholics believe that the security forces treat Protestants better, whereas a slight minority believes that they treat both groups equally. Some basis for these attitudes was provided by a survey by the Committee on the Administration of Justice (McVeigh, 1994). Broad sectors of Northern Ireland's citizens felt that the security forces were not policing their communities equally. Variation in beliefs about the evenhandedness of the security forces is greater among Catholics than among Protestants. Material factors such as social class, household income, and education were less important in explaining the findings than were perceptions of the relative positions of the two communities. Political and constitutional preferences were also important in determining attitudes, but the strongest factor was age, with younger Catholics and Protestants being highly likely to believe that the police favored Protestants. It has been suggested that this is as much a structural problem as an individual one and that it will not be remedied until the sectarian bias in the composition of the police is altered to include more Catholics.

Political Socialization of Youth

Given the complex cultural history and current state of conflict in Northern Ireland, it is important to understand what impact these experiences have had on children and young people's social development, including their attitudes toward violence, views about politics, and regard for authority and legal mandates. Here, we will report some of the findings on these issues and consider the mechanisms that may mediate political socialization – school, community, and family.

Attitudes toward Violence and Antisocial Behavior

Is violence viewed as an appropriate means to political ends among youth in Northern Ireland? Cairns (1996) comments that the question of what happens in the long run to children who are socialized into violence for political ends has inadequate empirical attention. The available evidence, however, offers only limited support for the hypothesis that children who see violence used successfully for political ends will develop an aberrant moral view of violence. Whereas earlier research appeared to support this view, more recent studies (Mercer & Bunting, 1980) have concluded that the motivations of young political demonstrators in Northern Ireland, who at times engaged in violence, were not really political. Lorenc and Branthwaite (1986) found that children in Northern Ireland were able to judge violence as wrong but also to make some qualification according to the circumstances; they were not more tolerant or accepting of violence than English children, and they also showed more respect for authority than English children. It seems that approval of violent behavior may be confined to the context of the political struggle and that children distinguish between violence for just or unjust causes. There is no evidence that youth in Northern Ireland are more approving of violence in interpersonal or broader social settings.

Focusing on youth's behavior, one of the most prominent concerns of adults in Northern Ireland is that their children who have been exposed to continuing aggression will think that violence is the only way to resolve social conflict. When presented with hypothetical situations, children in Northern Ireland do not endorse the use of violence any more than other children and are selective in their advocacy of it, just like children in other societies. What of actual, real-life situations? Has there been an increase in antisocial behavior in youth in Northern Ireland? Cairns (1996) reports that antisocial aggressive behavior by youth has increased since 1969, but he concludes that there has been only a fairly subtle effect, which is of concern to teachers perhaps and possibly to the children themselves. Neither psychiatrists nor magistrates have noted a rise in delinquency and there has not been a marked increase in the proportion of young people diagnosed as clinically ill or brought before the courts.

The Self-Reported Delinquency Study in Belfast, Northern Ireland (McQuoid, 1994) provides another way to address at the impact of social and political context in Northern Ireland on youth's behavior. It provides cross-national findings on antisocial behavior from cities in Northern Ireland and Spain and national samples from Britain, Switzerland, Portugal, and the Netherlands. Of the Belfast sample, 75% of the youth reported committing one delinquent act in their lives (ever). Percentages were higher for all comparison groups except youth in England and Wales. Nearly one-half of the Northern Ireland group admitted committing a delinquent act in the previous year; this percentage was slightly higher than in England and Wales, but lower than in the other areas. It should be noted that the data did not include alcohol consumption, which was popular among Northern Ireland youth, and some types of offense were more common in Northern Ireland. For example, car theft has become part of the subculture in some parts of Catholic West Belfast since the 1970s, when paramilitary groups encouraged young people to steal cars in order to create barricades and "no go" areas for the police. Northern Ireland has been found to have the highest car victimization rate of 15 countries but the lowest overall rate of victimization. In addition, the Belfast sample reported higher levels of property offenses, such as shoplifting or stealing, than were reported in England and Wales, Spain, and Portugal, but lower than in Switzerland and the Netherlands. The rate of violent offenses, such as vandalism, was higher in Northern Ireland than in England and Wales, but lower than in the other European regions. In terms of specific violent acts, the Northern Ireland sample was least likely of all the samples to engage in rioting, including fighting in a public place or carrying weapons such as knives or sticks. Finally, the Northern Ireland sample's rate of drug offense was lower than that in Switzerland, England, and Wales.

Youth's Attitudes toward Politics

The impact of growing up in Northern Ireland has produced youth attitudes toward violence and involvement in officially designated crime that are similar to, and in some instances more positive than, those of youth living in societies that have not been subjected to long-term civil strife. But what of their attitudes toward politics?

A recent survey of 1,300 youth, age 16 to 20, in Northern Ireland was carried out by the nonprofit organization Democratic Dialogue in 1996 (Democratic Dialogue, 1996). The findings on many issues agree mainly with those reported for adults. On identity, 70% of the Catholics in the sample described themselves as Irish, whereas 43% of the Presbyterians and 57% of those in the (Protestant) Church of Ireland said they were British. When asked about political identity, 88% of the Catholics described themselves as nationalist, whereas 60% of the Presbyterians and 65% of those in the Church of Ireland said that they were unionist; a little over 25% of the entire sample said that they were neither nationalist nor unionist. Very few of the youth were involved in political organizations; for example, 3% worked for a political party; 3% were in a trade union; and 12% worked on campaigns. Over half of the sample thought that politicians in Northern Ireland were not doing a good job and less than 2% thought that they were doing a good job. Only one in five youth thought that political parties did a reasonable job in addressing the needs of young people.

Older, compared with younger respondents; Catholics, compared with Protestants; and females, compared with males, were more negative in their views. And yet 75% of the respondents said that they were "very" or "fairly" interested in what is happening politically in Northern Ireland, and over half said that they would like to be more involved in the political process. There was a positive relationship between level of education and degree of interest in politics. Level of political knowledge was not investigated, but 79% of respondents thought that young people should have the opportunity to learn about the political process in school. The conclusions drawn from the study were that young people feel alienated and let down by politicians and political parties but that they would like to be more actively involved. There appears to be a willingness to be committed, but a lack of structures that might facilitate the process. On balance, youth in Northern Ireland do not appear alienated from the political system even though they recognize several of its faults.

Mechanisms That Mediate Political Socialization

Taken as a whole, empirical research on Northern Irish youth indicates that they do not differ from youth elsewhere in their engagement in their understanding of violence, antisocial behavior, and attitudes toward politics. Given the fact that they are growing up in a context of profound civil unrest, it is important to consider the role of mediating mechanisms that may buffer deleterious effects. The daily practices in which youth engage in their community, school, and family may help them avoid the development of extreme attitudes and forms of behavior. Recent programs reflect this view and have developed interventions to help youth through strengthening community relations, school, and family.

Community Context. Bell (1990) draws attention to the separate distinctive and strong subcultures permeating the lives of young people in Northern Ireland and describes the informal process of socialization by which cultural traditions become a powerful means of consolidating a sense of identity. For loyalists/unionists, for example, he identifies membership in marching bands that participate in parades during the "marching season" over the summer months as an important element of their subculture. These bands embody a whole cultural tradition that brings together religion and politics in identifiable pressure groups such as the Orange Order, the Royal Black Preceptory, or the Apprentice Boys. Parades sometimes take bands to a church for a service of thanksgiving or commemoration, or to an open space in which speeches, hymns, and religious services are held. Curbstones along the route are painted in patriotic colors of red, white, and blue, and murals on gable-end walls remind participants of episodes from past history when their ancestors stood firm or defeated an enemy. Banners are carried and enormous drums are beaten loudly, with the Lambeg drum particularly threatening to Catholics.

Although parades are partly intended as entertainment, the overtones of domination and the fact that many parades now pass through territory that is largely residential and Catholic generate among some Northern Irish resentment for a show of naked triumphalism. It is not unusual for Catholics to exhibit opposition to the parade, sometimes physically. Security forces have to be drafted in to keep the sides apart while Catholics are confined to their homes or excluded from the area for the duration of the parade. In 1995 and 1996 serious confrontations took place in Drumcree, a small village in County Armagh. The police initially banned a parade, because negotiations between Catholics and Orangemen to modify aspects of it or to prevent it from passing through Catholic territory broke down. Loyalists then set up roadblocks throughout the province, disrupting normal life and stretching the police and security forces beyond their resources. The police eventually gave in and protected the parade as it went through. This kind of event has serious implications for people's understanding of the purpose of authority, their own rights as citizens, and their sense of political efficacy and trust – with the message being different for each side.

On the Catholic-nationalist side, there is a strong adherence to Gaelic or Irish traditions and practices. There are parades there too and marching bands, but not through Protestant territory. The Gaelic games of football and hurling are played by nationalists, but not by unionists/ loyalists. Irish music, language, dancing, and song are part of the nationalist popular culture but not of that of the unionists/loyalists. And, of course, there is a degree of sympathy for the notion of a united Ireland, fed by the strong sense of grievance at the treatment of the community by the Stormont regime and the feeling of being treated as second-class citizens. Recreational activities and the spaces available to young people in their leisure time are linked inextricably with the subculture and reinforce the separateness of communities. Bell suggests that these cultural events have powerful political implications, showing that sectarianism permeates all aspects of life for most people and cannot be solved at a purely educational level.

A further element of the subculture that contributes to political socialization, particularly on the Catholic-nationalist side, arises from negative attitudes toward the forces of law and order. A consequence of this situation is the "informal justice system," which is a graduated system of sanctions, operated by the Provisional IRA and other paramilitary groups on both sides. This system of justice is put into effect by drug offenses, escalating from warnings through curfews, public humiliation, exile from the neighborhood, beating, and shooting with intent to wound (knee-capping) or, in exceptional circumstances, to kill. According to Thompson and Mulholland (1995), the actions of the paramilitary seem to be part of a self-maintaining cycle of action and reaction, fueled by fear, anger, revenge, frustration, and helplessness, since the community does not feel supported by the police. In such a context, young men, called "the hoods," feel that they have little to lose.

Community Programs. Since 1989, funding has been available from the government for local district councils to develop cross-community contact and cooperation, to promote mutual understanding, and to increase respect for different cultural traditions. A report in 1994 evaluated the program by providing an overview of the implementation of the initiative, assessing the effectiveness of the different types of projects and examining awareness of the program within councils. Ideological and logistical problems were found. They included, on the one hand, difficulties in actually making contact with members of one community because they were suspicious that community relations involve a hidden agenda and will force them to make political concessions (Knox, Hughes, Birrell, & McCready, 1994). On the other hand, there was difficulty locating neutral venues in which to locate projects. Intracommunity development, however, seems to be a necessary prerequisite since some groups have deeply entrenched negative social attitudes and sectarian prejudices. The process of repair will be lengthy, but findings of more positive attitudes toward community relations for local councils participating in the program are grounds for optimism.

Recent initiatives in the community setting also include the production of materials for youth and community leaders, women's groups, trade unions, and church groups to facilitate cross-community programs of work in community relations (Wilson & Morrow, 1996). Three broad themes encompassing nine subthemes inform the program: (1) understanding stable and divided societies (sharing a place, symbols and division, policing, transcendence); (2) coping with conflict (rituals, scapegoating, the best of a bad job); and (3) finding ways out (different approaches in different places, making a change). The authors report considerable interest in the materials, but a full evaluation of their effectiveness in changing attitudes and increasing tolerance will obviously take time.

Educational Systems. The Northern Ireland education system provides free education for all children of compulsory school age (4 to 16) as well as for those who choose to stay on until age 18. Secondary education is largely selective with pupils going to grammar schools or secondary high schools according to academic ability. Although there now is a small number of integrated schools that aim to have a balance of pupils from the Protestant and Catholic communities and these are attended at present by about 2% of the pupil population, over 90% of Catholics and Protestants are educated separately up to the school-leaving age. Teacher training colleges also operate on a segregated basis with separate colleges for the Catholic and Protestant communities. All other third-level education, which includes the 17 colleges of further education and the 2 universities, which enroll about 26,000 full- and part-time students, is integrated. Around 40% of eligible young people from Northern Ireland attend universities in Great Britain (Gallagher, 1989; 1992; Darby & Dunn, 1987).

Schools have potential for promoting attitudes of mutual respect across communities. The educational process, however, is complicated by the segregation that exists in other areas of life to varying extents in different parts of the country and within different sectors of the population. In 1991, for example, about half of the people in Northern Ireland lived in areas that were more than 90% Catholic or 90% Protestant, and only about 7% lived in areas with roughly equal numbers of Catholics and Protestants. Recent legislation has placed a statutory duty on the Department of Education in Northern Ireland to "encourage and facilitate" the development of integrated education. Beyond logistical problems, the process has been slow as a result of difficulties in setting up an integrated system that is not perceived as favoring one or the other group (Census data).

The task appears worthwhile, however, because there is evidence that stereotyping and prejudice may be promoted by segregated schooling and that political values may be communicated through the informal hidden curriculum. In the past, school systems differed in aspects of the curriculum, apart from the expected one of religious instruction. Perceptions of nationality and local history presented in schools of different traditions have been found to differ. There are also structural differences that occur through variations in school funding and provision of grammar school places for Catholic students. These were redressed in the early 1990s, but they seem to have an ongoing impact on people's perceptions of inequality in the educational system.

The existence of separate educational institutions to serve the two communities has focused attention on the relationship between social policies and the dynamics of the conflict. The Northern Ireland Department of Education appears to have taken the view that the core of the conflict is at the personal prejudice level and that schools should have a role in reducing prejudices. A series of programs has been developed to help students from the different communities to understand and become more tolerant of students of the "other" tradition and to prevent ignorance, fear, or hatred of those from whom they are educationally segregated. This program is intended to provide systematic curriculum-based opportunities for children from schools of different denominations to work together through two cross-curricular themes, known as Education for Mutual Understanding and Cultural Heritage.

Education for Mutual Understanding (EMU). EMU aims to promote self-respect and respect for others and to improve relations between people of different cultural traditions partly through activities undertaken together. Teachers are required to incorporate the theme into their subject areas. Legislation to include EMU in the curriculum was introduced in 1989 and became statutory and obligatory in September 1992. A recent report by Smith and Robinson (1996) discerned a need for a more specific focus, content, and approach, noting that the present approach was minimalist. They remarked on the absence of focus on issues involving human rights, lack of reference to ecumenism, and a missing emphasis on education for political participation. They also noted a failure to deal with gender issues. The authors were concerned at the lack of progress in developing a comprehensive plan for the education, training, and professional development of teachers, school governors, and ancillary staff plus weakness of institutional commitment to the program. Fewer than 50% of schools were participating in EMU in 1994–95 although it had been compulsory since 1990. They reported that only one pupil in nine had met a person of the other religion on the planned basis; this translates to just over 40,000 out of 350,000. Fewer than 1 in 5 primary and 1 in 10 secondary pupils were involved in the program. Clearly, greater school involvement and investment are required.

In mitigation of these conclusions, it is recognized that introduction of the program was not without controversy and was accompanied by charges of political interference in the curriculum through social engineering. Its implementation also depended on the perceptions of individuals and institutions within the system, which can mediate the way in which a policy is implemented. Bell (1990) encapsulated the issues by reminding us that teachers and youth workers in Northern Ireland experience a real dilemma of how to manage political argument and ethnic display in the educational setting. What is the school's responsibility for engaging with populist sectarianism and encouraging critical dialogue between and within the two traditions? Should schools provide a neutral haven by banishing all political discussion, or should young people be assisted in their critical interrogation of their culture of origin?

In fact, prohibition of political talk and evasion of controversial issues are the preferred strategies of most schools and youth clubs. Teachers believe EMU is too abstract, and few have received training to ease their own anxiety about dealing with the strong emotions these themes can arouse among people. Teachers also fear parental disapproval, as many parents want to keep politics out of schools. In addition, there exists a kind of denial that the problems of difference exist, and this adds to the forces that are ready to resist change.

On the positive side, the EMU theme has helped create a language that allows people to express their support for cultural pluralism and political dialogue as replacements for sectarianism and political violence. But the program needs to be developed further before it can stimulate young people to move beyond polite exchange toward engagement in meaningful discussion of controversial social, cultural, and political issues. As evaluators have noted, the program as now structured fails to address crucial themes, including ecumenism, political socialization, gender equality, and human rights.

Family Practices. What is known about the role of the family in political socialization of Northern Ireland's youth? Over a 1-year period, Taylor (1989) interviewed 14 families in Northern Ireland who had been active participants in the conflict and concluded that direct indoctrination was

Table 8.1. *Sample Sizes for Data Collection on Four Groups*

Year	West Belfast		East Belfast		Dublin		London		Total
	Girls	Boys	Girls	Boys	Girls	Boys	Girls	Boys	
1981	41	34	49	47	51	56	60	66	404
1992	64	56	52	78	44	71	51	60	476

insufficient to explain their activism. The families represented three "traditions" historically involved in the Irish conflict: the Protestant unionist community, the Catholic nationalist community, and the "mainland" British – represented by the British army. Each of the families had lost members who had been active participants in the conflict. The key events that moved individuals to become activists were previous family involvement, the teaching of history in school, and direct or vicarious experience of repression or of Troubles-related violence. According to the mother of Mairead Farrell, an IRA activist shot dead in Gibraltar in 1988, the incident that was instrumental in Farrell's decision to become involved in the IRA was the blinding of the mother of a school friend by a rubber bullet fired by a British soldier in Belfast. A history of family involvement can create an environment in which not to participate in the struggle, either physically or politically, would be seen as shirking one's duty. We know little, however, about what motivates the nonextremist, middle-of-the road individual to be active in politics.

Jean Whyte (1995) collected data on independence and commitment within families and knowledge of current affairs. The purpose of this study was to offer a baseline of information on family experiences and societal views of youth. Her sample comprised Catholic and Protestant 12-year-olds in Belfast as well as in Dublin and London. Data were collected from several schools serving socially disadvantaged areas in West Belfast (Catholic), East Belfast (Protestant), London, and Dublin (Table 8.1). Different students from the same schools participated in 1992 and completed the same questionnaire to establish whether there was change over time.

Participants completed self-report questionnaires in a classroom supervised by the researcher, usually within 50 to 60 min. Questions were modifications of the Manchester Scales of Social Adaptation (Lunzer, 1966). Information was obtained on youth's standard of living, such as whether they owned a bicycle and books, whether their family had a car and a telephone, what amount of discretionary spending money they had. Other sections addressed autonomy/independence, parental relationships, extracurricular and work activities, and access to information. Information on these variables seems important because they may contribute to aspects of youth's personal identity such as their sense of personal efficacy and self-esteem as well as to their declarative and procedural knowledge and their awareness of their status within the social system. These factors, in turn, might influence youth's perception of options, their interest in societal action, and their future aspirations.

Independence was assessed by the degree of responsibility youth had for making decisions in everyday matters and by the opportunities they had for traveling alone and for earning money by doing jobs outside the home. It was found that youth in Belfast were allowed less responsibility than were youth in Dublin and London. In addition, more support or nurturance was offered to Belfast youth by parents, particularly by mothers, in matters of personal hygiene, comforting, tucking in at night, and help with homework. Over time (1981–1992), there was some trend of increased independence in all the locations, but the Belfast youth were still more controlled. They were allowed less responsibility for decisions relating to their own activities than the Dublin or London youth with only small differences between East and West Belfast.

Commitment to the family was operationalized as helping with shopping and responsibilities for carrying out household chores as well as commitments outside the home and working for or helping others. The Dublin and West Belfast (Catholic) youth scored higher than the East Belfast (Protestant) and London youth. The same was true for some survival skills such as traveling alone by bus or taxi. On other survival skills such as making a telephone call from a public phone box, making a cup of tea, peeling a potato or apple there were no differences.

These differences are pertinent for further investigation because they may have implications for youth's autonomy and self-confidence, leaving the West Belfast Catholic youth perhaps feeling less competent to deal with public life in general. Such feelings could lead to an implicit conclusion that it is not worth bothering with politics because one cannot change the course of events. For the Belfast youth, the sociopolitical environment would clearly reinforce such a conclusion.

Further evidence on one aspect of political understanding is available in terms of youth's knowledge of current affairs, measured using 10 items from the Manchester Scales of Social Adaptation. Belfast youth scored lower than Dublin youth in both 1981 and 1992, and East Belfast

(Protestant) youth scored lower than the West Belfast (Catholic) youth. Although the calculation of statistical relationships was not appropriate given the nature of the scores on the socialization variables, it is nevertheless intriguing that the Belfast youth had lower scores on political questions and that they also were different from the Dublin youth on socialization variables related to independence and commitment. The consequences of lack of political knowledge at this age are potentially serious. Lack of factual knowledge about politics has been found to be related to lack of interest and opinions about politics (Raven & Whelan, 1983), and lack of interest in politics has been found to be a powerful predictor of unwillingness to vote in elections among 17- to 18-year-olds (Fife-Schaw & Breakwell, 1990). Future work should examine other aspects of political understanding and engagement such as participation in civic activities and relate these aspects to the measures of family relationships reported previously.

Conclusions

Cairns (1987) judged from the evidence available at the time that the form of political socialization of youth in Northern Ireland almost guaranteed the continuation of conflict and assured its escalation. Social institutions made little effort to encourage critical thinking about the conditions that caused the Troubles. As of 1998, the general situation had changed little despite the educational and government initiatives described. The problem with political apathy is that it leaves a vacuum ready to be filled by the politics of violence. Fortunately, violence has been relatively constrained. Moreover, the population is still attitudinally opposed to violence and crime has not increased. Community, educational, and family practices may have key roles in this constraint.

Youth in Northern Ireland tend to be protected more than their counterparts in Dublin or London; they are given less external responsibility and provided fewer opportunities to develop a sense of commitment. Parents and teachers tend to protect them also from the discussion of controversial issues. A positive outcome of this protection may be to assuage anxiety and discourage delinquency. But on the other side of the coin, this population of youth appears to show dependence on elders to make decisions and to be distrustful of government and other institutions.

The goal of this chapter has been to offer a fuller picture of youth's attitudes and behaviors and identify some of the key institutions that may influence their political beliefs and actions. Although some baseline information is available, there is much work to be done. In assessing the programming efforts and research in this area, there is a clear ideological distinction between those who emphasize personal solutions and others who focus on altering the social structure. The former define the problems underlying the conflict in terms of personal attitudes, which they then seek to change. The latter think in terms of societal structures, which they would then alter. A more productive approach may be to look at the interrelation of the two perspectives and also to address how personal attitudes are constructed in social contexts.

References

Bell, D. (1990). *Acts of union: Youth culture and sectarianism in Northern Ireland.* London: Macmillan.

Bronfenbrenner, U. (1986). Ecology of the family is a context for human development: Research perspectives. *Developmental Psychology, 22,* 723–742.

Burton, F. (1978). *The politics of legitimacy: Struggles in a Belfast community.* London: Routledge & Kegan Paul.

Cairns, E. (1987). *Caught in crossfire: Children and the Northern Ireland conflict.* Belfast: Appletree Press.

Cairns, E. (1996). *Children and political violence.* Oxford: Blackwell.

Darby, J., & Dunn, S. (1987). Segregated schools: The research evidence. In Osborne, R. D., Cormack, R. J., & Miller, R. L. (Eds.), *Education and policy in Northern Ireland.* Belfast: PRI.

Democratic Dialogue. (1996). *So what do you think? A survey of young people.* Belfast: Democratic Dialogue.

Fife-Schaw, C. & Breakwell, G. (1990). Predicting the intention not to vote in late teenage: A UK study of 17- and 18-year-olds. *Political Psychology, 11* (4), 739–755.

Fraser, M. (1973). *Children in conflict.* Harmondsworth: Penguin.

Gallagher, A. M. (1989), *The Majority Minority Review. No 1. Education and religion in Northern Ireland.* Ulster: Centre for the Study of Conflict, University of Ulster.

Gallagher, A. M. (1992). Education in a divided society. *The Psychologist, 5,* 353–356

Knox, C., Hughes, J., Birrell, D., & McCready, S. (1994). *Community relations and local government: A policy evaluation of the Northern Ireland District Council Community Relations Programme.* Coleraine, Northern Ireland: University of Ulster Centre for the Study of Conflict.

Lorenc, L., & Branthwaite, A. (1986). Evaluation of violence by English and Northern Ireland schoolchildren. *British Journal of Social Psychology, 25*(4), 349–352.

Lunzer, E. A. (1966). *The Manchester Scales of Social Adaptation.* Slough, U.K.: NFER.

McQuoid, J. (1994). The Self-Reported Delinquency Study in Belfast, Northern Ireland. In Jungertas, J., Terlouw, G. & Klein, M. W. (Eds.), *Delinquent be-*

havior among young people in the Western world: First results of the Inter-National Self-Report Delinquency Study. Amsterdam/New York: Kugler.

McVeigh, R. (1994). "It's part of life here": The Security Forces and harassment in Northern Ireland. Belfast: Committee for the Administration of Justice.

Mercer, G. W., & Bunting, B. (1980). Some motivations of adolescent demonstrators in the Northern Ireland civil disturbances. In J. Harbison and J. Harbison (Eds.), *A society under stress: Children and young people in Northern Ireland*. Somerset: Open Books.

NISA. (1992). *Social attitudes in Northern Ireland: The Second Report 1991–1992*. Belfast: Blackstaff Press.

NISA. (1995). *Social attitudes in Northern Ireland: The Fourth Report 1994–1995*. Belfast: Appletree Press.

NISA. (1996). *Social attitudes in Northern Ireland: The Fifth Report 1995–1996*. Belfast: Appletree Press

Raven, J. & Whelan, C. T. (1983). *Political culture in Ireland: The views of two generations*. Dublin: I. P. P.

Smith, A., & Robinson, A. (1996). *Education for mutual understanding: The initial statutory years*. Coleraine, Northern Ireland: University of Ulster Centre for the Study of Conflict.

Taylor, P. (1989). *Families at war: Voices from the Troubles*. London: BBC Books.

Thompson, W., & Mulholland, B. (1995). Juvenile offending and community tolerance. In W. McCarney (Ed.), *Growing through conflict: The impact of 25 years of violence on young people growing up in Northern Ireland*. Belfast: IAJFCM Conference.

Trew, K. (1980). Sectarianism in Northern Ireland: A research perspective. Paper presented at the British Psychological Society, Social Psychology Section, Canterbury, September.

Trew, K. (1996). Complementary or conflicting identities: The complexity of social identity in Northern Ireland. *The Psychologist*, Oct. 1996, 10–12.

Weinreich, P. (1992). Socio-psychological maintenance in Northern Ireland – a commentary. *The Psychologist*, 5, 345–346.

Whyte, Jean (1995). *Changing times, challenges to identity: 12-Year-olds in Belfast 1981 and 1992*. Aldershot: Avebury Press

Whyte, John (1990). *Interpreting Northern Ireland*. Oxford: Clarendon Press.

Wilson, D., & Morrow, D. (1996). *Future ways: Initiatives in community relations training*. Coleraine, Northern Ireland: University of Ulster/The Understanding Conflict Trust.

9. Youth Experience in the Palestinian Intifada: A Case Study in Intensity, Complexity, Paradox, and Competence

BRIAN K. BARBER

If anyone doubts the will and capability of adolescents to engage themselves fully in behalf of their society, one need look no further than the Palestinian Intifada to become convinced otherwise. Intifada is an Arabic word meaning an uprising or shaking off. It is used to refer to the popular revolution between 1987 and 1993 by Palestinian Arabs in the Occupied Territories of Israel (the West Bank and the Gaza Strip) against the Israeli military occupation that has been in place since 1967. The fervor and intensity with which the Palestinian youth in particular immersed themselves in this popular uprising – and then sustained this involvement over a period of several violent and traumatic years – are impressive and unique and illustrate the degree to which young people can commit themselves to the service of the larger society. Ironically, however, although the activities of Intifada youth are typically used to symbolize the popular uprising, the numerous volumes published on the movement contain very little about youth experience. The likely reason for this is that the Intifada involved all sectors of Palestinian society, and thus, there has been little reason to highlight any one particular age group. Nevertheless, there were specific activities in which adolescents participated most frequently (e.g., throwing stones, erecting barricades, burning tires), and because these were typically "front-line" actions, adolescents experienced the highest rates of victimization, including being harassed, beaten, shot at, arrested, detained, and imprisoned. For a pe-

I am very grateful to the College of Family, Home, and Social Sciences at Brigham Young University for its generosity in funding this study. I would like to thank the participants in this study for spending considerable hours with me discussing their very personal experiences. I thank also the three translators – Mohammed Abu Mallouh, Khalil Abu Shamalla, and Adnan Abed – for their rigorous and very valuable assistance. Finally, I thank the many Palestinian and American colleagues who read drafts of this chapter.

riod of 6 years (1987–1993), the lives of most Palestinian adolescents were affected, and often consumed, by deliberate quasi-violent and violent exchanges with a sophisticated military opponent, with all the accompanying intense experiences of danger, hope, trauma, unity, and discouragement.

The purpose of this chapter is to provide an initial view into the inner experience of these young people during this significant period of their development. The primary source of data for this chapter is a set of 1- to 2-hour semistructured interviews conducted in 1996 with 23 young adults in the Gaza Strip. These interviews were the first in a series of sets of interviews that intend to capture the essence of this social movement from the perspective of its key participants. The purpose of these interviews was to learn firsthand from participants about the Intifada: its meanings, the motives underlying involvement in it, its day-to-day characteristics, and its social and psychological impact. A snowball sampling technique was employed to select this initial sample, where referrals for participation were made by knowledgeable youth and adults with whom I have become acquainted during recent trips to the Gaza Strip.

Although no sample of this size can be comprehensive, efforts were made to achieve diversity that would permit a variety of perspectives. Participants (18 males, 5 females) resided in four of the eight refugee camps in the Gaza Strip: Khan Yunis, Deir El Ballah, Maghazi, and Nuseirat. Participants represented a range of political orientations: Fateh (5), independents (5), the Popular Front for the Liberation of Palestine (PFLP, 9), Hamas (2), Islamic Jihad (1), and Communist (1). The disproportionate representation of PFLP members is a function of the refugee camps I happened to live in during this first set of interviews. The educational background of sample participants ranged from less than high school to bachelor's degrees. Ages at the time of the interviews ranged from 17 to 35 (8–26 at the start of the Intifada). The majority of the sample (20) were adolescents during the Intifada.

I conducted all interviews with the assistance of three bilingual (Arabic/English) translators. All three were native Gazans who lived in the same camps as the participants. Two participants were fluent enough in English to be interviewed in English. Interviews were tape-recorded with the consent of the participant and were typically conducted in the participant's home. Most interviews were conducted privately with a single individual at a time. One group interview was held with six of the males. Participants were informed that the purpose of the interview was to gather data to write a book on the Intifada. It was made clear to all participants that they could decline to answer any question that made them uncomfortable in any way. None declined to answer any question. Participants were also given the option of using their real first name or a pseudonym. Four elected to use a pseudonym. I transcribed the tape-recorded interviews and used established techniques for the analysis of qualitative data (e.g., Lofland & Lofland, 1995). I edited the direct quotations used in this chapter for grammar and have occasionally inserted additional words in brackets to clarify meaning.

In preparation to maximize my ability as a non-Palestinian to present such an account, I have endeavored to immerse myself in the culture as much as has been possible. This has included eight extended visits over the past 30 months to Gaza and the West Bank, with a combined total residency of 7 months. All of this time was spent in Palestinian population centers, and several weeks were spent living with families in two of Gaza's refugee camps. I have visited 50 secondary schools and had discussions with hundreds of students, and my colleagues and I have surveyed over 7,000 students and their parents about the Intifada, family relationships, and social and psychological competence. Initial results from the survey work are reported in Barber, Chadwick, Heaton, Huntington, Fronk, and Torres (1996).

Several steps were taken to assure the credibility of the interview data, including using respected local contacts to select the sample and serve as translators, conducting the interviews in the native tongue of the participants, and having drafts of this chapter read and edited by numerous Palestinians, including the three translators and two of the participants. During the period of the interviews, the translators commented regularly – often with some surprise – on how open the participants were with their answers. It was clear that the participants valued the purpose of the interviews and appreciated the opportunity to relate their experiences. I was not able to detect any obvious patterns of exaggeration or stifling of response.

Despite the attempt to achieve diversity, the sample does not include all segments of the Palestinian youth population. For example, although one of the participants had been paralyzed by a soldier's bullet to the spine, the sample does not include youth who suffered serious psychological or emotional trauma as a result of their involvement in the Intifada. The sample also did not include any collaborators, Palestinians who were recruited by the Israeli authorities to spy and inform on Intifada participants. Several of the interviewed participants referred to collaborators in their portrayals of the Intifada.

Finally, although our recent survey data do not reveal dramatically higher Intifada involvement among Gaza youth compared to West Bank youth, limiting the sample to Gaza residents may have resulted in a somewhat more intense portrayal. The Intifada began in the Gaza Strip, which is a more socially and economically isolated area that is more tightly controlled economically and politically than many parts of the West Bank. Limiting the sample further to residents of refugee camps in Gaza, as opposed to residents of cities or villages, may have also contributed to a more intense account.

The chapter begins with a brief overview of the historical/political background of the Intifada. Next, reported motivations for youth participation and patterns of involvement in the Intifada are discussed, followed by the presentation of three general themes that highlight the complexity of Palestinian youth social and psychological experience during the Intifada. Finally, conclusions are made about the implications of the information from the interviews for the understanding of youth competence.

Historical–Political Background

The Intifada began officially on December 8, 1987, when an Israeli military vehicle crashed into a series of cars at the Erez border crossing into the Gaza Strip, killing four Palestinians and wounding several others. Massive protest demonstrations accompanied the funerals that evening. The protests, and accompanying confrontations between Palestinians and Israeli military, continued the following day and spread through the Strip. Shortly afterward, the uprising spread throughout the West Bank. The confrontations continued with varying levels of intensity until 1993. Despite its spontaneous ignition, the Intifada is best understood not only as a response to assorted conflicts and political events near in time to the car accident (see Tessler, 1994, for a thorough review), but also as an extension of a century-long political conflict between Arabs and Jews (Hunter, 1993). An awareness of the Palestinians' understanding of this political history is essential to grasping the meanings that the Intifada has had for them.

According to the Palestinian sociologist Abu-Lughod (1991, p. 3),

> The *intifada* is primarily a political act of resistance seeking the achievement of a political objective. It derives its major values, aspirations, and premises from the collective existential experiences of the Palestinian people, especially those who have encountered British and Israeli colonialism over the past seven decades; and in

carrying its purpose forward the *intifada* has benefitted from the previous militant experience of the Palestinians as they struggled for national independence.

The conflict took shape when Jewish nationalists decided late in the nineteenth century to mobilize the Jewish population – then scattered throughout Europe and Russia – to establish a homeland in Palestine. Although early relations between Arabs (representing 90% of the population of Palestine at the turn of the century) and Jewish immigrants were in part friendly and cooperative, it was not long before suspicion and mutual antagonism surfaced. Early disputes surrounded issues of continuing Jewish immigration, land purchases, and growing Jewish involvement and control of the commercial sectors of society. These and other economic issues continued as areas of strong contention and resentment, and the conflict deepened into issues of nationalism, autonomy, and survival for both sides (Tessler, 1994).

Although there were a number of mutual efforts toward cooperation and diplomacy throughout the period from the turn of the century to the Intifada, the period was marked mainly by the violence of numerous wars. All of these worsened the demographic, political, and economic condition of the Palestinian Arabs. Britain's victory in liberating Palestine from the Ottomans in World War I – but then retaining control over it – was perceived by the Palestinians as a betrayal of Britain's pledge to support the establishment of an independent Arab kingdom (Hunter, 1993). With dramatically increasing Jewish immigration in the 1930s, the Palestinians staged an unsuccessful 2-year-long violent insurrection (the Great Arab Revolt) that left them exhausted and demoralized (Tessler, 1994). Their condition worsened with their defeat in the 1947–1948 Arab – Israeli War, which the Palestinians refer to as *al-naqba* (the "catastrophe" or the "disaster"), and by which the establishment of the State of Israel was facilitated. Not only did this defeat deepen the sense of despair, but it also resulted in substantial demographic consequences for the Palestinians in the form of the displacement of as many as 760,000 Palestinian Arabs. The large majority of the displaced population fled to the West Bank and the Gaza Strip.

The situation worsened as a result of the 1967 war, in which Israel defeated Egypt, Syria, and Jordan and occupied the Sinai Peninsula, the Golan Heights, East Jerusalem, the West Bank, and the Gaza Strip. This, along with the later neutralization of Egypt as an ally to Palestinians through the 1979 peace treaty between Israel and Egypt, led the Palestinians to realize that they could not rely on their Arab neighbors and that they must take charge of their own cause (Hunter, 1993). The capture of the West Bank and the Gaza Strip by Israel placed hundreds of thousands of additional Palestinians under direct military control and thereby reset the stage of the Palestinian–Israeli conflict, which grew subtly yet systematically until the outbreak of the Intifada in 1987.

From the Palestinian perspective, the Intifada was a response to four types of subjugation inherent in the Israeli occupation of the West Bank and the Gaza Strip. The first was political suppression, which included Israeli control over legal, civil, and political rights. It also included the Israeli self-termed Iron Fist policy designed to put down growing Palestinian resistance through forceful means of collective punishments, arbitrary harassments, arrests, curfews, torture, home raids and demolitions, and deportations. The second form of subjugation was economic exploitation in the form of land and water resource confiscations, exploitation of Palestinian labor, restriction of external trade, annexation through confiscation of land, and establishment of settlements. Third was the intentional destructuring of social and financial institutions, affecting savings, investments, and trade unions. Fourth was ideological and cultural repression in the form of a requirement to license all publications; censorship; destruction of Arabic historic sites; expunging of the word *Palestine* from all textbooks; changing to Hebrew of Arabic names for towns, hills, and streets; and prohibition of festivals, exhibits, and public lectures (for a detailed review of this position, see Farsoun & Landis, 1991).

These conditions, although apparently designed to suppress the collective identity and will of the Palestinians, tended, paradoxically, not to subdue the Palestinians but to encourage resistance. Farsoun and Landis (1991, pp. 26–27) noted that

> grass-roots organizations sprang forth in all areas of communal life: medical relief, agricultural relief, local councils, professional associations, trade unions and even federations, women's committees, and all manner of self-help educational, cultural, welfare, and charitable societies . . . knitting the people together in a web of reciprocal relations, mutual cooperation, and solid politically conscious bonds.

Motivation for Participation

One of the most striking features of Palestinian youth is their awareness of political issues. In interviewing four male adolescents from East Jerusalem in 1994 in preparation for the survey study, I was struck with the extent to which political issues – carefully justified with relevant history – pervaded their experience. When I asked them to identify a man they admired in their society, all chose a political figure. When I asked them to describe the times in which they felt most happy, typical responses included "When the peace process is going well" or "When we get our autonomy." It took several probes before the young men realized that I was asking for a personal response. Finally, Tareq caught on and said with some enthusiasm, "I am happy when I run. I love to run." But then he followed immediately, with resignation, "But every time I run, the soldiers want to arrest me." This statement was a classic illustration of a fundamental characteristic of Palestinian youth in the Occupied Territories – that in their world there is no distinction between the personal and the political.

This acute sensitivity to history and politics, particularly as it related to the Intifada, was evident in the interviews of the young adults in Gaza. Their comments largely reflected the scholars' rendition of the historical and political background of the uprising summarized previously. At the beginning of every interview I asked all participants to "tell me what the Intifada was." All of the them defined it as a reaction against the military occupation, and their comments highlighted the historical, political, cultural, and psychological implications of the occupation. Hatim said, "I was 12 years old. I grew up during the Intifada. Before the Intifada we noticed all the arresting. We saw a main soldier [gives soldier's name]. We hated him very much because of his activities against the people. . . . The Intifada began. We saw the people who were older than us throwing stones. We saw that it was the best way to express our feelings. Especially, because we were still young."

It was very important to Khalil to define the movement in terms of its historical–political context. He said, "The Intifada came as a result of – not that accident that happened – no, definitely not. It came after 27 years of the occupation, and do you know what the occupation means? It means the most meaningful in terrorizing itself." Ghassan expanded on this same feeling of being terrorized when he said, "The Intifada was a public reaction against the Israeli hardness and inhuman actions against Palestinians; especially killing, harsh circumstances, bad economic situations, and other actions. I can't describe them exactly [the behaviors]. To them we were subhumans."

Saher's comments emphasized the history of frustration throughout the occupation: "It was the Israeli measures in the Occupied Territories including Gaza that created something like an express bomb that exploded. The Israeli measures accumulated inside the people here until they exploded."

Waheed was particularly indignant about violations of childhood and cultural norms during the occupation, saying, "For example, they used to stop youth, use bad language, and spit on them. Sometimes they beat them. Sometimes they told them to take off their clothes. Sometimes I saw them stop a girl and a boy and ask the boy to kiss the girl. These procedures created oppression and regression for Palestinians . . . and pushed the youth to face the Israeli occupation or troops with [the] simple possibilities they had . . . [e.g., stones]."

In defining the Intifada as an uprising against the "Israeli tough procedures," Mahmoud (3)[1] revealed the critical psychological impact of the occupation:

> The psychological effects result from different procedures, such as economic procedures, educational procedures, and actions against the political parties. The Israeli government used to use educational procedures. For example, the curriculum and the books were not adequate and not related to the Palestinians' settings and background. They punished the Islamic or nationalist people by preventing them from getting jobs at schools or hospitals or elsewhere. The classes are also full of students – 50 students in a class with one teacher. The classroom in the school is not adequate for learning, and it is not healthy sometimes. Also, there are economic and political procedures they follow, such as prisons, unemployment, and bad housing. All these things combine to produce a bad psychological effect on the people. The health procedures they follow also affect the psychological condition of the Palestinians. For example, there are not enough hospitals [or] medicine. Serious surgeries used to be done in Israel. Now few are done and most people die before the operations. Even the Palestinian expert doctors are not allowed to work in our hospitals. They [Israel] don't give them jobs in order to force them to leave the country or to make them useless or disappointed. You see, all these examples push the Palestinians towards the end.

In addition to this historical consciousness of antagonism toward the occupation, individual involvement in the Intifada seemed to be crystallized also by specific traumatic events. Often this was when someone known to the subject had been killed. For Waheed, it was when he saw the body of one of the members of his refugee camp returned to the camp after having been killed in the car accident that sparked the uprising. For Wael and Mahmoud (2) it was a common friend who was "martyred." Mahmoud (2) recalled, "He left big gaps in my life and also in the lives of my friends. I will not forget him forever because he was my close friend."

For others, these crystallizing events were the mistreatment of neighbors or family members during the frequent house raids by soldiers. Sami described soldiers entering the house and kicking his father and some women and said, "This affected me negatively." Wajdi recalled his mother's being shot when trying to stop soldiers from taking his brother during a house raid: "I could not help my mother. This was very, very bad in my emotions." Hatim recalled watching a 3-year-old child kick a soldier. He described, "The soldier then pushed him by his foot and all of the soldiers tried to pass over him by their feet. And this increased in me the belief in my cause."

Ibtisam detailed a moment she "will never forget":

> My home is located near the school. Always young people used to escape from the school to my house because the other side of my house goes to the other street where it was safe for them. Once, young people – students – scared from soldiers, passed my house and went to the other street. The soldiers came to my house where I was with my 12-year-old brother. They started to frustrate us by questioning us in Hebrew. I said that neither I nor my brother knew Hebrew. I asked whether they knew English or Arabic. But one of them shouted some dirty words in Arabic, and they started to kick us. They kicked my brother first, and when I tried to protect my brother they began to kick me also. At that time I felt that we needed to go on in our Intifada to achieve our target because we are suffering more and more, and if this occupation will remain in our land we will suffer more and more.

Ghassan's experience was similar. He said, "I saw a soldier hitting and kicking a woman in the street here. We could do nothing because there was a huge number of soldiers in the street. They began to besiege us so we couldn't do anything but flee. . . . We felt that our immortality, our supremacy was no more. In the eyes of the soldiers, we were animals that they wanted to hunt. So this created feelings of anger and revolution inside each one of us."

Maisirah volunteered the following story, which illustrates the intensity, fear, and sense of violation that these house raids produced:

> I was asleep and suddenly I realized that a soldier was seizing me from my shirt. He put a search light into my face. . . . He was

masked. In amazement and fear, I jumped off my bed. Another soldier took my brother and he separated us from each other. He took him into a separate room and locked the door on my mother and the other children in her room. Six soldiers besieged me and interrogated me about throwing stones on soldiers. One of the soldiers held me from my hair and the other put a dagger to my neck. At this moment [my father] saw what was happening to me and he began shouting at the soldiers to save me. They attacked my father and obliged him to shut up. But he didn't give up and he began shouting again. Then they threatened my father with a dagger. The incident lasted for about 20 minutes. I did not tell them anything and then, suddenly, they left the house.

Finally, events like this also served to escalate the type of participation. For example, soldiers suspected Mohammed's pregnant wife of hiding some stone throwers. He watched the soldiers drag her by her hair from their home into the street. Her injuries from this incident necessitated a stay in the hospital that lasted 25 days. Mohammed said, "I refused to continue using the traditional methods [e.g., stones]. So I sent a letter to the outside, to our political leadership outside, summoning or asking for the permit to use weapons."

Patterns of Intifada Involvement

Given the collective consciousness of long-term oppression and the frequency and intensity of experiences in which the youth felt their loved ones to be violated, it is not surprising that high numbers of them participated in the Intifada, which was clearly not an expression of a small, disgruntled minority. Our survey data indicate that at least 80% of adolescents were involved in the two most prominent forms of activity, demonstrating and throwing stones, with half involved in other activities such as protecting someone from soldiers and distributing leaflets to "reinforce people to go in their struggling" (interview with Hatim) and to announce the future conduct of the movement. Victimization rates, especially for males, were also very high with 86% reporting being harassed by soldiers, 73% beaten by soldiers, and 48% arrested by soldiers. For details on the prevalence and patterning of Intifada involvement and on their associations with youth and family functioning, see Barber 1997 and in press.

There were, of course, individual variations in participation, ranging from no involvement to daily involvement. Sami, who was 10 years old when the Intifada began, defended his nonparticipation on philosophical and rational grounds expressed in the form of both his and his father's belief that throwing stones was a "nonsense" [ineffective] way to resist the occupation. He said during the group interview, "I was like an intelligent side of the work. I was not active in the Intifada like this young Mahmoud [2]. I believed in rational questions about the events. . . . Mahmoud [2] knows many times young people came to me and asked me to help them and to participate with them in their activities. But my dead father, may Allah bless him, refused to let me."

Sami revealed his own sense of inner conflict about his role in the movement, commenting that after his father died toward the end of the Intifada, "I was hoping that this period [Intifada since his father's death] may be longer than what it was so that I could participate more with the young people than what I had done before . . . because I did not do what I should have done." Sami's repeated self-comparisons to Mahmoud (2) revealed some of the pressure felt by him to participate. His experience was echoed by Naji, who was paralyzed by a soldier's bullet in the spine. In response to a question whether he ever felt pressured to become involved when he didn't want to, he reported, "Yes, it happened once. There was a message to ask all of the students of the school to get out of their schools and to demonstrate. My point of view was that there was no reason for this. I was obliged to do this because it was just an order from upper authorities."

Generally, however, those interviewed described voluntary – usually eager – participation in the movement, for many, as a daily event. Ghassan spoke for others his age in the camp. "It was our life, every day. . . . Almost every day we were sitting in one home here or in another friend's home thinking about how to face the occupation: how, when to wait and how to wait, and what were the most certain ways to crush them [the soldiers] from the camp." Frequency of involvement was typically determined by the presence of soldiers. Waheed said, "My participation was a reaction to the Israelis – if they came in the camp and how severe their actions were. If they came once a day, then the confrontations would occur once a day. If they came once a week, then confrontations were once a week."

In the camp Abu Fida lives in, such confrontations occurred "three times a day. Whenever the army came to the camp there would be confrontations." Ghassan remembered, "Sometimes I walked in the street peacefully and calmly with my friends, laughing and remembering past moments. . . . Suddenly [a] jeep would emerge from a street and begin to chase us. The soldiers would be laughing and shooting. Sometimes we were sitting in a home like this, drinking tea or coffee, and watching

TV or exchanging opinions on the occupation. The soldiers would violate the house and begin to chase us on the roofs. . . . I can't remember everything, but actions or experiences like this would happen every day – 1 time, 2 times, 3 times, 10 times, every day."

In trying to characterize participation rates, Ahmed divided youth into two groups: those leaders who "were convinced of what they are doing" and who felt it was "their duty to do that" and those who did not seek leadership but were motivated simply by "something emotional inside themselves." He also provided insight into the toll the years of conflict took on some youth. "Some people were depressed in their self. For how long are we going to have this confrontation? What is our purpose? What are our resources to stand and for how long?"

In summary, the Intifada was a period of great intensity for these youth as they immersed themselves in the cause of their people. Their struggle against the military occupation was motivated by the pervasive historical and political consciousness among the whole society and by the personal experiences they had of mistreatment.

General Themes

The purpose of this section is to move beyond describing various facets of the Intifada to providing an interpretive characterization of the Intifada based on some themes that emerged during the interviews. There are numerous ways in which any set of interview data can be organized. I have chosen to concentrate on a pattern of contrasts that illustrate a rich and complex – often paradoxical – social and psychological experience of youth during and after the uprising. In studying the transcripts of the interviews, I was struck repeatedly not only with the raw intensity of the experience of these young people, but also with how often they were forced to confront and cope with seemingly contradictory or contrasting sets of feelings, attitudes, and experiences. Three illustrations will be given: (a) their attitudes simultaneously reflected defiance (to "illegitimate" authority) and deference (to "legitimate" authority); (b) they experienced substantial personal growth but have found little opportunity to exercise it; (c) the strong hope for the success of the movement has turned to discouragement and disappointment for many.

Defiance and Deference

The sociologist Tamari (1992, p. 18) has noted that "the image of young Palestinians using their slingshots against the Israeli army has been the most persistent image of youthful rebellion printed throughout the mass media in the Western world." The Intifada was a clear demonstration that adolescents, as well as much younger children, are capable of displaying blatant and sustained defiance against authority. Their behavior during the Intifada was often defensive, but it was also taunting, provocative, vengeful, full of emotion, and disrespectful. However, one of the greatest paradoxes of Palestinian youth is that such defiance emerged from young people who are otherwise quite passive and peaceful in temperament, who have strict standards of moral conduct, and who are also highly deferential to authority. Moreover, instead of a defiance that appeared to be wanton or reckless, they demonstrated a resourceful ability to plan and organize themselves with a sophisticated and methodical tactical competence. What emerges, therefore, is a portrait of youth capable of making discriminations about legitimacy of authority based on personal indignation and a sensitivity to the broader cultural consciousness, and then deliberately acting on these evaluations in circumstances of considerable selflessness and risk to their own safety.

The theme of defiance clearly ran through all of the interviews. It was evident in the way the participants defined the Intifada and in how they responded to the specific traumatic events discussed earlier. On the street, the resistance took both defensive and offensive forms including specific, often age-related actions (see also Kuttab, 1988), such as storing masks that would conceal identity, serving as lookouts, writing slogans and distributing leaflets (both forms of communiqués), burning tires and erecting barricades to impede soldier traffic, throwing stones and cocktail bombs, and, toward the latter end of the movement, using firearms in some groups. Ghassan responded to my request to talk about the relative balance of offensive and defensive actions:

> It depends. For example, during the first five years of the Intifada, the soldiers always instigated us. I read in the newspaper that they came in the camps in order to hunt people – to amuse themselves. Some of them wrote on their helmet, "Born to kill." The soldiers came at certain times near the schools, near the mosques, near the central market here in the camp. As soon as they came the youth were obliged to escape. They [the soldiers] began to chase them, to attack them, to arrest them which made it possible for other people to attack the soldiers. But at the end of the Intifada, things changed. People attacked the soldiers [who] were coming into the camp in order to kidnap persons. For example, they came for an hour to shoot people and went out directly without being in the camp for

further attacks by the people. They came, shot people, and went out. They came, arrested people, and went out directly. So the people became angry. What could they do? People were walking in the street. Then, suddenly, the soldiers came and arrested them and went out. When the people became angry they thought of one thing – that they had to initiate actions in order to prevent the soldiers from coming to attack them suddenly or overnight. Thus, initiation became the task of our people – not of the soldiers – in order to defend ourselves.

He remembered further one specific example of the offensive planning that took place:

> In the memory of [person], we planned to make a demonstration against the Israelis. It was not to be an ordinary demonstration, but a real revolution in the camp. So during the night of the day before, almost 50 persons hurried to plan for this. They put up barricades, they prepared tires [for burning], they put up Palestinian flags, some people arranged fire bombs, cocktail bombs. By the next morning, we were all prepared for this day. Some people went to the soldiers here near the camp in order to entice them to come inside the camp. The soldiers refused. It continued until almost three o'clock in the afternoon. But the people accumulated and increased and the soldiers were obliged to come into the camp. Attacks began soon – severe attacks. It was a day of which we are still proud.

With relish, Abdullah recalled the planning of one ambush. "In a hilly area in Nuseirat there is a general [public] bath for the people. It was used by the British army in the 1940s. We climbed on the roof of that place, and we divided the street in front of it into two parts. We put barriers in one half of the street, and nails in the other half. When the jeeps came down the road, they would get punctures. We waited for them on the roof of the bath. Then we would rain stones on them. The last jeep suffered the most."

As blatant and as frequent as this defiance was, youth actions during the Intifada did not appear to be chaotic, uncontrolled behavior fueled simply by unchecked passion. Instead, paradoxically, the defiance occurred simultaneously with substantial deference to recognized authority. Although one participant, Waheed, described his resistance activities as being relatively independent and solitary, most described their participation in faction-specific organizational systems characterized by clear hierarchies of authority. In answering my question, "How did you know what to do and when to do it?" most responded similarly to Abu Fida ("The people of higher rank instructed us what to do"); Naji ("There was an official. When we get a message from him we should carry out this message without any kind of objection"); or Ibtisam ("At the beginning, I involved myself spontaneously in the Intifada. But when the groups started to organize their activities, immediately I joined one of these organizations and I started to go on in an organized way"). Both Mahmoud (3) and Ahmed said that instructions and information were communicated by Palestinian authorities outside the territories to the local organizations.

Khalil detailed his process of integration into the organizational structures:

> Young people were searching and looking for organizations to join themselves.... As an example, at the beginning I did not know about the political program of any of the organizations. I knew some of the people here in my camp, or in neighboring camps, who were struggling before the Intifada. The first organization I belonged to was the movement [gives name]. I didn't know everything about them. After two or three months, I discovered where I was and who the people around me were. Because I realized that I did not believe in their political program ... I said to them that the moment has come that I must cut my relationship with you. I started to look for another organization – not the best organization, but a better one. (To me, there is no best organization. Even the organization I belong to now [gives name] is not the best. It might be better than any other organization, but it is not the best.) So, I went to my relative and told him that I wanted to join [gives name].

Ghassan summed up the general attitude of deference to older, more experienced persons in the community when he said, "We achieved respect from all of the people in our society through our actions. This urged me to achieve the confidence of the people. Always we asked them what to do. Should we do so or so? We listened to them carefully. For example, some people gave us advice during the clashes that erupted among some of the organizations here. In order to avoid these clashes, we asked some older people who are wise. And we always listened and attended to what they said in order to prevent suffering from these interfactional clashes."

He also spoke of deference to parents. "He [my father] didn't prevent me from doing anything. But always he said, 'Be aware. Just be aware, and maintain your studies during the actions.' So, in fact, after the actions, I always came home and began to study."

In sum, the Intifada was a time when young Palestinians displayed a paradoxical mix of strong defiance and clear deference. It seems they were able to make distinctions between illegitimate and legitimate authority, organizing themselves systematically and hierarchically under the latter in order to fight the former.

Growth and Stasis

Paradoxical conditions are also evident when considering how youth experiences in the Intifada reconcile with post-Intifada circumstances. Specifically, Intifada youth apparently experienced substantial personal growth from their involvement in the uprising. Current conditions in Gaza, however, do not provide opportunities for youth to demonstrate or use the growth. What has resulted is a frustrated condition wherein young people who accelerated their transition to the enactment of adult roles and who appear to have formed fairly solid and positive identity structures do not have regular access to conditions (e.g., employment, higher quality education, mobility) by which this maturity typically is transported into adulthood.

Comments relative to personal growth came in answer to a number of different interview questions, including those focusing on the perceived success of the Intifada, whether and how the Intifada shaped respondents' self-perceptions, whether involvement in the Intifada influenced the participants' attitudes toward conformity to social rules, and whether participation affected participants' level of commitment to social welfare. Various qualities were mentioned by respondents when describing the personal growth they underwent during the Intifada, such as personal satisfaction (Ghassan, Khalil), self-improvement (Sumaya), organization (Abu Fida), independence (Ibtisam), acceptance from peers and adults (Saher, Khalil, Waheed, Ghassan), and patience (Waheed). Several of the respondents cited their own personal growth by way of a discussion of needing to move beyond childhood. Ghassan said:

> Before the Intifada we were children. The only thing we thought about was football. Sometimes we studied, or watched TV, or did many things which were not so important. But during our actions or involvement in the Intifada, we began to think in another way. We began to have a role in our society. We changed the way people

thought. We become leaders when we were children, so we began to think that we had a great role to perform. . . . By this we achieved self-satisfaction, self-assertion. . . . We thought we could do something against the Israeli occupation . . . I am proud of myself to have lived such a life. Because what kind of life can a child have during the occupation? I think I lived my childhood in the kindergarten in the [refugee] camp. They were happy days. I also felt happy during my study in preparatory school. But during the Intifada it was our task to rebel and to fight, or to be engaged in conflict against the Israelis. . . . Yes, in fact, it was a good life. It was a good opportunity for us to become self-made men.

Similarly, Mahmoud (2) said, "Most of the people who were sharing in the Intifada were still in their childhood . . . it was as a result of their sharing in the Intifada that they lost their childhood. I think none of them regret that period. The Intifada provided many points of view to everyone. As an example, I struggled and I was active and I was in prison and I was injured two times. It might be abnormal in other countries, but for me, I am honored and I don't regret what I did."

Some of the respondents presented a more ambivalent picture of the loss of their childhood. Maisirah's response to the question about whether involvement in the movement affected how he feels about himself had both negative and positive components. "Sometimes yes and sometimes no. Concerning no, as a young man involved in a resistance movement, a lot of things like seeing blood, smoke, tear gas, and attacks made me very depressed. As a child, I wanted to live my childhood like children all over the world. Concerning yes, children here learned a lot of things which made them older and bigger as men. In contrast to children in other parts of the world, here children became responsible to do things which children in other countries don't do."

Both Waheed and Ahmed talked of losing their childhood. Ahmed said, "I lost my childhood . . . I see children playing and I want to go back to my childhood. A lot of our people – not a lot, I mean all of them – they lost their childhood. . . . My sympathy is that I want to see that my children, Palestinian children, can play freely in their own country in the future."

Ironically, much of the growth experienced by these young people came as a result of their experiences in prison. Imprisonment was a very common theme in the interviews. This method of trying to suppress resistance in large part backfired and encouraged substantial organization and growth. When Abu Fida's mother was begging the soldiers not to take her son to prison, he responded, "No, don't beg him. It is an honor for me to be in prison." Ghassan recalled the response he received from others: "Some of my friends often tell me nowadays that when I was arrested and went to prison my behavior changed. I mean older friends . . . friends who are now maybe 29 years old. They tell me that before I went to prison I was an ordinary child. But they say that when I came out of prison, they thought I was another man, another person; one who had exceeded his age."

Youth appeared to capitalize on the prison experience to train and organize themselves for further service in the Intifada. Khalil described the prison experience in detail:

> The first moment you enter prison, you see many tents and many people. After you enter, a group of prisoners come and welcome you. They say that you need to choose from a list of several political organizations. After you choose, members of your chosen organization take you to their tent and sit with you and have a welcoming party. They tell you which tents belong to which groups, and what the relationships are with the other groups, such as whether there are any conflicts between any groups, how you are to deal with the other groups – whether you should just say hello, or whether you can go to their tent and discuss or negotiate, or just to have social relations with them. . . .
>
> We had a main program within the prison. We got up at six o'clock, washed our faces and hands, and returned back to our tent for one or one-and-a-half hours to read and culture ourselves on any topic. After this was breakfast. After breakfast, the soldiers came to count us. Then the doctor came to see their patients or to see who wanted some tablets for headaches or other things like this. At ten o'clock, we started our lessons. We were classified into three levels: primary, middle, advanced. The primary level consisted of members who didn't know many things about their organization. The middle level members knew some things, but not enough. Advanced members studied [at the] theoretical [level]. After this we distributed ourselves among the others, finding a friend to sit with for many hours until lunch. After lunch, there was time for sleeping until the second count in the afternoon. We listened to radios. At the beginning of my first prison term, there was only one loudspeaker. There weren't any radios before 1990. But afterwards, in 1991, 1992, 1993, and still now, every group of prisoners has a special radio and T.V.

The second lessons were in the afternoon from about four or five o'clock until dinner at eight or nine o'clock. After dinner, we had the third set of lessons, in which we discussed different topics or continued discussing the previous lectures. The lesson lasted until the third role call. In the evening, we walked through the section, talking on any topic with anyone until 12 midnight when they told us on the loudspeaker, "Good Night, go to sleep; everybody needs to enter the tent."

Similarly, Ahmed reflected on the success of prisons in the development of the youth:

When the Israelis thought to have a prison, their intent was to kill us [the way we think]. They thought that when we would be freed after our prison term, we would return to our people and not want to resume our Intifada actions and be imprisoned again. We took this as a challenge. We began the challenge by improving the social circumstances. We spent a lot of time giving seminars, speeches, political speeches, reading books. We decided many times in prison to have a war against the prison's administration to achieve more of our rights as prisoners. We stopped eating food for long periods of time, I mean strikes.

I realized that prisons were becoming an academy for the Palestinian prisoners where the prisoners were educated. Sometimes the prisoners ran the Intifada from inside the prison. So, despite their goal to prevent the Palestinians from coming back to prison, the Palestinians decided indeed to come back.

All, or most, of my personality is due to the prison. I benefited a lot ... most of the prisoners ... they benefited a lot from life inside the prisons. It made them real men, and it taught them to depend on themselves, and to be good people. When the intelligence man said to me that he was going to throw me in the Negev prison for six months of administrative detention, I said, "You are serving me; I am going to the academy of the Palestinians in Negev."

Perhaps the most striking illustration of the capacity of these young people to capitalize on their detentions and incarcerations is that of Waheed, who was among 415 Palestinians deported to Lebanon in 1991. After describing a mock trial and prolonged mistreatment, Waheed talked about this experience of being "uprooted from my land, my family, my friends, my brother," and dropped in the middle of winter in a foreign country to stay for 1 year:

[In the bus] we had decided not to go inside Lebanon. It was a decision made by all of us, but they started shooting over our heads and we were afraid. We ran away... inside Lebanon, and we didn't know the way we were going. We met the journalists and the press men there. It was raining and snowing and we had no shelter, no house. It was an ugly feeling. We felt desperate. We met the Red Cross there who provided help and assistance and tents. We built our first camp. We decided to go back to our land, to our country, and not to stay in Lebanon, but they prevented us again by shooting bombs and bullets over our heads. So we decided to organize our days and time and work. We founded committees, for example, health committees to take care of the health of the deportees, a social committee and an engineering committee to take care of the tents and the houses and the shelters. We also founded a cultural and educational committee which took care of educating the deportees, giving them lectures and ceremonies. We built a mosque. Afterward, we started a university. There was a need for a university because there were 80 university students and 30 professors studying and teaching at universities in the West Bank and Gaza among the 415 deportees. So the students... continued their courses at this university. It was accredited and acknowledged by the home university. So, personally, I learned lab at that university. I took many courses there. I did many research projects there.... With the help of my professor, I founded a small museum for preserving snakes, animals, and foxes. As you know, this country is full of mountains and snakes. It was available and I made one small museum there. So, even though it was a severe and very difficult time, this experience changed my life from a misery to a gift, from deportation to a journey.

It is a strange and unsettling experience on the one hand to listen to such accounts of personal growth and potential, and on the other hand to look around at the context in which these statements were made – the tiny, crowded, deprived Gaza Strip – and to realize how little opportunity there is for this growth to be used or expressed in social structures there. I felt this paradox most intensely in the refugee camps, where living conditions are particularly impoverished. Aside from the inadequate physical and medical facilities and very high unemployment rates, Ibtisam characterized other static circumstances in which young Palestinians find themselves when she said, "Young people succeeded in improving themselves and becoming independent as a result of the

Intifada. But, as a result of this agreement – I mean the peace process – because of the closure, because of the bad economic and social situation, they cannot improve themselves. They have no say in the rules and the changes that exist. Also, there are no centers, no clubs, no places to meet each other. And, of course, young people have many creative feelings and energy, and they must work and practice and go ahead to improve themselves and to achieve their target."

One particular area of deprivation that many respondents cited was education. Not only did most of them mention the disruption in their secondary education through the frequent and prolonged Israeli-enforced school closures during the Intifada, but several also bemoaned the lack of opportunity to pursue good quality higher education since the Intifada. Their inability to pursue higher education, typically in the West Bank, is attributable both to continued Israeli control of movement out of Gaza and to restrictions from the new Palestinian Authority. Two of the participants described situations in which they lost their opportunity to study abroad because they did not belong to Fateh, the political faction most strongly represented in the Palestinian Authority. This latter issue introduces another recent source of contention and frustration, that of political factionalization and its effect on freedoms in the new "autonomous" Gaza Strip. This issue will be discussed in the next section.

Hatim's account of his concerns for education reveal both types of restrictions as well as his frustration at not being able to reach his goals:

> And now when I notice or see the situation – the present – I am trying to concern myself with my studies. I hope to study political science in order to be able to understand how this world is going on. But I have been prevented by Israeli soldiers, who refused to let me go to the West Bank. [In Gaza] I studied law after I had finished one year in chemistry. . . . Through my study at the university I was encouraging my friends, reminding them of the past, and especially the Intifada. I had an effect upon them. . . . But the university director belongs to the PA and it is a different system [from mine]. My cousin and I have had high marks. He was the second best student in his college. But the university director initiated a punishment council against him, and they failed him in his course. . . . I am suffering from that time until now. I think about emigrating and taking another identify.

In sum, Intifada experience appeared to facilitate important personal growth in youth, who reported growing in maturity, self-confidence, and effectiveness. At the same time, however, prevailing conditions in the

Gaza Strip – resulting from the continued effects of occupation and some of the practices of the new Palestinian Authority – frustrate substantially the expression or use of this growth. Specifically, the inability to pursue high quality higher education is a source of real frustration to many and is one of the numerous conditions contributing to a sense of discouragement currently evident in many youth.

Hope and Discouragement

The paradoxical theme of hope and discouragement introduced at the end of the preceding section can be used as a final illustration of the psychological condition of Palestinian youth after the Intifada. Any endeavor of intensity and duration surely is accompanied by high expectations and hopes for success. In the case of the Intifada, young people hoped and worked intensively to achieve some meaningful changes in the oppression that they had experienced personally and that pervaded the consciousness of their entire culture. Through much of the struggle, particularly the first 2 years, they reported an exhilarating sense of community cohesion that encouraged their hopes of making a lasting difference. Yet as certainly as there was hope and excitement for progress, the interviews revealed substantial ambivalence and discouragement as to the real effectiveness of the Intifada. All agreed that the Intifada was successful in drawing very important international attention to the plight of the Palestinians. But regarding the ultimate effectiveness of the movement at redressing long-standing deprivation and oppression, some respondents expressed cautious optimism, and others expressed uncertainty and confusion. Still others expressed a palpable sense of defeat and despair. Many bemoaned the loss of the unity they had felt throughout the society during the Intifada.

Not surprisingly, the difference in these viewpoints can be explained largely at a political level. As much as the Intifada created for these young people a powerful sense of cohesion and unity among their society at large – so much so that some expressed a sentimental desire to return to the movement just to reexperience the unity – the divergent political orientations and factions that emerged during, and have survived since, the Intifada are the source of friction and discouragement for many. The most positive attitudes came from members of Fateh, the party of most of the leadership of the Palestinian Authority. For Mohammed, the Intifada "succeeded a lot." Saher saw the ongoing peace negotiations as "a chance and if we are not going to benefit from this chance, surely we are going to lose a lot." Regarding the current situation under the Palestinian Authority, he elaborated, "We are here in the Occupied Territories. We were in prison. We were injured, our houses demolished, many people like [person] were wanted by the Israelis. We hope that the Authority will give us full rights. In fact, we evaluate the Authority here, and we look at it as a newborn baby. We sympathize with it, and in the long run, we hope the Authority will develop into a state and give us our own rights. [It is] a temporary stage, and after we reach the permanent stage, you see, we know that everyone will have all their rights." Similarly, referring to the Oslo Agreement as not being adequate, Ahmed still saw it "as a beginning and this is the first step of complete independence."

In contrast, two of the participants expressed real confusion about the overall effectiveness of the Intifada. Ibtisam said that the movement was not successful "because our people were dreaming to achieve a good target which is reparation and independence" but added that it "might be successful in social branches." She went on to say, "The Intifada was a long road and it had difficulties and many good things. But when we arrive to the end of this road we find ourselves in the front of many subroads and we stand without thinking. We don't know what to expect or how to decide which road to take to continue. We discover ourselves at one place."

Mahmoud (2) expressed similar confusion, with characteristic Palestinian optimism, self-reliance, and emphasis on the value of work and education. "I struggled and I was active and I was in prison and I was injured two times. It might be abnormal in other countries, but for me, I am honored and I do not regret what I have done. But there is a question if what is happening now is what I dreamed to achieve, or something else. At this moment, I find myself confused. Nevertheless, I make myself a program and a target, and I will achieve it by studying in college and through my work. With these two things I will trust myself."

Several others were clearly disappointed and disillusioned with the Intifada. Khalil, although granting that the Intifada helped his people become "conscious toward many things" and enabled them to "distinguish between the true and the wrong," concluded by saying that "what we were hoping, wishing to achieve, we could not achieve." Naji thought "with my other colleagues and my people as a whole that the Intifada would lead to a Palestinian state. But now I don't think that . . . this agreement with Israel is the end. I want more than this – to have a free and independent Palestinian state." Hatim said he "struggled during the Intifada to achieve my dreams through my people and my lands and to please my family and return back to my original village [gives name]. I was dedicated to that. But now, sometimes, I feel regret because all of our activities did not achieve our goals. The situation has increased suffering." Wajdi commented, "Our people had strong determination and courage because we hoped to achieve [our] rights. When I realized that my father and my grandmother lost their country, we hoped . . . to liberate our country. . . . We believed in many things, in principles, in moral principles, but the result came against our hope and our wish and that makes us very sad."

Ghassan summed up the tension between hope and discouragement:
> The Intifada made the Palestinian issue international. So many people came to know something about the Palestinians and their suffering. The Intifada destroyed the myth of the Israeli superman. It unified people. It made them confident in themselves. In other words, they learned they could fight and resist. They really can teach some lessons in resistance. These are the most important purposes. But in other domains, the Intifada failed. . . . Myself, I don't enjoy this peace. It is not a real peace. Real peace is peace which guarantees a real independent state; a comprehensive peace, to move freely from one country to another country; not to be subhumans.

Conclusion

The Palestinian Intifada opened a unique window through which to view some potentials of adolescent functioning. It was an extended period of intense rebellion and violence during which adolescents assumed responsible roles of leadership. The three themes identified in this chapter – defiance and deference, growth and stasis, and hope and discouragement – depict how intense, complex, and paradoxical Palestinian youth experience was. At a broader level, however, these three themes also illustrate how remarkably competent adolescents can be. This competence was evident not only at the behavioral level, in terms of the youth's ability to carry forth a carefully constructed, strategic opposition to a sophisticated military opponent, but also at cognitive and psychological levels.

Perhaps most impressive in this regard was the degree to which these young people saw beyond themselves to the concerns and needs of the broader society. Adopting their society's agenda of redressing historical oppression and inequity was clearly the driving motive behind adolescent involvement in the Intifada. Stereotypic adolescent thrill at risk and danger was evident only occasionally in the detailed portrayals of the movement. It was obvious that these young people had made fundamental ideological commitments regarding social and political needs. To assume this psychological commitment to events and concerns outside oneself during adolescence is impressive. To maintain it during years of sustained violence and trauma is extraordinary. Moreover, that these adolescents appeared to perceive that such involvement for social welfare was a marker of personal growth attests to an elevated level of moral reasoning. It is also a classic illustration of some of the earliest conceptualizations of identity formation that emphasized that there can be no differentiation between the personal and the historical in identity, as both define each other (Erikson, 1968).

Another phenomenon that speaks highly of adolescent competence is the way in which the Palestinian adolescents responded to specific conditions of punishment and control. The very common experience of imprisonment and the one exceptional experience of deportation that were reported in this set of interviews illustrate an impressive resourcefulness and maturity in dealing with conditions designed to extinguish opposition. In effect, under these conditions adolescents were able to create their own social world in which they united to maintain and fuel their commitments. The result for many was apparently an accelerated maturation and clarification of purpose that stood in direct contradiction to the purpose of their confinement.

The cognitive and psychological potential of adolescents was also evident in their ability to make a clear distinction between legitimate and illegitimate authority and then to construct their behavior accordingly. This distinction, which was obviously facilitated by the strength and clarity of the larger social agenda, enabled the adolescents to marshall their energies in unambiguous defiance against the perceived illegitimate authority. Yet despite the great amount of autonomy these young people exercised in their defiance, and despite the intensity with which they reacted to and acted against the illegitimate authority, they appeared to be able to keep these passions in check and not allow them to extend to all forms of authority. For the most part, adolescent participation in the Intifada appeared to be highly organized under clear hierarchies of authority. There was no consistent evidence in these interviews that Intifada involvement – despite its intensity – was a reckless display of uncontrolled adolescent passions. The very real passions associated with the uprising appeared to be expressed largely with deference to organization and authority.

This ability to express intense defiance against one authority but simultaneously maintain allegiance, respect, and deference for other authorities is perhaps most striking to the Western observer because media coverage of youth in the Intifada has only exposed us to the defiance, through videos and photographs depicting the masked youth throwing rocks, burning tires, and demonstrating. Therefore, it is easy for us to have concluded that the depicted behavior defines the general character of these youth – rebellious, violent, and undercontrolled. Such a conclusion reinforces long-standing negative stereotypes of adolescents and misrepresents their potential for highly competent psychological and social functioning and for social conformity. Beyond the deference to parents and organizational hierarchies during the Intifada that was reported by those interviewed, the contrast between the potential defiance and deference of these young people became very clear to me through spending time with them and experiencing the pervasive gentleness, shared affection, respect, and dignity that appear so basic to their personality and social interactions. My experience was similar to that of a visiting Western educator who toured schools in Gaza. He asked Ahmad Hillis, a noted Palestinian educator, with incredulity, "Can these be the same boys who were out throwing rocks?"

Finally, it remains to be seen what will come of this generation of adolescents. On the one hand, the growth and maturity that developed in them through their unusually intense and complex experiences appear solid, stable, and constructive in shaping their transition into adulthood. Now in their early adulthood, those interviewed reflected on those critical years with apparent reason, discernment, and appreciation for the growth they experienced. On the other hand – as with all matters Palestinian – political conditions will play an important role in the consolidation of past experiences and in the future development of these young adults. Many are very disappointed with the political fruits of the Intifada, some to the point of regretting their participation in it. Regardless of the future, however, adolescent experience during the Intifada has provided unique and valuable insights into the capability of youth in navigating the complexities of personal development and social responsibility.

Note

1. Three of the participants were named Mahmoud. This notation (3) refers to the third of the three.

References

Abu-Lughod, I. (1991). Introduction: On achieving independence. In J. R. Nassar & R. Heacock (Eds.), *Intifada: Palestine at the crossroads.* Birzeit, West Bank: Birzeit University Press and New York: Praeger.

Barber, B. K. (1997). Palestinian children and adolescents during and after the Intifada, *Palestine Israel Journal, IV,* 23–33.

Barber, B. K. (In press). Political violence, family relations, and Palestinian family functioning, *Journal of Adolescent Research, 13.*

Barber, B. K., Chadwick, B. C., Heaton, T. B., Huntington, R. L., Fronk, C., & Torres, J. C. (1996, November). Families in political context: The case of the Palestinians in the Occupied Territories. Paper presented at the annual meeting of the National Council on Family Relations, Kansas City, MO.

Erikson, E. H. (1968). *Identity: Youth and Crisis.* New York: W. W. Norton.

Farsoun, S. K., & Landis, J. M. (1991). The sociology of an uprising: The roots of the Intifada. In J. R. Nassar & R. Heacock (Eds.), *Intifada: Palestine at the crossroads.* Birzeit, West Bank: Birzeit Univeristy Press and New York: Praeger.

Hunter, F. R. (1993). *The Palestinian uprising: A war by other means.* Berkeley: University of California Press.

Kuttab, D. (1988). A profile of the stonethrowers. *Journal of Palestine Studies, 17,* 14–23.

Lofland, J., & Lofland, L. H. (1995). *Analyzing social settings: A guide to qualitative observation and analysis.* Belmont, CA: Wadsworth.

Tamari, S. (1992). The Intifada: Sociological perspectives. In N. Ateek, M. Ellis, & R. Ruether (Eds.), *Faith and the Intifada: Palestinian Christian voices.* New York: Orbis Books.

Tessler, M. (1994). *A history of the Israeli-Palestinian conflict.* Bloomington: Indiana University Press.

10. Beyond the Call of Duty: The Service of Israeli Youth in Military and Civic Contexts

RACHEL SEGINER

When Israeli males and females reach the age of 18, they are conscripted into compulsory military service. The Israeli defense service law has set a term of 3 years for men, and 2 for women. However, several surveys of the motivation of potential conscripts to serve in the Israeli army (Gal, 1986; Mayseless, Gal, & Fishoff, 1989; Ezrahi & Gal, 1995) show that for the vast majority of Israeli youth (around 90% in surveys taken since 1975), conscription has been subjectively construed as fulfillment of personal duty. As noted by Gal, military service has become "part of the Israeli ethos – an integral phase in the life of any Israeli youth" (1986, p. 59). Dissidence, when occurring, has been limited to a small number of reservists (86 during the war in Lebanon and 165 during the Intifada) who refused active military service on moral grounds (Linn, 1996) and viewed their refusal as an unavoidable expression of their sense of duty and continued contribution to Israeli society (Helman, 1993).

The Hebrew expression is "to go to the army." In practice not everybody "goes," and "army" is a generic term also embracing the air force and the navy. Excluded from service are *individuals* disqualified for physical or psychological reasons, and *groups* exempted by virtue of their nationality (Israeli Arabs), gender (Druze females), family status (married women, fathers of six or more children), and religiosity (orthodox Jewish females, ultraorthodox females and males). Of those eligible for conscription, 99% report to service (Gal, 1986). This high level of attendance, together with the finding that 90% would volunteer even if not drafted, the high ratio of candidates for voluntary units, the notable spirit of camaraderie in the military (Gal, 1986), all suggest that for many Israeli youth military service is performed beyond the call of duty.

I am grateful to Nurit Toren for her help in preparation of this manuscript, and to Dr. Yuval Dror – Head of the Oranim Teachers' College – for directing me to important references concerning the history of education in the prestate era.

205

The aim of this chapter is to explicate the meaning of military and civic service for Israeli Jewish adolescents. Toward this goal, the historic foundations of the development of military service in Israel will be first delineated. A description of historical background will focus on the structure of the military organization and the function of youth in the prestate era, as two compatible explanations for attitudes toward military service to date. This historical description will be followed by a report on current educational practices designed to involve youth in service to the community (civic service) and an assessment of processes underlying motivation for military service at three time points – before entering the army, during service, and after release from military service. The concluding remarks will focus on the meaning of military and civic service for Israeli Jewish adolescents by underlining its historic genesis, pointing to the interdependence of individualistic and collective value orientations and suggesting that effective service – be it civic or military – must always rely on intrinsic motivation. If this condition is fulfilled, service to the community is carried out "beyond the call of duty."

Historical Background

Self-Defense and Military Organization in the Prestate Era

The formation of the Israeli army on May 26, 1948, took place only 11 days after the declaration of the establishment of the State of Israel. These contiguous events reflect the extent to which the history of self-defense has been intertwined with the history of the Jewish settlement in Eretz Israel (Palestine) at the turn of the century. Historical research (e.g., Allon, 1970) has named the *Hashomer* (the watchmen) as the first organized defense group. Its historical significance lies not only in its status as the first voluntary self-defense group, but also in the influence of its ideology on the major clandestine organization of self-defense (the Hagana) and the Hagana's elite units in the prestate era. This ideology combined self-defense, Zionism, and socialism. The operative implications of this ideology were that the military had an active part in any Zionist endeavor to reconstruct Jewish life in Eretz Israel.

It is important to note that whereas in most known cases, a high involvement of the military in the civic system has ended up in a military regime, or at least in behind the scenes manipulation of power, the close bonds between the civic and the military in the prestate era resulted in non militaristic armed forces. Three factors led to this development: the *humanistic–socialistic* underpinnings of the Labor–Zionist movement (whose leaders founded the Hagana), the *voluntary* nature of participation, and, not least, the *part-time* nature of participation. In essence, the Hagana had been an "army" of reservists on call in case of emergency. Its elite units (the Palmach) were stationed and working in kibbutzim. The Palmach's emblem of wheat stalks and a sword signified its dual mission of work and defense

Such structure was highly receptive to a military doctrine emphasizing the principles of leadership by personal example, delegation of authority to subordinate commanders, and ideology-based motivation (Allon, 1970). As explicated in detail in Gal's (1986) *A portrait of the Israeli soldier*, each of these principles is still valued and practiced by the Israeli army. Another important principle ensuing from this military doctrine is the primacy of unit cohesion and morale. According to scholars of the Israeli army (see Gal, 1986), this quality has been a major factor in the army's high level of performance in the battlefield. Altogether, the heritage of the prestate clandestine military organizations that emphasized leading rather than sending soldiers to the battlefield, volunteering rather than being assigned, and basing of motivation on camaraderie, ideology, and commitment to defend one's home has been sustained in the Israeli army.

Youth Movements and Youth Organizations

During the prestate era, the ideological and practical preparation of youth for joining the military underground was assumed partly by schools (especially in the rural areas; see Dror, 1993), but even more so by youth movements (Adler, 1963; Alon, 1986; Shapira, Adler, Lerner, & Peleg, 1979). These youth movements were informal, nationwide organizations with local chapters, especially in urban areas. Their numbers are not known. Adler (1963) disputed the generally agreed upon figure of 20% of the 12- to 18-year-old Jewish population as an underestimation of the number of youth movement members during the prestate era. Regardless of their numbers, their impact on prestate youth was substantial. Studies of these youth movements (Alon, 1986; Shapira et al., 1979) have argued that they are a direct outgrowth of the European Jewish youth movements, founded during the 1920s after the German youth movements model. Shapira et al. (1979) suggest that in creating a new version of youth movements, their leaders drew from three traditions: the German, the English, and the European Jewish youth movements. The result was an emphasis on a youth culture distinguishing itself from the adult society (German youth movements), which had both a playful back-to-nature spirit (English Scouts) and a Zionist–collectivistic ideology (European Jewish youth movements).

However, although the form of Israeli youth movements might have been old, the content of their activities was new and was responsive to the Zionist–socialist ideology and goals reigning (but not without opposition) within the Jewish community in the prestate era. Recent historical research on Eretz Israeli youth at the turn of the century (Elboim-Dror, 1996) argues that the spirit of activist Zionism existed long before the prestate era youth movements came into being. These youths never formed a nationwide organization. Nevertheless, they had an important role in establishing Hebrew as the predominant language, as well as promoting other important components of the Eretz Israeli youth culture. These ranged from the development of a tradition of *know your country* – by hiking and learning about its history, archaeology, geology, and biology – to an Eretz Israeli identity. All these contributed to the development of a deep sense of devotion to the country, a commitment to defend it, and a spirit of fearlessness. Thus, the prestate youth movements' culture had its roots not only in the German and the European Jewish youth movements and the English scouts, but also in small Eretz Israeli youth organizations formed in rural communities and around urban high schools during the first two decades of the twentieth century. Moreover, the prestate youth movements' pattern of conforming to prevailing ideology while also demanding a more activist approach toward the materialization of that ideology (Adler, 1963; Alon, 1986) was modeled after earlier local organizations no less than after European youth movements.

In sum, the prestate era youth movements accepted the end but disputed the means by which adult society pursued its goals. Their adolescent zeal led them to demand greater activism at a faster pace and the right to pursue the materialization of the ideology in an autonomous manner. It is no small matter, however, that, as Adler concluded, these youth movements conformed in general to adult ideology: "There was no revolution here, but rather conservation of the fruits of the revolution of their parents' generation" (1963, p. 12).

A result of the Zionist–socialist underpinnings of the youth movements was that graduates were strongly encouraged to join kibbutz living, as the ultimate realization of the Zionist–socialist ideology. In reality, only a small fraction of youth movement graduates joined a kibbutz. However, according to Adler (1963), the importance of youth movements was not in the number of their graduates joining the kibbutz, but rather in its serving three national purposes: the preparation of youth for future roles, the identification with national values, and the participation of youth in social–collectivistic activities.

Thus, what mattered was the educational process rather than the materialization of its ultimate goals. It is important to note that in the discourse of prestate youth movements "preparing youth for its future roles" meant social–collectivistic roles only. The personal sphere roles pertaining to family and career were not at all considered. In reality that meant a balance between building the country and defending it. The message was "work, defense, and peace." Altogether these youth were carrying the great responsibility of building the country and defending it. This responsibility and the debt society owed them were succinctly expressed by one of Israel's noted poets, who described the youth as the silver plate on which the State of Israel was presented to the Jewish nation (Alterman, 1952).

Two other important features of youth movement activities were emphases on the experience of leadership and on the importance of the group (Adler, 1963). The experience of leadership involved primarily high school age members (9th–12th graders) who acted as leaders of elementary school age (4th–8th graders) children (Gat, 1974). Deliberately or incidentally, the inclusion of elementary school children allowed the high school youth to experience leadership, thus facilitating preparation for future roles.

Activities, be they for fun, ideology building, or service to the community, were always carried out by the group. These groups met twice a week and spent part of the summer together. The summer activities of the younger groups were limited to 1-week summer camp. The summer activities of the older groups consisted of two types of volunteer work: first as leader ("counselors") of the younger groups, and later in a 1-month work camp helping a kibbutz with its farming. Notably, although the act was one of volunteering (and money was never mentioned), the term *volunteering* was never used. Presumably, it was reserved for more noble actions. Thus, the tradition of voluntarily engaging in active service to the community – as a group – has roots in the ethos and practice of the prestate youth movements.

Contemporary Youth Civic Services

The previous discussion of the historic significance of youth organizations and youth movements to the development of youth in Israel might leave the incorrect impression that youth movements belong to the past. In fact, youth movements do exist and operate among children and adolescents in the present. However, since the 1950s their primacy in the life of Israeli youth has been declining. Sociologists (Adler, 1963) explained this decline in terms of institutionalization of voluntary processes by the State of Israel, leading to necessary changes in both content and structure.

Contemporary youth movements continue to emphasize youth leadership and centrality of the group. Although some sociological studies suggest that these elements of youth movements are outmoded (Adler, 1963), Gal (1986) reports that they are important to the development of leadership and group cohesion in the army, and hence crucial to adaptive military service. These elements have also been adopted by other youth organizations formed in recent years for various specific purposes. One example is a youth program called *Exploration Circles*, which has as a main objective promoting nature loving and concern for ecological issues among 7th to 12th graders.

The weakening of youth movements, the transition of Israeli Jewish society from more collectivistic to more individualistic orientation (Horowitz & Lisak, 1990), and the concern of educators that Israeli youth might drift away from a tradition of community orientation have all led to the creation of several forms of youth community service. In the following sections, four models of youth service to the community, which have operated in Israel for some time, are described. One feature that these programs share is that all four have been adult initiated and operated. Beyond that, they each have a unique structure, activities, and duration.

The first program is mandatory and universal. All Jewish senior high school students are required to participate in volunteer work for one academic year. Youth are allowed to choose the type of service to which they will commit themselves. The second and the third programs apply only to select groups of volunteers, or at least (in the third program described) of adolescents who have agreed to participate. The second program is an after-school program and usually involves a long-term commitment (of 1 year or more), and the third is a short-term curricular program. The fourth program is also voluntary but applies to high school graduates and pertains to a specific segment of the Israeli society: children of the kibbutz. Despite their diversity, these programs emphasize the role of meaningful participation and the interdependence of individualistic and collectivistic goals. Explication of these two themes will follow the description of each of the four programs.

Four Models of Civic Service

1. *Mandatory Volunteer Work.* Voluntary activities become mandatory when a system can no longer trust the intrinsic motivation of enough of its members. The November 1981 circular (No. 42) of the director general of the Israeli Ministry of Education included an item on service to the community. In it, the director general adopted the recommendation of an ad hoc committee on requirements for high school graduation (Schild, 1979) that academic achievement emphases should be counterbalanced by values education. Toward this goal, senior high school students would be required to participate actively in service to the community. Consequently, the director general circular stipulated that participation in service to the community was a necessary condition for high school graduation.

Guidelines for implementation of the program have been outlined in the educational document *Toward activity: Service to the other – personal commitment* (Israeli Ministry of Education, 1986). Its preamble is pertinent to the present report. It lists expected benefits for both individual students and the entire society. Foremost among them is the belief that the Personal Commitment Program will lead to the revival of new–old norms like helping other people and volunteering.

Altogether, the program has two major aims: (a) to promote students' awareness of social and community needs and recruit them to participate actively in satisfying these needs and (b) to offer students personal gains pertaining to four major aspects of growth and development. These gains are in coping strategies and interpersonal communication skills, as well as in acquainting oneself with the world of work by exploring inner resources (inclinations, strengths, and weaknesses) and occupational opportunities. It was also hoped that by implementing the Personal Commitment Program, student–school, school–community, and student–recipient of help relationships would improve.

In most high schools, the program has been included in the 10th grade requirements, so that for one school year students engage themselves in one of a variety of after school activities initiated, organized, and supervised by the school. Among the most prevalent service activities are working with children (e.g., disabled children), teaching (e.g., teaching of Hebrew to new immigrant children), and community services (e.g., help to senior citizens; work in hospitals).

Zur (1986) has studied the implementation of the Personal Commitment Program and its meaning to participating students. Of special relevance to the present discussion is her analysis of students' initial motivation to participate in the program and their subsequent evaluation of subjective gains. The majority – but not all – joined the program willingly and were not disturbed by it mandatory nature. Rather, they accepted it as a legitimate educational technique, especially because they believed that individuals are not self-motivated: "It is necessary to educate us, youths, to give to others," or "This activity starts as a requirement, the rest depends on the person" (Zur, 1986, p. 72). Presenting a different view, students who indicated they were not motivated complained about the mandatory volunteer program contradiction in terms and indicated that they complied only because of pressure from the school. Thus, they may have confirmed the need for the mandatory nature of the program. Overall, Zur (1986) found that 30% of the students who were initially highly motivated lost interest in their projects, but she also found that 30% of the students chose to continue working on their projects for the following year, after they had fulfilled program requirements.

Employing the case study method, Zur's data do not allow for analyses at the individual level. Instead, she evaluated the role of the participating parties (school, the homes, and the recipient agencies) in promoting and sustaining the students' motivation to participate in the program and experience intrinsic gains. Her overall conclusion was that the school did not accept the project as an important part of the curriculum. Moreover, by treating the program as any other subject in the curriculum and listing it on the students' school report, the school forsook the uniqueness of the program. The response of parents varied. Some proudly reported that their son or daughter had followed a family tradition of volunteering. Other parents rejected any activity that interfered with school work and achievement. The recipient agency played a decisive role in sustaining the students' motivation. To the extent that an agency was willing and able to give the students a sense of personal responsibility, participation was meaningful and satisfaction was high. Where agencies failed to communicate to the students the importance of their work and kept them as "outsider," the students' motivation dwindled.

In terms of subjective gains, 40% of the students regarded their volunteer activity as a source of inner reward, 50% valued it as a source of external reward achieved by their school report evaluation, and 10% felt no reward whatsoever. Given that the majority of students described themselves as highly motivated to participate in the Personal Commitment Program, their motivation was in fact extrinsic rather than intrinsic.

Psychologists studying the effect of external reward have reported the deleterious effects of external rewards on intrinsic motivation for some time. The same two factors – adult surveillance and extrinsic rewards – identified by Lepper and Greene (1975; see also Lepper, Keavney, & Drake, 1996) as interfering with children's curiosity and intrinsic motivation, may be also operating in the case of the Personal Commitment Program.

2. *Voluntary Community Service: Transpersonal Commitment.* The work of Magen and her colleagues (Magen, 1995; Magen, Birenbaum & Illovich, 1992) has lent some empirical support to the conclusion that the mandatory nature of the Personal Commitment Program diminishes its subjective gains. Drawing upon the perspective of humanistic psychology that commitment beyond self is a central characteristic of the healthy personality, Magen and her colleagues have conducted a series of studies on the relationship between adolescents' commitment beyond self and several aspects of the healthy personality. Her earlier studies (Magen & Aharoni, 1991) focused on adolescents' desire for transpersonal commitment, indicating the interdependence between active involvement in voluntary organizations and desire for transpersonal commitment (e.g., contribute to others, serve my country).

Since the direction of these relationships could not be uncovered in a correlational design, her subsequent research (Magen et al., 1992) focused on the effect of active participation in volunteer activities. To this end, she compared three groups of adolescents: active volunteers, signed-up but not yet active volunteers, and nonvolunteers. Results indicated that the active volunteers scored higher on the desire to commit themselves to help others, as well as on two measures of healthy personality (Positive Experience Questionnaire and Sense of Coherence Scale) than the two nonactive groups. Hence, she concluded that the crucial factor was not the disposition to volunteer (the committed but not yet active) but rather the activity itself.

Although that study needs to be replicated under more stringent conditions (e.g., a 2 × 2 × 2 design of involvement versus noninvolvement, individual versus group activity, and nonaltruistic versus nonaltruistic behavior; a before–after design), its preliminary results indicate the importance of the activity relative to the disposition. On the basis of these findings, Magen and her colleagues recommend that the educational implementation of these findings should be carefully planned and introduced. This recommendation is especially important because the effect of participation in a Personal Commitment Program (in a before–after design) was found only for volunteers and *not* for students who were required to participate (Magen, 1995). Although these findings are of a preliminary nature, they do point in the direction of problematic aspects of a program combining the mandatory with the voluntary.

3. Peer Leading Programs: The Case of Drug Prevention. This program, unlike the other programs presented in this section, was initiated by the Israeli Ministry of Education counseling services for the specific purpose of drug prevention. The decision to use the peer leader method was not guided by considerations of leadership development nor by the opportunity for service to the school community. Rather, the method has been implemented because of program effectiveness. Erhard (1995) studied the effectiveness of this program by focusing on three main criteria: satisfaction, outcomes, and participants' recommendations of employment of peer leaders in subsequent programs.

Analysis of the responses of 1,106 students (who did not act as discussion leaders) from 46 classrooms (8th–12th grade) indicated that participants expressed a high degree of satisfaction from the program and recommended that subsequent programs be led by students. The effects of the program were especially favorable when cognitive outcomes were considered. Participants felt that after the program they had a better understanding of problems related to drugs and alcohol than they did before (46% understood better and thought that their classmates understood better, and 38% thought they knew more about the issue). However, fewer students (only 24%) thought the program also had an effect on the behavior of students, so that fewer of them would use drugs.

Of special importance to the present analysis are the indirect outcomes of the program. The program developers had expected that it would promote the program leaders to become confidants or counselors to their fellow students. This outcome did not occur. The fact that students carried out a specific adult-initiated leadership role for a limited period of time did not change their social status among their peers. It is also notable that in this program, as in others of its kind, the students who gained the most were the 157 who acted as leaders. Altogether, the evaluation of this program suggested that when students are actively involved in a project that is meaningful to them, they benefit from it even more than do the recipients of their services. It thus further supports Magen's (1995) proposition concerning transpersonal commitment and attests to the importance of introducing personal meaning to school-initiated programs.

4. One-Year Societal Service of Kibbutz High School Graduates. Like the three previous models, the kibbutz youth program is a "top down" initiative of kibbutz leadership rather than of youths themselves. Launched in the late fifties (Avrahami, 1997), it has been steadily recruiting 30% of all kibbutz high school graduates. Youth may join one of three programs; they become youth movement leaders, work for voluntary organizations (both programs are set in urban areas), or help young kibbutzim. The majority (70%) opt for the youth movement leadership tasks, and only a small minority choose to help a young kibbutz. Following the 1-year service, participants start their military service.

This program is shaped by the idea that the 1-year service will help both the kibbutz community and the individual youth. Its importance to the kibbutz ensues from the kibbutz's reliance on urban youth for growth and expansion. By acting as leaders of youth movements, these kibbutz high school graduates become messengers of kibbutz ideology and lifestyle. Thus, they may recruit new candidates to the kibbutz and, by activation of the dissonance principle (Festinger, 1957), also strengthen their own commitment to the kibbutz way of life.

Analysis of the importance of the 1-year service for its participants (Avrahami & Dar, 1993) suggests that kibbutz high school graduates enroll in the program with both collectivistic and individualistic motives. Their collectivistic motives are articulated as a desire to serve others and contribute to society. Their individualistic motives focus on the opportunity to practice independence, initiative, and responsibility and to examine kibbutz ideology and way of life vis-à-vis other alternatives. The high endorsement of the explorative–nonconformist motive factor – consisting of three items: to examine alternatives to kibbutz life, to be independent among age mates, and to expand horizons and experiences – has led researchers (Avrahami & Dar, 1993) to conclude that the 1-year service experience has an important function in the transition to adulthood for its participants. Thus, this essentially collectivistic task has resulted in an individualistic outcome of facilitating transition to adulthood.

Summary of Four Models. Altogether, the four youth civic service programs suggest two important conclusions. One concerns the nature of the motivation to engage in service to the community. The programs presented here suggest that external motives (such as satisfying school requirements) do not necessarily interfere with the adequate performance of service to the community activities. If a community recruits its youth to carry out certain routine services, external rewards may suffice. However, if the premise underlying a youth service program is to strengthen community orientation in participants and instigate greater sensitivity and responsiveness to community needs, then external rewards may not be enough. Rather, such programs rely on the intrinsic meaning that service to the community has for the person. Arousing intrinsic motivation is a complex task. The present report indicates that the organizers and recipients of services could have a decisive role in promoting intrinsic motivation by entrusting youth with responsibilities and conveying their value.

The second conclusion pertains to the interdependence of individualistic and collectivistic orientations in relation to service. As noted by Waterman (1981) and demonstrated by the empirical results of Magen and her colleagues (Magen et al., 1992), the simplistic correspondence between collectivistic orientations and community orientation does not hold true. Although a collectivistic orientation may render community needs more salient, readiness to engage in service activities ensues from the personal meaning such activities inspire. The interplay between these two orientations will be reiterated in the discussion on military service.

Military Service: Mandatory and Voluntary

This section will examine motivation to engage in military service from several angles. The first focuses on the army practices to promote motivation to serve in the army prior to induction. The second examines motivations prior to service, during military service, and in retrospect after completion of active military service. Although military service in Israel applies to both men and women, the majority of analyses of military service in Israel have focused on the service of men. For this reason, the third angle from which motivation to serve in the army is discussed focuses on women.

Preparation for Military Service: Facilitating the Induction Process

In its attempt to cushion entry into the army, the military – in cooperation with the Ministry of Education – have developed a program for preparing high school students for their forthcoming military service (Israelashvili, 1992). Following a circular from the Director General of the Ministry of Education (October, 1990), this program has become mandatory and under the responsibility of the school's psychological counseling services and homeroom teachers. This structured program consists of multiple steps and a set timetable. It starts at the middle of 11th grade, when many students already have received their first notice to report for military registration (age 17), and continues through the first part of 12th grade.

The preparatory program has three major components pertaining to *values* (why is meaningful service in the IDF important?); *information* on different units, military courses and training; and *adaptation* (improvement of physical fitness, coping and adaptation techniques, and a week's tryout at an army base). Cognizant of the changing, but nevertheless close relationships between parents and their adolescent children and the important role parents serve in their adolescent children's lives, the targets of this program are both high school students and their parents.

In addition to the school-based program, the army has initiated special TV and radio programs. These programs take place at the beginning of summer and are devoted to information concerning the different corps and service courses. They consist of a series of 1-hour open line programs broadcast on prime time for 10 consecutive days. They traditionally open with the chief of staff, followed by commanders of the various military corps. The general message of the program is that the army demands coping with personal challenges and hard work, offers high social support and attention to soldiers' needs, and views the families as partners in that support effort.

Although the army has been attempting to inoculate its prospective conscripts against the stress of the initial stages in military service (Israelashvili, 1992), the effectiveness of the program is to date not known. However, preliminary evidence suggests that the program may be effective in communicating a positive message. Luski (1988) carried out a preliminary investigation of the school-based preparatory program. His findings suggest that following participation in the program, participants ($N = 100$) have more information on military service, better understanding of the reasons for mandatory military service in Israel, and higher motivation to serve in the army (more would volunteer for military service even if it were not mandatory, and fewer would try to change their assignment to a noncombat unit). Thus, given the army's reliance on its soldiers' strong morale and sense of inner duty, the message to prospective conscripts and their families might be of high value indeed.

Youth's Motivation to Serve in the Army: Stable or Changing?

According to Gal (1986), 99% of eligible conscripts report for recruitment, and the mean attrition rate over 3 years of military service is less than 10% (compared to 30% to 40% during the first year of service in the United States and Canadian armed forces). Another indicator of motivation to serve in the army is the willingness of potential conscripts to serve in the army if military service were not mandatory. As noted earlier, this question has been repeated in several surveys since first being asked in 1975. Over the years, the rate of respondents (males only) who would not serve at all has fluctuated from 6% to 12%. At the same time, there has been a notable change in respondents' tendency to qualify their positive response. The rate of potential conscripts who would serve a full term (3 years) declined from 67% in 1975 (2 years after the arduous war of the Day of Atonement) to 34% in 1994 (while peace talks with Palestinian Arabs were going on).

The demographic composition of those with strong motivation to serve in the army and in its elite voluntary units has also changed (Ezrahi & Gal, 1995). Whereas in former years, kibbutz youth were noted for their high motivation to serve in the army and were overrepresented in elite voluntary units, Ezrahi and Gal's (1995) recent survey shows a shift from secular kibbutz youth to the religious Zionist youth, and particularly religious kibbutz youth.

These shifts are even more pronounced when the question pertains to serving in combat units and to becoming an officer (which adds another year of service and more responsibilities on active reserve service). Similar changes are also noted by Seginer and Schlesinger (1998). In comparing the future orientation of two cohorts of kibbutz and urban high school students (the classes of 1984 and 1992), Seginer and Schlesinger found that the relative importance of two prospective life domains pertaining to military service and work and career has been reversed over the years. Whereas the class of 1984 invested in the prospective domain of military service more than in any other life domain, and its investment in work and career fell behind, the class of 1992 invested in work and career more than in any other domain, and military service lagged behind.

As important as these phenomena are in themselves, their correlates are even more telling. Ezrahi and Gal's (1995) analysis shows that overall, motivation to serve in the army has been positively related to two factors: strong belief in the importance of contributing to society (transpersonal commitment, $r = .50$. $p < .001$) and strong national identity (collectivistic orientation, $r = .31$, $p < .001$). In addition, motivation for military service has been negatively correlated with one personal factor pertaining to worries concerning military service ($r = .29$, $p < .001$).

Thus, the relationships between motivation to serve in the army and volunteer for its elite combat units and transpersonal commitment values are still viable. However, adherence to those values has declined over recent years, and its heralds can be found now more among religious Zionist youth than among kibbutz youth. Although no data are available, the weakened motivation of conscripts has been acknowledged by the army in the last year. A recent television news report (Barkai, 1997) that after a long period of eroded motivation, a larger number of highly qualified conscripts volunteered for elite units may signal that this erosion has been curbed.

Active Service Motivation

Obviously, there is relatively little public information on the motivation of active service soldiers. Analyses carried out by historians and military analysts had focused on the end results, that is, battlefield performance of the Israeli army. The relevance of this indicator for the entire army has been confirmed by Gal (1986), who noted that the Israeli army standards are set by the combat units.

Gal (1986) found that although motivations of potential conscripts have been associated mainly with collectivistic orientations, motivations of soldiers in active service are only secondarily collectivistic. Primary motives center on the *self* (self-preservation and self-concept) and the *immediate unit* and its commanders (unit cohesion and "follow me" leadership) (Gal, 1986).

Military Service in Retrospect

Two pertinent issues have been investigated by students of active military service outcomes. One focuses on motivation to serve in the army and contribute to collectivistic causes (Mayseless, 1992), and the other on appraisal of personal growth and development (Lieblich & Perlow, 1988). By asking her respondents to reflect on whether they would volunteer for military service (had it not been compulsory) and to evaluate the effect of military service on their willingness to serve civic collectivistic causes, Mayseless (1992) offers a rather complex picture of released soldiers.

Her results show that recently released (6 months) and veteran reservists (3 years after release) reflect on their experience in the military differently. More of the recently released (14% vs. 7% of the older veterans) would not volunteer to military service, but more of them (31% vs. 15% of the older group) also felt military service increased their motivation to serve civic collectivistic goals. These results may indicate that the recently released made a clearer distinction between military and civic service than did their older counterparts. The validity of this interpretation and the extent to which it points to historical changes in the meaning of service among younger cohorts should be examined in a longitudinal study of young reservists.

Lieblich and Perlow (1988) studied developmental opportunities offered by Israeli military service. Whereas Elder (1986) examined the effects of military service by comparing the life histories of U.S. veterans and nonveterans, such a research design was impractical in a study conducted in a universal conscription setting. Instead, Lieblich focused on subjective accounts of military experience. Her interviewees were 30 male students who participated in the Lebanon war in 1982 and had recently (no more than 6 months before) completed active service.

Their narratives suggested a unique pattern of transition to adulthood. Pertinent to the present analysis is the men's sense of personal growth and development. Lieblich and Perlow (1988) conceptualized it in terms of two types of subjective gains: greater capacity for active coping and overcoming difficulties ("doing") and expansion of personal boundaries reflected in a better understanding of life's vicissitudes and complexities ("being"). Both gains have led these young men to view themselves as more mature and ready to enter the world of adulthood, and they attribute this growth to their military service. Altogether, findings on the motivation of preinduction youth to serve in the army and the retrospective gains observed by recently released men suggest a developmental process by which as youth move from the preinduction to the post–active military service stage, the locus of personal meaning moves from collectivistic to individualistic orientation.

Women's Military and Civic Services

As noted earlier, military service is universal for both males and females. However, armies are masculine institutions. Consequently, the army is more selective in the recruitment of females and more willing to exempt them from military service, and females' motivation to join the army has also been somewhat lower. In the 1995 survey of potential conscripts (Ezrahi & Gal, 1995), 18% of the females and 12% of the males would not serve in the army had it not been compulsory; in the 1989 survey (Mayseless, Gal, & Fishof, 1989) the figures were 11% of the females and 6% of the males. The list of military occupations open to females has been expanding in recent years, but females are still excluded from combat occupations (Gal, 1986).

The close bonds between the military and the civic system has resulted in a unique service opportunity for females: soldier–teachers. This military occupation is almost as old as the Israeli army and was created in response to teacher shortage following the mass immigration in the 1950s. To date, it is voluntary and open only to a select group, trained by the army to act in one of several educational tasks: as teacher assistants, counselors in youth boarding schools, and instructors in community centers and nature reserves.

A recent evaluation study (Spector & Findling-Andy, 1995) showed that boarding school and school principals were highly satisfied with the work of soldier–teachers in their schools. The researchers noted that these young soldier–teachers' limited professional knowledge was compensated for by high personal ability, dedication to the job, and commitment to their pupils. The soldier–teachers themselves ($N = 280$) thought their work contributed to the national cause (97%) and to the educational system (100%). However, only 77% agreed or highly agreed that their job should be included in the list of military occupations for females. This may be another sign of the loosening of the close ties between the military and civic systems.

Conclusion

This chapter has focused on the two avenues through which Israeli youth serve their society: the civic and the military. The experience and meaning of the military and civic service of Israeli Jewish youth draw on the historical heritage created by the prestate clandestine military organizations and youth movements. For this reason, a short description of their development, structure, and function was presented. This description emphasized the role played by clandestine military organizations and youth movement in developing the ethos of voluntarism and the commitment of youth to defending the civilian society. Persistence of this spirit, reflected in high willingness to serve in the army and its voluntary units and low rate of attrition, supports the conclusion that for many Israeli youth military service is carried out beyond the call of duty.

The weakening of youth movements and a growing emphasis on individualistic orientations in Israeli society, however, have prompted the Israeli educational system to develop a mandatory 1-year program of service to the community. The administration and meaning of this program, as well as other voluntary programs offered to high school students and graduates, have been analyzed by several studies reviewed in this chapter.

These studies of civic service, together with research on motivation for military service and the retrospective accounts of young men recently released from military service, lead to two conclusions germane to future youth programs. First and most important is that, although service to the community may be made mandatory, its value for the provider and recipient of service depends on its personal significance.

A second, and related, conclusion is that as collectivistic orientations give way to individualistic orientations, collectivistic goals such as community service can be served by individualistic motives. The tension is not between collectivistic (i.e., community-centered) and individualistic (person-centered) orientations, but rather between extrinsic and intrinsic gains. In our review of civic and military service, both recipients and providers gained when providers of services had a sense of meaningfulness. Meaningfulness was derived from a continuum of collectivistic and individualistic gains, ranging from ideological commitment and a sense of group cohesion to happiness, self-worth, and a sense of growing more independent, mature, and able to cope more effectively with the world around. Such intrinsic gains constitute an important condition for performing a service to the community – be it of a military or civic nature – "beyond the call of duty."

References

Adler, C. (1963). *Tnuat Hnoar bachevra hayisraelit* [The youth movement in Israeli society]. Jerusalem: Israeli Ministry of Education and culture.
Allon, Y. (1970). *The making of Israel's army*. New York: Bantam Books.

Alon, M. (1986). *Hsikui hanitzchi: Noar veshinui chevrati* [The eternal prospect: Youth and social change]. Tel Aviv: Sifriat Hapoalim.

Alterman, N. (1952). Magash Hacessef [The silver tray]. In *Hatur hashevi'ee; Shirim laet velaeeton* [The seventh column: Poems for their time and newspaper]. Tel Aviv: Am Oved.

Avrahami, A. (1997). Bnei kibbutz hamitnadvim leshnat shirut betnuat hanoar ba'eer: Ofi hahitnasut vehashpa'ata al tahalich habigur [Kibbutz youth volunteer for one year service in an urban youth movement: The nature of the experience and its effect on transition to adulthood]. In Y. Dror (Ed.), *Hachinuch hakibbutzi besvivato.* (pp. 83–104) [Kibbutz education in context]. Tel Aviv: Ramot.

Avrahami, A., & Dar, Y. (1993). Collectivistic and individualistic motives among kibbutz youth volunteering for community service. *Journal of Youth and Adolescence, 22,* 697–714.

Barkai, A. (Executive Producer). (1997, March 5). *Mabat* [View news]. Jerusalem: Channel 1, The Israeli Television Broadcasting.

Dror, Y. (1993). The new rural school in Upper Galilee (Eretz Israel) at the beginning of the 20th century. *Journal of Research in Rural Education, 9,* 179–190.

Elboim-Dror, R. (1996). "Hu holech uva, mikirbenu hu ba haivree hachadash": Al tarbut hanoar shel ha'aliot harishonot [He is coming and going, one of us he is, the new Jew: Youth culture in the early waves of immigration]. *Alpae'em, 12,* 104–135

Elder, G. H. (1986). Military times and turning points in men's lives. *Developmental Psychology, 22,* 233–245.

Erhard, R. (1995). *Hanchayat amitim: Tfisot talmidim et hatochnit vetozareha* [Peer leadership program: How students perceive the program and its outcomes]. Jerusalem: Israeli Ministry of Education, Culture & Sports, Psychological Counseling Services.

Ezrahi, Y., & Gal, R. (1995). *Tfisot olam veamadot shel talmidim bevatei sefer tichone'em clapei nos'ay chevra, bitachon veshalom* [World views and attitudes of high school students toward social, security and peace issues]. Zichron Ya'akov, Israel: The Carmel Institute for Social Studies.

Festinger, L. (1957). *A theory of cognitive dissonance.* New York: Row, Peterson.

Gal, R. (1986). *A portrait of the Israeli soldier.* New York: Greenwood Press.

Gat, R. (1974). *Tnuot hanoar shel Eretz Israel Ha'ovedet 1930–1945: hitavutan umeoravutan hapolitit* [Youth movements affiliated with socialistic parties in Eretz Israel in 1930–1945: Their genesis and political involvement]. Unpublished doctoral dissertation, University of Tel Aviv, Tel Aviv, Israel.

Helman, S. (1993). *Haseruv lesharet hazava kenisaion lehagdara mechudeshet shel haezrachut* [Conscientious objection to military service as an attempt to redefine the contents of citizenship]. Unpublished doctoral dissertation, Hebrew University of Jerusalem, Jerusalem, Israel.

Horowitz, D., & Lisak, M. (1990). *Mezukot beotopia* [Troubled Utopia]. Tel Aviv: Am Oved Publishing.

Israelashvili, M. (1992). Counseling in the Israeli high school: Particular focus on preparation for military recruitment. *International Journal for the Advancement of Counseling, 15,* 175–186.

Israeli Ministry of Education and Culture (1986). *Likrat Pe'elut: Sheirut lazulat – mechuyavut ishit* [Toward activity: Service to the other – personal commitment]. Jerusalem: Ministry of Education, Youth Division.

Lepper, M. R., & Greene, D. (1975). Turning play into work: Effects of adult surveillance and extrinsic rewards on children's intrinsic motivation. *Journal of Personality and Social Psychology, 31,* 479–486.

Lepper, M. R., Keavney, M., & Drake, M. (1996). Intrinsic motivation and extrinsic rewards: A commentary on Cameron & Pierce's meta-analysis. *Review of Educational Research, 66,* 5–32.

Lieblich, A., & Perlow, M. (1988). Transition to adulthood during military service. *The Jerusalem Quarterly, 47,* 40–76.

Linn, R. (1996). When the individual soldier says 'no' to war: A look at selective refusal during the intifada. *Journal of Peace Research, 33,* 421–431.

Luski, A. (1988). *Hachanat bnei no'ar lekrat gius lazava: tochnit veha'aracha* [The preparation of adolescents for recruitment into military service: Program and evaluation]. Unpublished master's thesis, University of Tel Aviv, Tel Aviv, Israel

Magen, Z. (1995). Mechuyavut al-ishit ucmiha leosher bekerev mitbagrim [Transpersonal commitment and search for happiness among adolescents]. In A. Yogev, R. Shapira, & D. Chen (Eds.) *Hachinuch likrat hame'aa ha'esrim veachat* [Education toward the 21st century]. Tel Aviv: Ramot.

Magen, Z., & Aharoni, R. (1991. Adolescents contributing toward others: Relationships to positive experiences and transpersonal commitments. *Journal of Humanistic Psychology, 31,* 126–143.

Magen, Z., Birenbaum, M., & Illovich, T. (1992). Adolescents from disadvantaged neighborhoods: Personal characteristics as related to volunteer involvement. *International Journal for the Advancement of Counseling, 15,* 47–59.

Mayseless, O. (1992). *Nituach hashva'ati shel kvutzot gil shonot benos'ay amadot utfisot clapei zahal vehamedina* [Comparative analysis of different age groups perceptions and attitudes toward the army and the State of Israel]. Zichron Ya'akov, Israel: The Carmel Institute for Social Studies.

Mayseless, O., Gal, R., & Fishoff, E. (1989). *Tfisot olam veamadot shel talmidim clapei nos'ay chevra ubitachon* [Students' world views and attitudes of high school students toward social, defense and peace issues]. Zichron Ya'akov, Israel: The Carmel Institute for Social Studies.

Schild, E. O. (1979). *Dean vecheshbon hava'ada lebdikat sugiat bechinot habagrut vete'udot habagrut* [Report of the committee on matriculation examinations and matriculation certificate]. Jerusalem: Israeli Ministry of Education and Culture.

Seginer, R., & Schlesinger, R. 1998. Adolescent future orientation in time and place. *International Journal of Behavioral Development, 22,* 151–167.

Shapira, R., Adler, C., Lerner, M. & Peleg, R. (1979). *Hulza khula vezavaron lavan: Mechkar al olamam hachevrati shel bogrei tnuot noar beisrael* [Blue shirt and white collar: A study of the social world of Israeli youth movements graduates]. Tel Aviv: Am Oved.

Spector, A., & Findling-Andy L. (1995). *Ha'arachat tafkidan shel hamorot hachayalot bama'arach hachinuchi* [Evaluation of the functioning of soldier-teachers in educational settings]. Jerusalem: The Szold Institute for Behavioral Science Research.

Waterman, A. S. (1981). Individualism and interdependence. *American Psychologist, 36,* 762–773.

Zur, V. (1986). *"Mechuyavut ishit-sheirut lazulat":* Mechkar ha'aracha etnographi al haf'alat tochnit chadasha bachinuch hachevrati beveit sfer tichon ["Personal commitment – service to the other": An ethnographic evaluation study of a new high school program in social education]. Unpublished master's thesis, University of Haifa, Haifa, Israel.

11. Recent Trends in Civic Engagement among Japanese Youth

KEIKO TAKAHASHI AND GIYOO HATANO

Contemporary Japan is an economically successful, well-educated, aging society with a high level of public safety. Recent statistics support this characterization. First, Japan accounted for 13.2% of the gross national product (GNP) of the world in fiscal 1991 (Economic Planning Agency, 1996). The unemployment rate stood at 3.3% as of 1996 (Management and Coordination Agency, 1996). Second, more than 99% of the Japanese are literate; over 95% of adolescents of both sexes are in high school, and nearly 40% of 18-year-olds are in educational institutions of higher learning, including colleges and universities (Ministry of Education, 1996). Third, the low fertility rate (an average of 1.43 per females 15–49 years old in 1995) and the longest average life expectancy of the world (82.8 years for women and 76.4 years for men in 1995) have rapidly brought about an aging society (Ministry of Health and Welfare, 1996). Fourth and finally, in 1995, there were 1,281 homicides. Arrest rates, mostly for theft, were 9.2 per 1,000 among 10- to 20-year-olds in 1995 (National Policy Agency, 1996).

Historical Review of Civic Activities and Movements

Civic and Political Movements

After opening the country to trade and commerce with the West in the 1860s, the Japanese government made movements toward adopting democratic social systems such as voting rights for citizens and establishing an elected Diet. By 1890, however, only 1% of males, those who were able to pay 15 yen or more in tax, had voting rights. Through active protests, all males over 25, but not females, won enfranchisement in 1925. The government reluctantly accepted the new democracy, but, at the same time, tried hard to develop a strong centralized bureaucratic system. From the beginning of the Meiji era, critics of government expressed their discontent through labor disputes and demonstrations and in articles and books. However, it was very difficult to gain support for their progressive views, especially during World War II, when all democratic and civic movements were suppressed by the military government.

The conclusion of the war in 1945 allowed a fresh start for civic and political movements. During the 1950s and 1960s, college students' political movements were very active both on and off campuses in all parts of Japan. Students had many grievances against "the Establishment." For example, they protested against U.S. military aggression in Vietnam, American military bases in Japan, the Japanese government's policies in South Asia, the revised Japan–U.S. Security Treaty, and the introduction of atomic weapons to Japan. On campuses, students sought democratic innovations in college administration, asking for self-management in dormitories, enriched curricula and improved ways of teaching, and disclosure of school finances. When the revised Security Treaty was ratified in 1960, many Japanese people, including high school as well as college students, were involved in expressing strong objections.

After the end of the Vietnam War and some success with democratization of universities and colleges, students lost their targets of protest. In the 1970s and thereafter, students indulged themselves in conservative ways of living. At present, it is believed that Japanese adolescents and young adults are conservative and not interested in politics in general. In fact, it was reported that two-thirds of the 20- to 29-year-olds stayed away from the polls in the Lower House election of 1996 (Kono & Aramaki, 1997).

However, even today, there are many specific problems in Japanese society, which some groups of people are trying to address in a range of ways from public protest to local, personal help. In the remaining part of this section, we review the three most prominent areas of civic engagement, namely, feminist movements, community service, and environmental protection. Though we will not discuss them in detail, we note that there have been other areas of engagement as well. One concerns the government's policy toward issues of ethnicity. Some minority groups within Japan, such as the Buraku-min, have for decades protested their treatment as scapegoats for social problems. There has also been recent active protest for the rights of native Japanese (Ainu) and other minorities such as Koreans. The government has been criticized for its treatment of foreigners, which includes the use of fingerprints for identification.

Feminist Movements

During the twentieth century, significant change in women's status in Japanese society has occurred. Although the conservative government, enterprises, and males were reluctant to accept and sometimes even obstructed progress, women's movements slowly but steadily have influenced social systems and laws and, thus, affected the everyday lives of women and men.

The first ripple of women's movements in Japan can be found as early as the late nineteenth century. In the 1880s, a few female groups organized associations of women that became engaged in civic activities for female independence, equality, and fair treatment of females. Through sustained efforts, some improvements were made. With the onset of World War II, however, such activities were suppressed by the government and the militaristic atmosphere of the society.

In 1945, the ballot was extended to females by the Occupation officials, and in 1946, 39 females were elected as representatives (8.4% of the Lower House members). Both the New Constitution, established in 1946, and the New Civic Law, established in 1947, declared that all men and women were equal before law and that females were to be treated without discrimination in family and society. However, the reality was, and has been, quite different.

In the 1970s, a number of small groups of women in different parts of Japan jointly organized the first meeting of a women's liberation group in Japan. In those days, the male-dominated mass media attacked, made fun of, and minimized the movements. However, we believe that the movements heightened females' awareness of their condition. Many females started to question their traditional gender role and to assert themselves against social norms. They became reluctant to stay home, and more than half of them worked outside the home after 1984; today, over 60% of married women are employed (Ministry of Labor, 1996).

The first Japanese book on women's studies was published in 1979 (Iwao & Hara, 1979), and, since then, there have been many more publications. Betty Friedan's *The Feminine Mystique* was translated into Japanese in 1965 and was widely read. Research on gender has begun to enter the mainstream of Japanese academic society. Feminists mostly in the social sciences strive for equality and fairness in schools, companies, and homes. Researchers in education criticize the Ministry of Education for inequalities in schooling and textbooks. Feminist psychologists have started to examine traditional theories and methods in psychology. Universities and colleges have addressed gender issues in seminars and lectures that many female students, but only a small number of male students, attend. Empirical research indicates that older and younger females are much less engaged in gender issues than older and younger males (e.g., Azuma & Suzuki, 1991; Yukawa, 1996).

In conjunction with the "Decade of the United Nations for Women" program, which ran from 1976 to 1985, gender issues have become one of the main foci for government agencies. In 1986, the Law of Equal Employment Opportunity for both males and females was enacted. Nonetheless, it is reported that there are many violations of the principle of "equal pay and equal work" in job opportunity, promotion, and payment even today. In 1991, the Child-Care Leave Law was established, so that one parent can take an unpaid leave from work during their child's first year. Although the two laws are not sufficient to protect women's rights, they are regarded as first steps toward future equality and fairness, and already there are court cases based on these matters.

Although numerous gender problems remain unresolved, Japanese citizens are making progress in social and political reform. For example, females speak out about sexual harassment in companies and schools, and mass media often expose gender inequalities in wages and promotions. Although the feminist movements are not conspicuous, they are supported by many female adolescents and young adults, who are engaging in these movements in their own mild, but still effective and persistent ways.

Community Service. Traditionally civic service was based on religious concepts of Buddhism or Christianity. In the seventh century, institutions based on the Buddhist ethic were established to assist poor people and orphans, and ever since, some monks and wealthy Buddhist believers have devoted themselves to helping the needy. In the sixteenth century, Christianity was introduced into Japan, and thereafter missionaries and Christians also worked for people in need.

During World War II, about 658,000 civilians were killed. Children and adolescents suffered severely because of the loss of their parents. There are no formal records accounting for how many children were helped and by whom. However, there are many well-known cases of service to those in need. For example, a young female Christian from Tokyo, named "Maria in Ant's Town," worked for homeless people and children in the 1940s. For more than 30 years, beginning in 1946, another

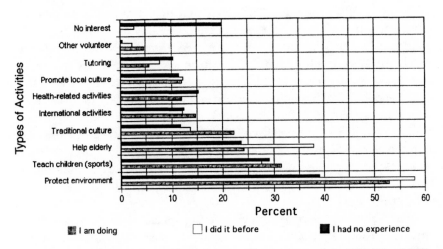

Figure 11.1. Volunteer activities among Japanese youth in 1993 (*N* = 2,052).

Christian woman devoted herself to the care of children born to Japanese mothers and American fathers.

In other countries, community service is often instigated by churches. However, because Japanese do not typically affiliate with formal churches, we wonder how citizens' active involvement in voluntary helping behaviors is promoted. In fact, a 1993 survey of over 2,000 13- to 25-year-olds indicated that although 81% of adolescents wanted to participate in community activities, only 33% had some experience and only 5% were at that time involved in community service such as protecting the earth's resources (58%), taking care of the elderly and handicapped (38%), and teaching children (28%) (see Figure 11.1; Management and Coordination Agency, 1994).

A Japanese alternative may be to provide school-based service opportunities. In 1989, the Ministry of Education started to promote community service in schools. Specifically, high schools began to encourage subjects such as social welfare, community service, and voluntary activity, and in 1994, it was reported that 11,000 elementary and high schools had special programs for community service (Management and Coordination Agency, 1994). Our survey of female students at a private college indicated that 85% had been involved in community service during high school and that 65% of the service participants were involved through school programs. After graduation, only 9% continued to do service, but 74% of students indicated that they would like to resume service activities if they had the opportunity (Takahashi, 1996).

Actions by the Ministry of Education may have had some cumulative effects. In 1995, the Hanshin-Awaji earthquake struck Japan and more than 6,000 citizens were killed. Surprisingly, numerous adults and students responded by traveling to the area and volunteering their services. An estimated 60,000 volunteers worked each day, and a total of one million citizens participated. Sixty-three percent of them came from outside the city. Half of the volunteers did not belong to any organization, and most of them were young people who were novices in such activities. Many high school age and college age people volunteered (Honma & Deguchi, 1996).

Some volunteers participated by offering special skills. Several college students from communication departments worked to establish communication networks via e-mail or Internet. Graduate students in clinical psychology addressed the mental health concerns and posttraumatic stress of children and the elderly. Follow-up research indicated that after their involvement with earthquake victims, youth often continued to be engaged in service activities in their home towns and cities (Honma & Deguchi, 1996). Some youth are now working in a variety of projects run by nongovernmental organizations, and two monthly magazines for volunteers were initiated in 1996.

Environmental Protection. There are three major types of environmental protection efforts in Japan: protests against pollution by particular enterprises, protests against nuclear weapon testing and nuclear power plants, and, with increasing interest, preservation of the natural environment.

Protests against pollution started in 1890s. A Diet member, Shozo Tanaka, pointed out that the copper poisoning from one mine contaminated nearby rivers, and people who ate fish of the rivers either died or became sick from the mineral poisoning. Over 2,000 farmers joined Tanaka in protest, asking the government to close the mine, but to no avail.

In 1956, a doctor found victims of mercury poisoning in Minamata Bay. The bay was polluted by mercury from the waste discharged into the Minamata River from plants of a chemical enterprise. When mercury accumulated in the human body via the food chain, it caused severe symptoms, which were named *Minamata disease*. Victims and their voluntary supporters protested against the chemical company. In 1963, the government agreed to give a warning to the enterprise, and in 1995, after more than 40 years of protests, victims finally won their case. It is not easy for victims to win against big enterprises, which are typically supported by government. In fact, the enterprise that caused Minamata disease contributed 24% of the income of the Minamata city budget in 1961 (Kurihara, 1996).

Antinuclear protests started in 1954. Twenty-three fishermen who had been working near the prohibited area of Bikini Atoll were contaminated by the "Death Ash" from U.S. nuclear testing. One of them died and others suffered from cancer. Since the death of the fisherman, who was called the "third victim of atomic bombing," after Hiroshima and Nagasaki, Japanese people, including youngsters, consistently protested against nuclear tests, and often against the construction or expansion of nuclear power plants. As mentioned before, this was one of the most political movements for students and young workers in the 1950s and 1960s. Although the government wants to build more nuclear plants, citizens who live nearby strongly object to such plans. In one small town, citizens won a referendum in 1996 against a nuclear plant. This victory embarrassed the government as well as the electric power company that owned the plant.

Unlike members of the two preceding types of environmental movements, supporters of environmental protection in Japan are generally apolitical. They have mainly been focused on consumer behaviors. Many people are interested in food additives, natural food, and organic agriculture. Food enterprises, farmers, and customers have participated in those movements.

Other activities are directed toward saving the earth's resources by reducing energy consumption, recycling, and protesting against the misuse or abuse of the natural environment. Citizens including children are participating in many kinds of recycling. Since the 1980s, the government has started to worry about the depletion of energy resources and environmental deterioration. In 1992, environmental education was introduced into schools. Although environmental problems are closely related to politics and economics, as suggested by the Earth Summit in 1992, government-led environmental education focuses mostly on encouraging children to engage in recycling, nurture flowers, and respect nature.

However, some people rightly insist that environmental problems are economic and political issues, and some economists criticize Japanese multinational enterprises, for example, in South Asia and South Africa.

Some schoolteachers are developing educational programs to foster societal understanding among children in classrooms. The effects of these programs on students' environmental attitudes are yet to be examined.

Understanding the Economic Structure of Society

Japanese youth's civic engagement may be greatly inhibited by their lack of knowledge about the economic structure of society. As discussed in the previous section, Japanese youth are willing to help people in need such as the poor, the physically handicapped, and the suffering. They do not ignore unfair or inhumane treatment of others. However, a great majority of youth are indifferent to politics because they do not feel that political parties represent their interests and concerns. Moreover, they often lack knowledge needed to influence big businesses and the government, which tends to favor the interests of big businesses. In general, youth do not seem aware that business enterprise by definition tries to maximize profit. Very few know that business enterprises require capital for their activities and are, thus, driven by a fear of losing fund-raising capability.

Understanding the economic structure of modern society is highly complicated and challenging. In mass societies including contemporary Japan, ordinary people can feel alienated from the economic system. Adolescents have even fewer opportunities than adults to participate in economic activities in society and, thus, tend to possess even less knowledge. In addition, in the Japanese culture there has been no tradition of encouraging less mature members of society to earn money or to use it intelligently. In a sense, Japan's culture is far behind its advanced economic system.

In this section, we present findings from our studies on youth's folk knowledge of economics. More specifically, we discuss (1) Japanese youth's conceptions of a bank, (2) their humanistic bias about the banking business, and (3) induced changes due to the presentation of critical pieces of information regarding the banking business. There have been a number of studies on understanding of the banking business as representative of understanding of social institutions or societal cognition (e.g., Furth, 1980; Jahoda, 1981). Throughout this section, we emphasize that Japanese adolescents are rather ignorant of the societal economic structure, and this lack of knowledge may make their civic activities less effective.

Conceptions of a Bank

The first study examined how accurately Japanese children and youth understand the role played by a bank in Japanese society (Takahashi & Hatano, 1989; 1994). Three groups with a total of 80 participants were included: 20 8- to 10-year-old children, 36 11- to 16-year old adolescents, and 24 young adults (college students). They were individually interviewed with questions, as in Jahoda (1981), about a bank's deposit and loan functions and the relationship between deposited and loaned money, including the difference in the interest rates. Specific wording of the questions is provided in the protocols to be described.

The interviews lasted 30 to 40 minutes and were recorded and transcribed verbatim. The transcripts were analyzed with a focus on how the participants conceptualized a bank's functions. Three alternative conceptions were expected. They ranged from simple to complex and were labeled as "safe-deposit box," "governmental agency," and "ordinary enterprise." The first type supposed that deposited money was not lent but stored at the bank safely. The second characterized the bank as a nonprofit organization that loaned money only for public purposes. The third assumed that the bank did business for itself, as well as loan money for business. In addition we coded responses as "correct" or "near correct." The correct conception was coded when a participant answered accurately about the bank's deposit function and interest paid, its loan function and the interest charged, and relationships between the two functions and the difference in the interest rates; a near correct conception was coded when the participant made just one minor inaccurate response. Prototypical responses were prepared for the different conceptions and used for identifying them among the participants. Intercoder agreement was 71.4% for whether or not interviews were classifiable into one of four specified categories (the three alternative conceptions and correct and nearly correct combined) and 84.2% for whether response was classifiable or not.

It was revealed that participants, even 3rd to 4th graders, generally responded coherently and seemed to have their own conceptions about the banking business. As shown in Table 11.1, in addition to the correct and nearly correct conceptions, the expected three types of alternative conceptions of banks were evident. About 38% of the participants offered alternative conceptions, and about 32% could not be classified at all because their responses were not coherent or detailed enough. Here, we describe the three alternative conceptions in more detail.

Table 11.1. *Number of Subjects Holding Correct or Alternative Conceptions of the Banking Business*

Conceptions	8- to 10-Year-olds ($n = 20$)	11- to 16-Year-olds ($n = 36$)	College students ($n = 24$)
Correct conception	0	3	11
Nearly correct conception[a]	0	7	3
Total alternative conceptions	12	13	6
Ordinary enterprise	3	2	5
Governmental agency	1	5	0
Safe-deposit box	8	6	1
Unclassifiable	8	13	4

[a]Committing only one error in responses and offering no false explanations were classified as having a "nearly correct" conception.

Bank as Safe-Deposit Box. Participants holding this conception assume that a bank safely keeps deposited money; accordingly, it seeks funds for paying interest and for loans from such outside sources as the government or the tax bureau. What follows is a typical protocol for a child holding this conception. Though it was uncommon, we note that a few adolescents and young adults expressed similar views. We note also that in the following protocols the symbol // before the beginning of a question indicates that we are not presenting some questions that preceded this question.

Miz (8:3, Grade 3):
What does a bank do?
"It keeps your money, and it's the place you go when you want to get your money back."

If banks disappeared, would there be a problem?
"There would be trouble if I had lots of money and a robber or someone came and stole it."

Let's say, I put 100,000 yen in the bank. After 1 year when I withdraw it, how much money do I receive? 100,000 yen? More than 100,000 yen? Less than 100,000 yen? About how much do you think I will get?
"100,000 yen."

Why is that?
"Because a bank is a place that keeps people's money, so if the people in the bank took the money, we'd be in trouble."

//What does the bank do with everybody's money?
"It writes the exact amount of money it keeps in a person's passbook, and it puts the money in a cash register it makes for the person or in a safe."

//Let's say, I borrowed 100,000 yen from the bank. After 1 year when it's time to return it, how much should I give back? 100,000 yen, more than 100,000 yen? Less than 100,000 yen? About how much do you think?
"100,000 yen."

Why is that?
"Because if you give back less than you borrowed, the bank will be in trouble, and because you got exactly 100,000 yen from the bank and you borrowed it, so if you don't give back just the same amount of money, [the bank will have] trouble."

//Do banks make a profit?
"No, they don't make money."

Bank as Governmental Agency. This conception can be characterized by such constituent beliefs as that a bank uses deposited money for public services; that it is a nonprofit organization; and that interest for deposit is paid by the government or the Mint Bureau. The following protocol illustrates this type of conception.

> **Nat** (13:7, Grade 7):
> What does a bank do?
> "It takes money from other people and stores it."
>
> If banks disappeared, would there be a problem?
> "If you had lots of money, it wouldn't be safe to keep it yourself."
>
> Let's say I put 100,000 yen in the bank. After 1 year when I withdraw it, how much money do I receive? 100,000 yen? More than 100,000 yen? Less than 100,000 yen? About how much do you think I will get?
> "100,000 yen."
>
> Why is that?
> "If you had a long-term deposit, it would grow; I don't know if it's the usual way. Since you put in your own 100,000 yen, that's what you'd get. Because if it increased, someone would have to put out more money."
>
> Even if you deposit your money in a regular bank it increases. After 1 year for 100,000 yen, you get about 3,000 yen in interest. Why is that, do you suppose?
> "[She thinks for a while]. The people at the bank keep the money . . . and then . . . I don't know."
>
> Where does the money for interest come from?
> "From the government."
>
> What do banks do with the money they keep for people?
> "They give it out when the country or the city builds something."

Where does the money that the bank lends to people come from?
"From a place called the tax office."

//How does the bank pay the salaries of the people that work in the bank?
"[without much confidence] The people who said they'd built the bank, or
the bank president [and all], they get the money from the government and
the city."

Bank as an Ordinary Enterprise. This conception was coded using two
subtypes. The first equates a bank to the financing section of a big business. A bank gathers money, and its parent company uses the money
for some business to pay interest for deposit. The second portrays a bank
as a stock company. A bank not only loans money with interest, but also
sells and buys stocks and, in this way, makes a profit. The following
protocol illustrates the first subtype.

  Tag (20:9, College student):
  What does a bank do?
  "If a big company is running the bank, there is a large profit, and when
  they decide they'd like to do something big with that money, they collect
  money from us and use it. We also get interest. So it's good for both sides."

  Does a bank manage anything?
  "It doesn't manage. It lends to big companies, and big companies . . . like
  Sumitomo, or Mitsubishi . . . have banks."

  //Why do banks give interest, do you suppose?
  "Since a deposit is loaning money to a bank, the bank adds interest and
  returns it. When a large company undertakes a big project and gets returns,
  it comes from that. And also, it comes from the Bank of Japan."

  How does the Bank of Japan relate to this?
  "It's the same as a bank. The Bank of Japan is a national, public institution
  and issues currency and sends it to all the banks and collects it from all
  the banks. It's connected with the Diet."

  How is it connected with the interest we receive?
  "There isn't a direct connection."

  Where does the bank get the money it lends out?
  "From every business."

  Do banks make profits?
  "They don't make money. They don't earn profits; they're a convenience.
  They are institutions for acquiring a lot of money for the common good.
  They're run by big companies. Or by the Bank of Japan maybe. A pipeline.
  It's a pipeline connecting us and business. It's okay if they don't make
  money."

Finally, in order to clarify further the nature of those alternative conceptions, the following protocol exemplifies the response of participants who held the correct conception.

> **Kom** (20:8, College student):
> What does a bank do?
> "For the part that we come into contact with, deposits and loans, for individuals and for companies."
> //Why does a bank pay interest for deposit?
> "When a bank lends money to another company, it charges interest and part of that it takes for itself, but since it is using its customers' money, it charges a little of the interest for them."
> //Which is more, the interest the bank pays when it keeps your money or the interest it takes from people when they borrow? Or are they the same?
> "The interest is higher for borrowing."
> Why?
> "If they don't do that, they wouldn't be able to run the bank."
> //Do banks make a profit?
> "Yes, they do."
> How?
> "A bank makes a profit on the difference between the interest charged on money lent and the interest paid to depositors."

We conclude that a majority of Japanese adolescents and young adults, including college students, do not fully understand the banking business. Although the frequencies of immature alternative conceptions decreased as the participants grew older, all age groups of students showed the same kinds of alternative conceptions and they did so fairly frequently. However, we would add that two fifth graders, who had special experience with banks through parents' borrowing money from the bank for housing and through discourse with the father, who was a banker, had the correct conception.

Humanistic Bias

It is likely that when people have limited knowledge about social institutions, they construct an alternative conception of it by borrowing rules from everyday personal interactions, which are basically governed by ethical and humanistic rules. Our study aimed to investigate whether college students would apply ethical and humanistic rules in understanding of a bank's behavior when customers would like to borrow money (Takahashi & Hatano, 1996). Two studies were conducted, focusing on (1) whether participants would apply ethical/humanistic rules when they inferred reasons for a bank's decision on customers' loan applications and (2) whether they would more readily attribute a bank's decision to those ethical/humanistic considerations when the customers had personal reasons for borrowing money.

Fifty-four female college students in an introductory psychology class participated in the first study. None had taken a class in economics at college. The participants were asked to respond to a questionnaire about (1) whether a bank would lend money to eight hypothetical loan applicants, each of whom had specific reasons for borrowing money. The participants were asked to predict a bank's decision (unconditional approval, conditional approval, or disapproval); and (2) if they selected "conditional" or "no approval," they were asked to offer inferred reasons for the decision. Half of the applicants were characterized as persons who needed the money because of personal difficulties such as alcoholic addiction, and the other half needed the money because of accidental circumstances such as traffic accident or depression in business. Each participant responded to four cases. These cases were presented in mixed order with two representing personal circumstances and two representing accidental circumstances.

The inferred reasons for a bank's decisions were coded into nine categories representing two main groups: Economic and Ethical/Humanistic. Economic reasons included the necessities of a mortgage and certainty of repayment. Ethical/humanistic reasons included a bank's sympathetic understanding of a borrower's situation or personality. Although they were encouraged to write as much as they wanted, each participant usually wrote one reason for each case.

The results were as follows: (1) 80% (for Personal) and 85% (for Accidental) of the responses were classified as Economic reasons. For both types of cases, more than 30% of the participants referred to the possession of real estate (e.g., a house) as a security or a guarantor for Personal and Accidental circumstances, another 30% wrote that a bank would demand certainty of repayment on a debt, and nearly 10% implicitly referred to possibilities of repayment. For example, one student mentioned that as the yen was overvalued, the applicant would have difficulty in continuing the business transaction. (2) 15% (for Accidental) and 19% (for Personal) of the responses were identified as ethical/humanistic reasons. For both types of cases, 10% of responses were coded as both "economic and humanistic" because they assumed the bank's goodwill in negotiating the interest rate or extension of the loan period with sympathetic consideration of the borrower's economic circumstances. For example, some students believed that the bank would help and encourage such persons to earn money and the bank would extend the repayment period or lend money free of interest. In addition, 3% (for Accidental) and 8% (for Personal) of the reasons were identified as purely "Personal." Some participants assumed that to avoid risk of a bad debt, a bank would not lend money to a person who had a difficult disposition such as alcoholic addiction. Some others supposed that a bank would loan because of a sympathetic understanding of a victim of an accident. (3) Forty-five percent of the students anticipated the bank's humanistic consideration of the applicant in at least one of the four hypothetical cases.

This study indicated ethical/humanistic biases in understanding of a bank's behaviors, but it did not clarify how the students conceptualize a bank's loan decisions. In the second study, participants were urged to infer in detail a bank's reasons for approving or disapproving a loan. Thirty-five college female students in another introductory psychology class participated. None had taken a class in economics in college. The participants were asked to respond to the same eight cases as in Study 1, but participants were asked to infer reasons for a bank's loan decision. We told the participants that the bank employee should primarily consider the bank's profit and maintain good relations with the bank's customers. The participants were asked to infer reasons for the bank employee's decision in four cases: 2 circumstances (personal, accidental) × 2 loan decisions (approval, disapproval).

The inferred reasons were coded into the same nine categories as in Study 1. On average, participants gave two reasons for each case. (1) From 54% to 79% of the reasons were identified as "Economic," but only 1% to 8% of the participants pointed out the necessity of having collateral and/or a guarantor for the loan, although those are the most important criteria for bankers. Instead, most of the economic reasons were classified as "explicit or implicit certainty of repayment" or "other reasons," in which, for example, the participants referred to limitations on the amount of money loaned or on the loan period for the bank's safety. The participants were mostly concerned with direct collection of a debt rather than guarantee of the principal. (2) Of the reasons given 21%–45% were identified as "ethical/humanistic." Especially when hypothetical applicants had personal difficulties, 43% of the disapprovals and 21% of the approvals were attributed to the applicants' personal disposition. When applicants were accidentally put in difficult circumstances and were approved for loans, 11% of the participants assumed "sympathetic" reasoning of the banker. (3) All but three of the students mentioned "ethical/humanistic" reasoning in at least one of their responses.

To conclude, these two studies indicate that many college students applied ethical/humanistic rules to understanding a bank's behaviors. When the participants were forced to infer the reasons for a bank's loan decisions, their ethical and humanistic biases were more clearly revealed.

Spontaneous and Induced Changes in Conceptions

We observed that two of the junior high school students and one college student changed their conceptions during the interview. One initially answered that a bank did not make a profit because it had to pay as much interest for the deposited money as for the loaned money. However, when she was asked how a bank paid salaries to employees, she answered, "From the profit it makes . . . it makes a little profit," and recognized the contradiction with her previous answer. She decided to change her previous answer and said, "The bank makes a little profit, by getting interest for loaned money."

In the second case, the participant recognized a contradiction in her previous answers, which equated interest rates for deposits and loans. This realization occurred when, after some consideration, she gave an affirmative answer to the question "Does the bank make a profit?" She then spontaneously changed her previous answer and claimed that the interest rate for loans must be higher than that for deposits because she thought the bank made a profit.

Encouraged by these observations of the effect of pieces of factual knowledge on understanding of the banking business, we tried to induce changes in alternative conceptions by presenting critical information about banks (Takahashi & Hatano, 1993). We examined whether when presented some critical pieces of factual information, students would change their conceptions of banking.

Four students, who had articulated a clear alternative conception of a bank in the study on conceptions of a bank, one holding the "safe-deposit box" conception and three holding the "government agency" conception, were, 3 months later, individually given a set of four critical pieces of information about the major banks in Japan. They were then immediately given a second interview.

The information given was the following: (1) Banks collect money from a large number of people in Japan. For example, Daiichi-kanngyo Bank collects about 40 trillion yen per year in deposits. They use this money for their business activities. (2) Banks are nongovernment companies. (3)

They make an outstandingly large amount of profit every year. More than half of the top 10 most profitable companies were banks last year. (4) Bank employees are paid better than employees of other companies and public officials. The average salary of bank employees is larger than that of employees of other big companies by up to 170,000 yen.

The postintervention assessment of the participants' conceptions showed that the holder of the "safe-deposit" box conception, a 9th grader, did not learn to comprehend profit-making mechanisms of the banking business at all. She believed that money for loans was a bank's own money and interest rates were the same for deposits and loans, even after the intervention. She replied correctly that a bank loans money, but this was the only change the information made in her understanding. The other three students who had possessed the "government agency" conception (one 9th grader and two 10th graders) increased the number of correct responses to those questions concerning profit-making mechanisms of the banking business. They no longer answered that money for loans came from the government. However, two of them believed that money for loans was provided by a company running a bank or interest for deposits was paid by the company. They did not understand that banks are themselves profit-seeking companies. Only one participant revealed more or less complete understanding of the banking business, discarding her earlier conception of a bank as a governmental agency.

To summarize, it seems that for each alternative conception, there are critical facts that make this conception no longer tenable. In their attempt to find a better model, some youth will be led to the correct conception, whereas others will develop another inaccurate conception. Needless to say, presenting the critical facts alone may not induce conceptual change. Like misconceptions in other domains, alternative conceptions of banks are certainly resistant to change. For example, the first participant could have kept her prior conception intact, as many of her age mates and younger participants did, by assigning the source of salaries for employees to the government. However, the results of the studies among college students suggest that without intervention, we must expect development in societal cognition to be very limited. This is why conscientious schoolteachers (e.g., Suzuki, 1986; Yasui, 1986) have tried very hard to inform their students of the facts of economics.

Conclusion

As shown in our historical review, many Japanese people, including adolescents, have engaged in several kinds of civic movements and community service. On the basis of the observation that people often complain that it is difficult to find opportunities and that they would like to participate, it can be assumed that many more people would participate in such activities if given the chance. This assumption is bolstered by the case of the Hanshin-Awaji earthquake in 1995, when a surprising number of people rushed to the area as volunteers. Thus, the goodwill of Japanese citizens has generally been untapped.

Another problem our review suggests is that the Japanese have insufficient knowledge about economic and political structures and mechanisms. As indicated by our research on the understanding of the banking business, ordinary people's knowledge of the society is very limited. This may make people's civic activities less effective and less geared toward contributing to the welfare of all.

Unfortunately, the government and the so-called power elite are often reluctant to promote accurate and detailed knowledge among the masses of society's workings. They tend to hide important facts and treat highly political and economic issues as if they were apolitical, neutral, and ethical/humanistic. This situation is made worse in Japan because the Japanese have traditionally viewed the government as dependable and trustworthy as well as dominating and controlling. A large majority of citizens do not think that they have to watch the government and leave everything in its hands. The government, in response to such expectations, has developed apparently "boundless" and "warmhearted" social systems. As an embodiment of the "interdependent" relationship between citizens and the government, the Ministry of Education has introduced environmental programs and community service in schools. The Ministry of Social Welfare has developed similar social programs for more mature citizens. We admit that these government interventions have helped the society to some extent. For example, Japan has almost no street children and a smaller number of homeless people than most other developed countries. However, as we have already mentioned, Japanese citizens seem to have become less spontaneous and less independent in engaging in civic activities.

We need more nongovernmental citizens' organizations to promote civic engagement. Some conscientious teachers are developing educational programs for enhancing students' understanding of social mechanisms. One teacher has constructed a series of programs to help high school students to understand the actions of multinational enterprises (Ohtsu, 1987). Another teacher in an elementary school has developed a program focusing on war (Kutsumi, 1989). Although within the limit of public schooling, these and other attempts may encourage more active citizens.

Outside public schooling, some active and sensible citizens are establishing nonprofit organizations and developing citizens' networks. It is reported that in 1970, there were more than 3,000 groups for civic movements, and in the 1990s, meetings of network leaders have been organized (Kurihara, 1996). These organizations are drawing not only upon each other's strengths, but also upon international resources, such as the expanding number of books on citizens' networking that are translated into Japanese. As happened with the volunteers in the earthquake of 1995, these networks are also increasingly making use of e-mail and the Internet, as a means of building their membership and strengthening their organization. Thus, despite the negative anticipation of the Japanese intelligentsia, who had claimed that civic activities could not attract nonreligious Japanese people, ordinary citizens, including youngsters, have begun to involve themselves in a variety of civic activities. The disastrous damage by the Hanshin-Awaji earthquake has revealed people's "latent" goodwill. We can say that support for civic activities is increasing. Civic activities seem to heighten self-confidence and give a sense of meaning to individuals' lives, which is difficult to find in this rich and highly technological society.

Let us conclude this chapter by quoting a female college student majoring in clinical psychology who worked as a volunteer for victims of the earthquake. After her first participation in voluntary activities, she started to think about herself differently:

> I had lived in Kobe City before. I felt guilty when I heard of the earthquake. It was a very good chance for me to join the activities. However, at the beginning, I was obsessed by the idea that I was doing such activities because of self-satisfaction or for my own feeling of guilt . . . I worked hard every day in the city, and persuaded myself that I was doing nothing special. . . . Yes, I did natural things. Now, I am sure that the next time I will feel more free and natural   (Center for Information of Family Problems, 1995).

References

Azuma, S., & Suzuki, J. (1991). A review of studies of sex role. *Journal of Japanese Psychology, 62,* 270–276 [In Japanese].

Center for Information on Family Problems (1995). The Earthquake, volunteers, and children. *Familio, 8,* 1–3 [In Japanese].

Economic Planning Agency (1996). *International financial statistics*. Tokyo: Author [In Japanese].

Furth, H. G. (1980). *The world of grown-ups: Children's conceptions of society*. New York: Elsevier.

Honma, M., & Deguchi, M. (1996). *Volunteers revolution*. Tokyo: Toyo-Keizai-Shinpo-sha [in Japanese].

Iwao, S., & Hara, H. (1979). *Introduction to women's studies*. Tokyo: Kodansya [In Japanese].

Jahoda, G. (1981). The development of thinking about economic institutions: The bank. *Cahiers de Psychologie Cognitive, 1,* 55–73.

Kono, K., & Aramaki, H. (1997). How did voters cast their ballots under the new electoral system? *The NHK Monthly Report on Broadcast Research, 1,* 26–43.

Kurihara, A. (1996). *Evidence of good-will: Interface between young people and social institutions*. Tokyo: Shinyosya [In Japanese].

Kutsumi, N. (1989). *Human beings are wonderful: Social studies classroom co-constructed with children*. Tokyo: Jyugyo-wo-tukuru-sya [In Japanese].

Management and Coordination Agency (1994). *Survey of voluntary activities among youth*. Tokyo: Author [In Japanese].

Management and Coordination Agency (1996). *Survey of labor power*. Tokyo: Author [In Japanese].

Ministry of Education (1996). *Survey of schooling*. Tokyo: Author [In Japanese].

Ministry of Health and Welfare (1996). *Tables of life*. Tokyo: Author [In Japanese].

Ministry of Labor (1996). *Report of working women*. Tokyo: Author [In Japanese].

National Police Agency (1996). *Statistics of national police agency*. Tokyo: Author. [In Japanese].

Ohtsu, K. (1987). *Social studies: Viewed from a piece of banana*. Tokyo: Kokudo-sya [In Japanese].

Suzuki, M. (1986). *Social studies lesson for invisible world: Children support each other in a classroom*. Tokyo: Shin-nippon-syuppan-sya [In Japanese].

Takahashi, K. [1996]. Voluntary activities among college students. Unpublished manuscript [In Japanese], Tokyo Sacred Heart University.

Takahashi, K., & Hatano, G. (1989). Conceptions of the bank: A developmental study. *Technical Report 11*. Tokyo: Japanese Cognitive Science Society.

Takahashi, K., & Hatano, G. (1993, October). Induced changes of naive theory by giving key conceptions: A case of banking business. Paper presented at the Japanese Educational Psychological Meeting, Nagoya, Japan.

Takahashi, K., & Hatano, G. (1994). Understanding of the banking business in Japan: Is economic property accompanied by economic literacy? *British Journal of Developmental Psychology, 12,* 585–590.

Takahashi, K., & Hatano, G. (1996, August). *A naive theory of banking business: Humanistic rules applied to societal understanding*. Paper presented at the Biennial International Society for the Study of Behavioral Development, Quebec, Canada.

Yasui, T. (1986). *Teaching students to understand civic rights*. Tokyo: Ayumi-shuppan [in Japanese].

Yukawa, T. (1996, August). *Stereotypes of sex-roles among Japanese college students*. Paper presented at the Biennial International Society for the Study of Behavioral Development, Quebec, Canada.

12. Learning Politics in the Crucible: The Socialization of Taiwan High School Students as Citizens in a New Democracy

PERRI STRAWN

> Reading Taiwan's history is painful. It seems as though everyone has just used this piece of earth as a stepping-stone. I'm suspicious how many people really would be willing to put themselves out for the sake of this piece of earth, no matter whether you're talking about Han Chinese, the Japanese, or the Republican government. People are always opposing something, but they don't know what it is they want. . . . Sometimes I read books from the China mainland, and I can see that they are so confident and proud of their country. When are people in Taiwan going to be able to face up to the past and find their own road?
>
> (from a 17-year-old Taibei high school senior, 1994[1])

Introduction: Taiwan as a Frontier Political Space

This chapter discusses how students at college-preparatory high schools in Taiwan have engaged with the island's political transformation from an authoritarian regime to democracy. Any discussion of political activity by Taiwan students must take into account the larger historical framework of Taiwan society in the past 50 years, and Taiwan's place in the larger spatial and temporal orbit of modern China's history (Shepherd, 1993).

Chiang Kai-shek and his Nationalist partisans (KMT) gained control of Taiwan, a Japanese colony since 1895, at the end of World War II. Civil war broke out on the mainland between the KMT and Mao Zedong's Communists soon after the Japanese surrender, and refugees from the mainland began pouring onto Taiwan. In April 1948, the newly elected National Assembly on the mainland approved temporary amendments to the ROC Constitution, which resulted in the imposition of martial law in Taiwan. Chiang and his troops retreated to the island after their defeat by the Communists in 1949. During the period of martial law on Taiwan (1948–1987), the KMT under Chiang Kai-shek and his successors imposed its view of national identity and history on Taiwan as plans were formulated and tested for an eventual takeover of the mainland.

The curriculum and much of the daily ritual in Taiwan's schools during martial law went according to KMT regulations. All military instructors and most teachers were KMT party members, and political expression other than support for the ruling regime was forbidden. This meant that in addition to rules to ensure the smooth running of the school, such as requirements to be on time, be in proper attire, do homework, and sit attentively in class, there were also rules (not always written, but always understood) to ensure that students maintained the correct political orientation. Students heard speaking Taiwanese instead of Mandarin Chinese were fined and made to wear placards. Discussion of Taiwan independence or of the KMT's right to rule Taiwan were not allowed.

The end of Taiwan's martial law on July 15, 1987, marked the beginning of an open debate about Taiwan's social, political, and cultural identity. The KMT finally acknowledged that the ROC government would never retake the mainland by force. And more than a decade of agitation for political reform on the island culminated in the legalization of Taiwan's first opposition political party, which had been fielding successful candidates for elections since the late 1970s. By September 1987, the government lifted the ban on new political parties and independent media outlets. Newspapers and magazines representing every color of the political spectrum began to flood corner groceries, and radio stations began broadcasting out of basements and storefronts. Change reached schools more slowly, but shifts in policy, curriculum, and texts gradually began to reflect the larger social changes. However, many of the structures of authority implemented in schools during martial law remain. The justification for continued control of the student body (and bodies) is the maintenance of a certain social stability, which is believed to foster economic growth and peaceful political reform.

In the following sections, I will first discuss the political involvement of Taiwan's high school students, including a brief historical overview of twentieth-century student protest in China and of Taiwan's 1980s student movement. This will provide an opportunity to discuss the ways students find to negotiate meanings within their highly structured school environments. In conclusion, I will argue that Taiwan's status as an "economic miracle," the high value placed on educational credentials in Taiwan, and the importance of "harmony" as an ideal are all factors affecting the level of political involvement by Taiwan's high school students and their willingness to challenge authority.

Student Involvement in the Politics of China and Taiwan

China has a rich tradition of student protest dating from its nineteenth-century political upheavals. These student protests were in turn rooted in the Confucian tradition in which scholars were identified as the arbiters of morality and the accepted critics of the imperial state.[2] In Taiwan, intellectuals in general and students in particular were in a difficult position during martial law. Since even the smallest gestures of defiance against the regime, such as speaking Taiwanese on campus, were punishable, larger gestures of dissent were unthinkable unless someone was willing to risk jail, or worse.

Students as Actors in Changing China

By the turn of the century, Chinese students were regularly traveling abroad for advanced training and study. China's defeats in the Sino–Japanese War and the Boxer Rebellion (1900) and the continuing exploitation of China's territory by other nations angered students and intellectuals familiar with nationalistic movements around the world.

The goal of protecting China's sovereignty motivated and shaped China's student movements in the first half of the twentieth century. In spring 1901, "progressive teachers and their students joined with members of other classes to take part in public meetings denouncing Russia for refusing to cede control of Manchuria to China" (Wasserstrom, 1991, p. 39). Shanghai students united to form "student armies" dedicated to protecting China. China's 1905 boycott of American goods to protest American immigration policy was supported by "the patriotic excitement of Chinese students – many recently returned from studies in Japan" (Spence, 1990, p. 238). Japan's "Twenty-One Demands" of 1915, seeking economic and political concessions in northern and eastern China, sparked nationwide anti-Japanese student protests and a boycott of Japanese goods.

But it was the Treaty of Versailles ending World War I that ignited China's most famous student movement and changed forever China's social, political, and cultural landscape. The treaty gave control of German's Shandong concessions to Japan, instead of returning control to China. When news reached students in Beijing, several thousand demonstrated, violating a police ban. Demonstrations occurred throughout China over the next few days. Though the title "May Fourth Movement" refers to this specific event, it came to be associated with a larger movement in China from 1915 to about 1922, involving a range of cultural and political developments. Many scholars see this "as a pivotal period of intellectual ferment comparable to the European Enlightenment or Renaissance" (Wasserstrom, 1991, p. 51). Significant student mobilizations in 1925 and 1931 further demonstrated the power of students to garner public support and affect China's political course.

Students and the State in the ROC

By the 1930s, the KMT viewed students not as potential revolutionaries but rather as potential troublemakers whose energy and passions must be properly directed (Israel, 1966). After the numerous large outbreaks of independent student activity in the 1920s and 1930s, the KMT systematically clamped down. During the 1930s, mandatory military training was instituted in the high school and university under the National Military Training Commission. Junior middle-school students were required to join the Boy Scouts (Eastman, 1990).

These institutions traveled with the KMT to Taiwan in the late 1940s, with profound ramifications for social developments there. The ROC government instituted military training for students in Taiwan from the late 1940s. After the imposition of martial law in 1948, the island's population was on constant alert to defend against mainland attacks and to prepare for the eventual recapture of the mainland.

Lack of resources, the need for skilled labor, and a deep faith in the power of tests to rank students more fairly than school admissions officers led to the implementation of a rigid tracking system based on competitive entrance exams. Entrance to high school and then university, vocational academies, or teachers' colleges was determined by scores on the islandwide entrance exams. Since 1981, the ratio of adolescents continuing past the mandatory 9 years of schooling has been 3:7 college-prep/vocational.[3] In this way, the number of students attending college has been restricted, and a large pool of trained labor has been available to fuel Taiwan's economic growth.

The strictures of martial law provided a focal point for Taiwan's large-scale student demonstrations of the 1980s. Students at National Taiwan University began demanding the right to elect their student body head, instead of having the position filled by appointment. Other major student demonstrations of the 1980s and early 1990s involved protest of construction of a Dupont chemical factory, demands that the National Assembly uphold the constitution, and protest of the arrest of a graduate student who was head of a student group supporting Taiwan independence. Although it is impossible to go into detail about the social and political events that led to the end of martial law in 1987, it is important to note that these university student mobilizations played a crucial role up to and after the end of martial law, by forcing issues into public dialogue and by familiarizing people in Taiwan with the rituals of protest.

Since martial law's end, street demonstrations have become a main outlet for public sentiment in Taiwan. Hardly a day goes by in Taibei without at least one rally outside the National Assembly building, and on Sundays, people crowd the streets marching for acquired immunodeficiency syndrome (AIDS) awareness, women's rights, educational freedom, political parties, environmental issues, and other causes. But in contrast to that in those earlier student-led demonstrations, leadership is much more widespread. Students and professors still participate, but they often join other groups rather than themselves forming the core. In fact, a recent article reflecting on Taiwan's last 15 years of university student activity noted that students are beginning to turn inward, focusing more on issues in the school setting or on "finding themselves," rather than trying to implement large-scale social change. The end of martial law removed the obvious target for opposition, according to some former student leaders quoted in the article, and now students are identifying more with issues that have immediate impact on their lives (*Lianhe Bao*, 1994).

A Study of High School Student Political Involvement in Post–Martial Law Taiwan

The data for this article were collected as part of my dissertation fieldwork from September 1993 to July 1995. The primary research sites were two top girls' college-prep high schools, one in an urban setting and the other in a rural area. I spent a semester at the urban school and 6 weeks at the rural site, during which I attended certain classes with the same groups of girls for the entire period. I ate lunch with the students, observed extracurricular activities, conducted group and individual interviews, and administered detailed surveys. I also interviewed teachers and administrators and collected material on the schools' histories. In addition to these primary sites, I collected data from top boys' schools in both urban and rural locations. Finally, I gathered data from a mixed-sex school and two vocational schools near Taibei.

The study had three main objectives. The first was to identify the multiple layers of meaning that national identity comprises in Taiwan. The second was to identify the explicit and implicit mechanisms through which high school students in Taiwan are taught about what it means to be Chinese in Taiwan, and to examine how teaching about national identity is differentiated across gender, class, and ethnic lines. Finally, the study asked to what extent the explicit aims of the Ministry of Education, the KMT, opposition political parties, and other groups with the power to shape policy become internalized and conventionalized by students. To what extent are those aims subverted, altered, or transformed in the process of identity formation by Taiwan's youth? In other words, is it possible to evaluate the "success" of government and school attempts to socialize students into a particular worldview?

During my stay, Taiwan experienced two major elections. The second, in December 1994, was the first in the island's history in which the provincial governor and mayors of the major municipalities were elected in direct democratic elections. The rising strength of the opposition Democratic Progressive party (DPP) and the emergence of the conservative New party created a lively and intense campaign atmosphere, providing rich opportunities to observe the debate about Taiwan's future. Political rallies and debates created an excellent background for discussions with students, teachers, taxi drivers, and nearly everyone else I met about who, and what, is Taiwan.

Training for Life: Learning to Live in Harmony

With the end of martial law, the KMT's rigid control of curriculum relaxed. Students who want to go to college must still spend school years mastering the test material, and many spend evenings at cram schools. However, students are allowed to read books from mainland China and to report on some of the KMT's darker history. Military training instructors spend more time discussing first-aid techniques and less talking about PRC troop strength. But many of the structural aspects designed to regulate students' lives have not changed so much. Taiwan students still exist within a series of concentric and nested circles of control, in which they are fitted into groups and chains of hierarchy that facilitate the accomplishment of specific educational and social goals.

A main objective of socialization through education in Taiwan is to train students about the importance of maintaining harmony in groups,[4] or *tuanjie*. Fostering a sense of group identity among students is a primary goal of most teachers and administrators, who regularly cite *tuanjie* or *tuanti de guannian* ("the idea of the group") as motivation for a range of policies and practices.

The notion of group harmony is in dialectical relationship with a concept that most Chinese offer as a defining aspect of Chinese culture, filiality. Being filial often means sacrificing personal desires, needs, and goals to maintain the overall harmony of the family. Decisions about a career, a spouse, a course of study, a place to live, or a hairstyle are all subject to family pressure. In general, women worry more about preserving the family harmony and are expected to do so.[5] Such expectations are in part related to traditional ideas about gender roles in China, which the educational system in Taiwan until recently has done little to challenge (Wilson, 1970).

From the narrow confines of the family, the notion of group unity expands to encompass society and the nation, an embodiment of the Confucian view of the world. Confucianism emphasizes the importance of harmonious relationships – starting with that between father and son – as the key to maintaining a larger social harmony. The KMT's recourse to Confucian tradition and its emphasis on filial piety have "actually [been] an attempt to extend feelings of family solidarity to the level of the nation" (Chun, 1996, p. 138). Thus, *tuanjie* links the physical and mental routines of discipline that students experience to larger social and historical frameworks.

The lack of *tuanjie* in China over the centuries is a defining characteristic of China's history as students have been taught it. But they are most familiar with the lack of *tuanjie* that has characterized China in *this* century – from the fall of the Qing, to the rocky founding of the republic, the warlord era, the war with Japan, and the civil war, which resulted in their own separation from the China mainland. This separation constantly reminds them of China's people's apparent inability to live together peacefully. Students often told me they feared China would never be whole again, "because it is very difficult for Chinese people to unite." Thus they attribute the cross-strait dilemma to what they understand to be a national character flaw.[6] Students have such beliefs in part because of the way history is taught. But the idea of a "national *tuanjie*" or national unity continues to be part of KMT rhetoric, as seen in slogans that decorate some school gateways, such as "Harmony and self-strength will save the country."

In addition to teaching students how to march and wield a gun, one mission of high school military training instructors is to teach students that what they learn about military life and training can be applied in any group in the wider society. During classroom instruction, the focus is on implanting the idea that no matter what group a person is a member of (class, family, team, company, or military), maintaining the harmony of the group is more important than anything else. One section of the text is devoted to explaining what "absolutely following authority" means. Always it comes back to protecting the harmony of the group and working to achieve the group's greatest potential. Only in this way can the ultimate potential of the group's individual members be reached.

Inculcating the idea of KMT authority as powerful, competent, and legitimate has always been a core goal of KMT education policies. This strategy has been an important part of Nationalist attempts to maintain control in Taiwan, and it proved remarkably effective for some 40 years. Many restrictive policies and practices took root in Taiwan during the period of martial law under the guise of preventing social chaos, which was portrayed as a real threat to national security. Censorship of the media and literature, travel restrictions, repression of political dissent, and an education curriculum dedicated to reinforcing the inalienable connection of Taiwan to the China mainland and the KMT's right to rule were all attributed to the need for unity in the face of the mainland threat. Only by presenting a unified front to the outside world could Taiwan ever hope to maintain its security, went the argument.

Since martial law's end, the issue of whether Taiwan will declare independence has entered the public dialogue.[7] Taiwanese language and history are now taught in schools, and promotion of local culture is a cornerstone of President Lee's education policy. However, the rhetoric about the need for harmony continues. President Lee speaks frequently about the need for *zuqun hexie* – "ethnic harmony." Aborigines, native Taiwanese, and descendants of mainlanders should all consider themselves both Taiwanese *and* Chinese, Lee says. This rhetoric is deployed in part to defuse independence sentiment and to demonstrate the KMT's identification with Taiwan. But the underlying justification for the social stability rhetoric is that it allows Taiwan's continued economic success.

It is here that we can see how effective the KMT has been at getting people to internalize a fear of social disorder. People on Taiwan enjoy a high material standard of living, with a per capita income in 1994 of $10,000 and huge foreign exchange reserves that are now legendary. For decades, the fear of a mainland attack was used by the KMT to justify harsh social control. As that fear has receded, the KMT has instead focused on the need to safeguard a certain level of social stability, which will in turn continue to foster Taiwan's economic success. Despite daily public debate about whether Taiwan should claim independence, most people prefer the status quo to any political upheavals that might jeopardize foreign investment. An additional concern is that Taiwan's role as a significant economic player guarantees its place on the world stage. The majority of people in Taiwan do not wish to jeopardize that status, since Taiwan's awkward political position has meant that few countries recognize it diplomatically.

Opportunities for Student Political Involvement

In my research I found that high school students only occasionally join street demonstrations, and usually for causes with less explicit connections to specific political causes, such as AIDS awareness and the environment. Most teachers discourage students from participating, hoping to keep them focused on more immediate goals such as preparing for the college entrance exam or work. There is also some residue of anxiety among parents who remember the Taiwan they grew up in, where criticizing the government could lead to jail. Better for students to shelter themselves at home and school than to be concerned with politics, which might only bring trouble.

Historically, high school students in Taiwan have had few opportunities to express their own views about anything within the school setting. Large lecture classes lasting 50 minutes leave little time for group discussion. Furthermore, the relationship between students and teachers puts students in a passive, receptive role, in which they are expected to memorize all the crucial information that comes their way. The ability to form and express opinions holds little value since it would neither score points on the college entrance exam nor help in finding a job. Students also fear that they will look foolish if they speak out in class. Years of being reprimanded for giving an incorrect answer when called upon have left this legacy to Taiwan students.

Not all students heed their teachers' admonishments to avoid street demonstrations, however, and not all teachers discourage students from getting involved. Two teachers at the top boys' school in Ilan County are famous throughout the county (some would say infamous) for organizing student participation in antinuclear protests. Teachers at the neighboring girls' school for the most part disapproved, believing that the politically active teachers not only were imposing their views unfairly on the boys, but were also distracting them from studying. In my experience, such large-scale involvement by Taiwan high school students in public demonstrations is rare.

Instead, what I found to be a more typical pattern was for students to find ways *within* their highly structured school environments to explore "alternative" political or cultural issues. Club activities in particular can provide outlets for students to consider current events and popular culture in meaningful ways. The range of club activities available varies from school to school. The top college-prep schools tend to give the students the most flexibility in forming clubs and freedom in deciding how much time to spend on club activities, since such students are assumed to be capable of managing time and of keeping up with work. The types of clubs at a school reflected students' interests and backgrounds. In the vocational schools I visited, clubs tended to cluster around activities such as break dancing, cartoon drawing, and target shooting, whereas the college-prep schools were more likely to have clubs that taught students how to play traditional Chinese musical instruments, for example.

In 1993, I was surprised to hear that some of the schools I was visiting had "Three Principles of the People" clubs. *The Three Principles of the People* is a collection of essays by Sun Yat-sen compiled after his death, and it forms the underlying ideology of the ROC government. The "three principles" are nationalism, democracy, and the people's livelihood. A year-long course in the doctrine is required of senior high school students, and it is tested on the college entrance exam. My understanding was that most students studied it only because it was required, that they found the class boring, and that many were put off by the comments of Chiang Kai-shek that had been inserted throughout the text. That they would voluntarily join a club devoted to its study intrigued me. As it turned out, neither of the "Three Principles" clubs I visited had much to do with *The Three Principles* anymore; both clubs had been formed to help students prepare for the entrance exam, but both had gradually dropped it as subject matter. What the students discussed at their club meetings shed some light on how they manage to make sense of the political change going on around them.

The "Three Principles" club located at a top urban boys' school had about 20 members who met once a week, more or less. Copies of *The Three Principles* were stacked on bookshelves in their meeting room, dusty. Their roster of activities included a combination of lessons in parliamentary procedure and a systematic review of current films. Jane

Campion's films were under study when I visited. Students from a nearby university were invited to discuss the minute details of *Robert's Rules of Order*. Club members explained to me that understanding the rules of parliamentary procedure was critical to implementing democracy. As it turned out, their study of democracy in the abstract had soured them on Taiwan's current political scene. Corruption in the KMT bothered them, and they also found the DPP's occasional outbursts in the National Assembly disheartening. When pressed to explain where they might have need of so much expertise in the minutiae of parliamentary procedure, if not through participation in Taiwan's national politics, they suggested maybe at class meetings or school government sessions. Meanwhile, they used their group discussions of current films and books to keep abreast of international cultural trends.

The situation at the neighboring girls' school was quite different. Dusty copies of *The Three Principles* occupied shelves in their meeting space, too, but alongside stood novels by Taiwanese authors and books on Taiwan history. After the end of martial law, that club's leader had decided it was time for students to start learning something about Taiwanese history and culture. The club read literature by Taiwanese authors and discussed essays by Taiwanese dissidents. They studied the history of Taiwan's aborigines and discussed Taiwan's prehistory. They even invited a DPP politician to speak to their group, though he was turned away at the school gate. It was among this small group of students that I heard the most critical accounts of the KMT-controlled curriculum, which they regularly referred to as "brainwashing."

In both of these cases, students were purposefully trying to make sense of Taiwan's ongoing democratization. Even the example of high school boys watching Jane Campion films fits that categorization, since greater access to foreign media has been an important aspect of Taiwan's political reform. These examples were only a few of many I found of students experimenting with alternative frameworks of understanding.

"Everyday Forms of Resistance"

Not only do students assert themselves in behind-the-scenes, indirect ways that reveal their attempts to make sense of and embrace the tremendous social and political changes Taiwan has experienced in the last decade. Another broad category of student resistance includes direct challenges to school and public authority through violating rules or norms in a public fashion. These public challenges in turn range from minor infringements of school rules to law-breaking, the former far more common among Taiwan students than the latter.

In the course of a day, students constantly challenge school restraints in small ways, by what could be called "everyday forms of resistance" (Scott, 1985, p. xvi). Arriving tardy to school, doing homework during class, sleeping in class, failing to prepare for class, and doing homework during an assembly are the most common forms of routine rule breaking. Punishments vary. Tardy to school means standing apart during the flag raising and possibly standing outside the military training instructor's office for 10 or 20 minutes later in the day. Doing work for one class while another goes on is the only way most students can keep up with the constant tests and homework assignments, and teachers will often ignore it unless the student is unable to answer a question when called on or is sitting in the front row. Students frequently sleep in class but this is not looked on kindly by teachers, and once caught a student is often made to stand for the rest of class. Students' behavior at school assemblies is often criticized, especially if they are not paying attention while an invited guest speaks. Books will be confiscated by military instructors and talkative students might receive demerits.

More major infringements involve student extracurricular activities. School authorities struggle to keep tabs on extracurricular activities because students often find ways to circumvent rules at those times. Club activities provide students with excellent opportunities to bend rules. At the all-girl schools I attended, for example, contact with boys was discouraged. But members of the debate club often managed to hook up with members of the opposite sex during competitions with other schools. At one school such interactions were ended by an administrator who felt trouble might grow out of the occasional contact with boys. At some schools certain clubs are allotted space outside classrooms for their activities. Yearbook staffs generally have their own small offices, for example. Students take advantage of these semiprivate spaces to skip class, discuss politics or trade gossip, or engage in forbidden activities such as smoking. Off-campus club activities must get school approval. On one occasion I learned of a group in which a member was injured while on a weekend hiking trip that had not received prior approval. In addition, boys from a neighboring school had joined the girls on the hike. The students had to face the wrath of the administrator, who in turn had to assuage angry parents.

In the tradition of *carnivale*, many schools provide students with a sanctioned opportunity to turn the established order on its head, though briefly. One high school has become famous throughout Taiwan for its annual water-balloon fight between students and teachers at graduation. Usually the approved chaos occurs during a school's annual birthday celebration, when students dress up in costumes, wander about the school freely, and spend the day running races and putting on performances. Occasionally, as in the account that follows, students take advantage of the chaotic atmosphere to bend or break rules, figuring they will not be caught or school authorities will look the other way.

The Birthday Party. I had the opportunity to observe the festivities at a rural girls' college-prep school in spring 1995. Since it was not a major anniversary, the audience would be small, but the students nevertheless felt excited. They begged teachers for a break to finish elaborate costumes and practice performances. The nature of each group's costumes remained a closely guarded secret until the morning of the anniversary celebration, and students worked late at school both nights before and early on the day of the event to finish preparations.

Waiting to parade before the reviewing stand, students looked like a giant Halloween party. First came the "American Indians," whooping and stamping their feet. Then, a giant bowling game, a basketball game, and the "rock group" – girls in brown-paper miniskirts who could have just stepped out of Fred Flintstone's living room. "Health" was all dressed up as vegetables and milk, followed by pirates, Spanish bullfighters and dancers, Japanese geisha, Korean "dolls," princesses, hoodlums, prisoners, mummies, and a group mocking the recent elections.

Each class had its own booth covered by a tarp, where they spent the rest of the day, competing in races and cheering on classmates. By the next morning, practically all traces of the celebration were gone. But one item remained to be resolved.

On the morning of the celebration, one class had agreed to meet especially early, at 6:30 a.m., because they still had so much to do. The class leader discovered she had locked her keys in the room the night before. She called the section adviser, who called the school sentry, who agreed to hurry over to unlock the room. Fearing the delay would make it impossible to complete their costumes, a student broke a window and unlocked the door from the inside. Someone swept up the glass while everyone hurried to finish. When the section adviser discovered the broken window, she told the students to get it fixed quickly. The window was not fixed before the school discipline administrator found out about it, and she became furious. The students refused to reveal who had decided to break the window, so the class leader had to bear the responsibility, and the brunt of the administrator's dressing-down in front of the whole class.

When the school discipline head found out I would be observing the class the day she planned to scold the students, she asked whether I wanted to attend. "You know I'm going to scold the students today. They committed a serious moral error," she said. She feared the students would be embarrassed if I attended, but I persisted. Before class, students warned each other to straighten uniforms and be quiet.

When she entered, the tension in the room was palpable. Everyone sat with head slightly bowed and eyes cast down. First the administrator pointed out that other classes finished their preparations on time. She criticized the class leader for not taking responsibility for her group and was angry no one would reveal the culprit. She called the willful destruction of public property a serious error, and she expressed surprise students at this school would find it acceptable. She noted that she was willing to ignore it when many students stayed late to finish their preparations. However, if students were going to flaunt rules *seriously*, then perhaps the school should consider canceling the event.

She reminded the students that they were one of the top classes in the whole school, and asked how the school's brightest students could have such an idea. She asked whether they had any comment, whether she had given an unfair account of events, and then whether any felt she bore personal responsibility for what happened. Everyone raised her hand. With that simple action, the tension in the room relaxed. Heads that had been bowed lifted, and people began glancing around. In a more conciliatory tone, the administrator assured the students her actions were in their best interest – she was concerned for their sense of values, and its impact on their future. "Our country, this society, is chaotic, it's true," she said. "If we want to unite with them [the mainland], we must have greater progress."

The Value of Education. One of the striking aspects of the nature of student resistance to authority in Taiwan is that the response to the total institution of the schools does not break down along class lines in quite the way it has been observed to do in other situations. In his study of working-class British youth, Willis (1977) argued that a central difference in the school experience of working-class and middle-class students was their attitude toward the value of school learning. Willis's "lads" valorized a masculine roughness, intense physicality, and disdain for institutionalized authority that traced the patterns of lives in the working-class communities they grew up in. Since school learning held little social capital for Willis's lads, they refused to allow themselves to be controlled, instead spending their time and energy figuring out ways to challenge school authority. Attending school drunk, playing pranks, and cruising for girls were only a few of their regular activities. Such behavior was supported or at least tolerated by their families and friends.

In Taiwan, the value placed on education transcends class differences. Even among students who are unlikely to excel in Taiwan's system, the desire for educational credentials is fierce. Evidence for this can be found in the lucrative and widespread cram-school business; the constant demand for English-language instruction among young people, who believe it will help them attain high enough TOEFL scores to gain admission to a U.S. school; and the hiring of foreigners to edit or write U.S. college applications. Education was the first route to mobility in postwar Taiwan, and it has continued to be a highly sought-after objective even as acquisition of big money through business, crime, and the stock market has also become a channel of mobility. Competition for spots in top high schools is tough because their students are virtually guaranteed college entry. A college degree is still a fair guarantee of white-collar employment in Taiwan or the chance to study abroad. Students at second-tier college-prep schools or good vocational schools often spend the year after they graduate at cram schools in hopes of faring well enough on the next entrance exam to gain university admission. Students at lesser schools might focus on getting out of school as soon as possible and finding a job. Some others manage to go abroad to the United States, New Zealand, Belize, or other places where access to advanced training is generally less restricted so long as the applicant can pay tuition.

I am not arguing that no class differences exist among Taiwan students. To the contrary, social classes among students separate along the vocational/college-prep dividing line. In general, the further a person's present and future are away from manual labor, the more prestigious the educational setting in Taiwan. Vocational high schools that train students in industrial arts such as die-making and welding, for example, have the lowest prestige, though perhaps not as low as that of the worst college-prep high schools. Second-tier college-prep and vocational schools that train students in business skills (accounting and business management, for example) are somewhere in the middle, while the top college-prep high schools have the highest prestige.

Most people in Taiwan would argue that whether students attend college-prep or vocational schools is not related to any class differences that exist in larger Taiwan society. Belief in the fairness of Taiwan's entrance-exam system is widespread among students, teachers, parents, and school officials. By "fair," they mean the test is the best available method of tracking students into appropriate educational paths without regard to economic background, political connections, or other social factors.

My own observations among students supported the conclusion that in spite of what most people in Taiwan believe, the entrance-exam system contains an inherent bias toward children who grow up in financially and socially stable environments. In addition, children who are surrounded by educated relatives and who have access to the resources available in urban areas have an advantage over rural youth or children from families where few people have achieved educational success. I did find children of elementary school graduates and of fruit salesmen attending the top college-prep schools. But it was rare to find the children of well-educated parents at lower-tier vocational schools or children of aborigine extraction at the top college-prep schools.

The fact that there is differential access to educational resources in Taiwan raises a question of more importance here: Do these differences result in varying levels of "rebellious" or disruptive behavior among students? A small, emergent counterculture does exist among urban Taiwan youth, including children who race motorcycles, use drugs, go to bars and dance clubs, and hang out on the streets (Shaw, 1994). However, the number of Taiwanese teenagers engaged in such behavior is still relatively small.[8]

In my experience at both college-prep and vocational schools, I found that students at the top college-prep schools are more motivated to adopt behaviors and attitudes conducive to furthering their chances of success on the college entrance exam. Those students are aware of how much they have to lose if they fail, and how much to gain if they succeed, and usually avoid direct challenges to school or public officials that might result in severe punishment and long-term demerits on their records. On the other hand, students at vocational schools, particularly the lower-tier schools, have less to gain from their educational experience, and perhaps more to gain from bonding with their peers. In this way they resemble

Willis's lads. But the crucial difference between them and Willis's lads is that the Taiwan youth do not find support among their parents and communities for the disruptive behavior they engage in; there is little valorization of a working-class culture in Taiwan. Educational credentials remain a valued objective worth tremendous sacrifice of time, energy, and money, and people who lack such credentials still wish their children would obtain them. Thus, attitudes in Taiwan toward education closely resemble what Willis presented as the middle-class experience among his British students, in which children find at home a "reinforcement of a certain view of the social importance and value of knowledge" (Willis, 1977, p. 76). Middle-class British parents, like their Taiwan counterparts, are also likely to view school as a source of qualifications that would translate into social mobility.

Conclusion

During the period of martial law on Taiwan, students learned that taking an overt interest in politics might get them in trouble. But a definition of political activity must be broad enough to incorporate the often constricted outlets students have for self-expression. When the people primarily responsible for school discipline are all assumed to be members of a ruling regime's political party, even routine rule breaking becomes a potentially political act. Thus, school discipline became broadly entangled with ideological mandates, and the school's power to punish was used to make students follow the KMT line. The emphasis on maintenance of order and control in Taiwan society as a whole meant that even small expressions of dissent or disorder could be interpreted as having political ramifications.

With the democratization of politics and education in Taiwan, school officials can no longer punish students for speaking Taiwanese or advocating Taiwan independence. But, as the example of the broken window illustrates, students' misdeeds are still interpreted in light of larger national policy goals, adding a political element to what might otherwise be considered routine rule breaking. Even today, therefore, students' attempts to understand Taiwan's changes and to engage with the process of democratization can come into conflict with what is perceived to be appropriate behavior for students, as the following example shows.

A student at a top urban high school proposed a yearbook essay about Taiwan's aborigines. According to the students who recounted the story, the yearbook adviser rejected the essay because it described how Taiwan's aborigines had suffered under KMT rule. The essay's author angrily faxed a letter to a journalist, complaining that the school restricted students' free speech. The school contacted the student's father, who traveled to the school from a distant suburb to take her home. Since she was living away from home to attend a prestigious school, her parents had been unaware of her interest and involvement in the aborigine political movement. The principal's account was that the yearbook adviser had only suggested the student make some organizational changes in the essay. According to the principal, the student had reacted to the criticism inappropriately, by throwing a fit and then making public accusations against the school. This is what prompted the school to contact her parents.

In the end, the article was published in the 1991 yearbook, some 50 pages including photographs. It contains a scathing critique of Taiwan's education policies, the publication of which would have been impossible during martial law. A section of the essay discusses the gap in achievement between Taiwan's aborigine children, many of whom live in isolated mountain areas, and Chinese children. One reason for this gap is that the poorest quality teachers are sent to those remote areas, the author says. Furthermore, the essay argues, though the characteristics, values, life-styles, and environment of aborigine communities differ from those of the Chinese, aborigine children are forced to study the "unfamiliar history, culture and language" of China, and are subjected to an "underlying Han [Chinese] chauvinism" in standardized school texts.

Whether the student was reprimanded because of her breach of authority or the essay's anti-KMT tone is difficult to judge. However, the school apparently decided it could not punish her for the essay's content, instead targeting her noncompliant attitude. In post–martial law Taiwan, students are unlikely to be disciplined for previously punishable offenses such as speaking Taiwanese on campus or advocating Taiwan independence. Instead, it is episodes in which students threaten the harmony either of the school or of the larger community that attract disciplinary action.

The students who demonstrated for social change in China earlier this century saw themselves as part of a well-established tradition in which scholars were viewed as "the conscience of the nation" (Wasserstrom, 1991, p. 281). Even with the new political freedoms enacted since 1987, however, it is unlikely that Taiwan high school students will feel motivated or capable of assuming that mantle. Though martial law has ended, high school students are still socialized in ways meant to inscribe particular understandings of authority in their patterns of behavior. Students' need for some form of political expression is often worked out through small acts of resistance that occur within the constraints imposed both by school and KMT authorities, and within the frameworks of cultural values about education and what is appropriate behavior for children.

Notes

1. I have used the pinyin romanization of Chinese words here, except in cases where English romanizations are so common that a different spelling would be awkward, such as the spelling of Chiang Kai-shek's name.
2. Scholars ranked above all others in Confucius's list of professions because they spent their lives seeking truth and knowledge in pursuit of the ultimate Confucian ideal of moral perfection, rather than in pursuit of financial gain. The civil service exam system through which officials were selected developed into a rigorous test of candidates' knowledge of the Confucian classics and other literary and philosophical works. This meant that scholars not only had moral authority by virtue of their knowledge, but occupied real positions of power throughout the empire. Theoretically, officials could speak freely about local dissatisfaction with state policies, and some did so. Imperial Beijing relied on these communications for news of the huge empire (Israel, 1969; Wakeman, 1975).
3. The government decided to increase the ratio of students attending vocational high schools to students attending academic high schools gradually from 4:6 in the 1960s to 7:3 in 1981, "in order to keep education consistent with economic development" (Sun, 1994, p. 98).
4. Much has been written on the subject of group identity in Asian societies, to the point where Asians and non-Asians alike accept the stereotype of Asians as more group-oriented than Westerners. Often the idea of group identity or group harmony is idealized and romanticized, masking calculated strategies for controlling members of a group and its competitors or opponents.
5. I analyzed the letters to a personal advice column in a Taiwan housewives' magazine over the 20-year period from 1960 to 1980. The single point that remained constant in the letters was the writers' concern with maintaining the harmony of their family or work groups. They based life decisions on their own predictions as to which course of action would least disrupt the group (Strawn, 1989).
6. The governments on both sides of the Taiwan Strait have claimed the right to govern all of China. The PRC claims sovereignty over Taiwan, even though Taiwan and the PRC have lived under separate governments for 50 years. For decades the ROC government on Taiwan claimed to be the legitimate government of all China, maintaining seats in the National Assembly on Taiwan that supposedly represented every province in China and consistently referring to the PRC government as "Communist bandits." The ROC government finally gave up this claim in 1991, acknowledging that it has no sovereignty over the mainland, but it has not abandoned the goal of eventual reunification.
7. Independence supporters, who are for the most part native Taiwanese, advocate the right of Taiwan's citizens to self-determination. At the other end of the scale are people who believe in the right of the Republic of China

264   Perri Strawn

government to rule the complete physical territory of China. Most people in Taiwan occupy positions between these two poles (Wachman, 1994).

8. A series of 1993 articles indicated that juvenile delinquency is on the rise in Taiwan, and troubled youth do not always come from "bad" backgrounds as they once did. According to statistics compiled by the National Police Administration, there was a sharp increase in youth (children aged 12 to 18) crime between 1983 and 1993: from 45 juvenile criminals for every 10,000 children in 1983 to 130 per 10,000 in 1993. In 1992, theft (mainly of automobiles and motorcycles) accounted for 46% of juvenile crimes and drug offenses (mainly amphetamine use), for 36% (Wu, 1993: pp. 4–6).

References

Chun, Allen (1996). From nationalism to nationalizing: Cultural imagination and state formation in postwar Taiwan. In J. Uher, ed. *Chinese nationalism* (pp. 126–147). Armonk, NY: M. E. Sharpe.

Eastman, Lloyd (1990). *The abortive revolution.* Cambridge, MA: Harvard Council on East Asian Studies.

Israel, John (1966). *Student nationalism in China 1927–1937.* Stanford, CA: Stanford University Press for the Hoover Institution on War, Revolution, and Peace.

Israel, John (1969). Reflections on the modern Chinese student movement. In S. M. Lipset & P. G. Altbach, eds. *Students in revolt* (pp. 310–333). Boston: Houghton Mifflin.

Lianhe Bao [United Daily News]. (1994, December 30). The hibernating lily (*Dongmin de Yebaihe*). p. 39.

Scott, James (1985). *Weapons of the weak: Everyday forms of peasant resistance.* New Haven, CT: Yale University Press.

Shaw, Thomas (1994). Learning to be an individual: The education of Taiwan's new middle class. Paper presented at the Association for Asian Studies annual meeting, Boston, MA.

Shepherd, John (1993). *Statecraft and political economy on the Taiwan frontier, 1600–1800.* Stanford, CA: Stanford University Press.

Spence, Jonathan (1990). *The search for modern China.* New York: Norton.

Strawn, Perri (1989). Harmony above all else: Women in Taiwan as portrayed in the advice column of *The Woman* magazine. Unpublished seminar paper, Yale University.

Sun, Chen (1994). Investment in education and human resource development in Postwar Taiwan. In S. Harrell & H. Chün-Chieh, eds. *Cultural change in postwar Taiwan* (pp. 91–110). Taipei: SMC.

Wachman, Alan M. (1994). *Taiwan: National identity and democratization.* Armonk, NY: M. E. Sharpe.

Wakeman, Frederic (1975). *The fall of Imperial China.* New York: The Free Press.

Wasserstrom, Jeffrey (1991). *Student protests in twentieth-century China.* Stanford, CA: Stanford University Press.

Willis, Paul (1977). *Learning to labor.* Westmead, England: Saxon House.

Wilson, Richard W. (1970). *Learning to be Chinese: The political socialization of children in Taiwan.* Cambridge, MA: M.I.T. Press.

Wu, Emma (1993, December). Adolescent blues. *Free China Review*, pp. 4–11.

Conclusion: Transcending Themes

MIRANDA YATES AND JAMES YOUNISS

The chapters in this volume offer portraits of youth's participation in community and civic activities in a range of social–historical contexts. The fresh empirical data presented in these chapters indicate that youth's participation in society varies considerably across time and location. In each context, youth are characterized as active decision makers seeking to understand and find their place in the society in which they were born. But youth do not seek simply to fit themselves within the status quo. As several chapters show, youth in many countries play pivotal roles in challenging the existing order and working to improve social conditions.

In this concluding chapter, we identify recurring themes that transcend the varying contexts presented in this volume. Our purpose is to illustrate the emergence of a more adequate approach to political socialization that goes beyond the simplicity of the internalization model and that accounts for human development occurring within social contexts often filled with ambiguous and conflicting perspectives. Our challenge is to understand how youth come to terms with the complexity of society and its political order and also, ideally, come to believe that they can play a role in shaping its future.

The presentation of themes begins with the concern expressed in many countries that contemporary youth are disconnected from political processes and lack a sense of social responsibility. From here, we tie together findings that present adolescents as active participants in figuring out the workings of society and that pertain to the role of social–historical opportunity in this process, particularly as it is instantiated through adolescents' social relationships with community organizations, family, and friends. These findings lead us to discuss the insights the chapters offer on the meaning of the concept of "society" and, ultimately, on how community service and civic engagement in youth can be seen as integrally connected to identity formation.

Theme 1: Public Discourse on Youth's Civic Engagement

A striking number of chapters describe a general mood of concern about contemporary youth's disconnection from political processes and the workings of society. Roker et al. (chapter 3) begin with headlines from British newspapers portraying youth as politically apathetic and morally suspect. This portrayal fits with Flanagan et al.'s (chapter 7), Seginer's (chapter 10), and Yates's (chapter 1) assertions that at the end of the twentieth century, discussion about rising individualism and self-interest in youth prevails in the countries they studied. Indeed, concerns about this trend in youth have motivated national programming efforts to promote service participation and increase service opportunities, most notably in Israel, Japan, the United States, and the United Kingdom.

The authors, however, make the point that criticisms of youth's attitudes toward society are misdirected and that contemporary problems of alienation and social disconnection are probably more reflective of the general state of some modern cultures than of the particular state of the current generation of youth. This does not mean that service and civic opportunities for youth should not be promoted; it simply highlights the need for a positive rationale for promoting these opportunities, a rationale that recognizes youth's talents and their desire to have a meaningful role in society. The chapters indicate that youth in many cultures are spending their time in productive ways, engaged in such activities as educating younger children, coordinating sports and religious events, protecting the environment, and delivering health and social services (see Flanagan et al. [chapter 7]; Marta et al. [chapter 4]; Pancer & Pratt [chapter 2]; and Roker et al. [chapter 3]). Rather than viewing these activities as a process of imposing normative values on youth's antisocial tendencies, it seems more productive and realistic to view service programs as responding to youth's yearning to be a part of society and to be respected for their contributions.

Theme 2: Adolescents as Constructive Agents

In any country, the political and social world in which adolescents live is complex and often riddled with ambiguous messages. Youth are challenged to make sense of this world as it relates to their own lives in the present and future. For example, Barber (chapter 9) highlights the contradictory feelings, attitudes, and experiences with which Palestinian youth must grapple. By delineating youth's simultaneous experiences of defiance and deference, growth and stasis, and hope and discouragement, he builds a case for youth's competence and active participation in their own identity formation.

Other chapters also offer insight into how youth grapple with the complexity of the political realm. Oswald (chapter 5) describes how youth in former East Germany may develop different political attitudes by reviewing variations in orientation related to educational level, socioeconomic status, gender, parenting styles, and political party status. Pancer and Pratt's model of volunteer involvement (chapter 2) illuminates the varieties of paths youth take by identifying several initiating and sustaining factors associated with volunteerism. These chapters indicate that no single factor can adequately explain youth's understanding of political events and of participation in community and civic activities. Rather, a confluence of factors and experiences plays a role in youth's developing political awareness.

The constructive nature of this process is highlighted by youth's participation in social and political change. Takahashi and Hatano (chapter 11) describe youth's efforts to become more involved in service, despite a traditional lack of opportunity for this kind of activity. Barber (chapter 9), Seginer (chapter 10), and Strawn (chapter 12) all describe the past and present roles of youth in leading political protest and practicing "everyday forms of resistance." To these chapters, we could add accounts of youth protest and reform efforts in Latin America and Africa. These chapters show that the process of political socialization entails not simply learning how the present political and social order is structured, but rather aspiring to an ideal of how things could be improved. Thus, youth are constructing something new that is the nexus of their sense of societal connectedness and agency with the social–historical conditions of their country.

Theme 3: Learning through Doing

The chapters emphasize that to understand political development in youth, we need to focus on the community and civic activities in which they participate and to examine how political understandings emerge through these activities. This approach reflects a broadened definition of the term *political* that extends beyond the typical considerations of party affiliation and projected voting. A broadened definition of what is political seems necessary for at least two reasons. First, in some countries the strict term *political* has taken on negative connotations. Some people who are active in their communities and have positive attitudes toward this activism indicate disdain for political involvement. In the chapters, this phenomenon was revealed in some discussions of volunteer motivations. For instance, Marta et al. (chapter 4) report that a series of scandals in Italy may have influenced volunteers to conceptualize their volunteerism in more interpersonal than political terms. In a related way, Flanagan et al. (chapter 7) describe how youth in several countries framed their community service as doing something for society, their country, other people, or their community, rather than as political. A second reason for connecting the practice of community and civic activities to political engagement is that despite this trend toward separating community and civic involvement from the political, mounting evidence indicates a compelling pattern of continuity between engagement in a range of community and civic activities in youth and direct political activism – in the forms of political party membership and leadership and voting rates – in adulthood. This continuity suggests these types of activities are part of a continuum of social–political integration. It is, therefore, productive to examine community and civic activities in youth.

What do we learn when we look at youth's participation in these activities? The chapters indicate that participation in community and civic activities encourages the development of leadership and organizational skills and promotes a sense of connectedness, agency, and realism, all of which seem to be important aspects of mature political identity. Marta et al. (chapter 4) discuss the potential for concrete skills development through volunteerism. The Palestinian youth in Barber's study (chapter 9) indicate that their experience in the Intifada made them leaders. In this study, the youth's sense of moving away from childhood and becoming leaders is most likely played out not only in the learning of concrete skills, but also in the development of a sense of social responsibility and agency. Supporting this point, Pancer and Pratt (chapter 2) and Roker et al. (chapter 3) emphasize the emergence of a heightened sense of social connection and efficacy through community service and volunteerism. Taking a slightly different perspective, Yates's chapter (chapter 1) indicates that service experiences also offer the chance for youth to form realistic appraisals of what they can contribute. So although community service experiences can help to engage youth in social change efforts, they also help them to figure out the most effective avenues of effort. All of the changes specified by the authors depend on actual experiences in which youth sometimes do well and sometimes make mistakes and in which they learn and become more engaged in their community and society at large.

Theme 4: Participation Framed by Political and Historical Conditions

Assessing the chapters together illustrates the argument that it is crucial to consider how political and historical conditions frame service and civic participation. Clearly, we knew from the outset that there would be substantial differences in which kinds of activities Canadian, Taiwanese, and former East German youth – to name just three examples – participate. This volume allows us to consider more specifically issues pertinent to the influence of political–historical context on the provision of opportunities and the development of individual citizens. As shown, for example, in the chapters on Ireland (chapter 8), Israel (chapter 10), and Italy (chapter 4), religious beliefs and practices and the historical events surrounding the establishment of a country have very real implications for the shape and degree of service and civic participation in youth. Whereas some countries such as Canada and the United States have long traditions and expectations of citizen voluntarism dating back to these countries' inception, other countries such as former East and West Germany are undergoing substantial changes that necessitate renegotiation of citizen involvement. Flanagan et al. (chapter 7) make the point that history and political conditions are connected to how service is framed. Whereas service in the United States, for example, is often oriented toward charity, in Eastern and Central Europe voluntarism has different political connotations because it has historically been viewed as a "free" and uncensored space in which to organize political opposition.

The chapters help us to identify four different political situations pertinent to understanding the degree and form of community and civic participation. First, Flanagan et al. (chapter 7) and Oswald (chapter 5) depict countries undergoing rapid political change involving the renegotiation of the relationship between state and citizen (or of the "social contract") and increased freedom and need for direct citizen involvement. Second, Takahashi and Hatano (chapter 11) and Strawn (chapter 12) describe youth's current efforts to challenge what they view as the paternalistic actions of government. In Taiwan this takes the form of subtle acts of subversion and minor rule breaking. In Japan, youth are actively seeking to harness technology to create social networks of informed citizens who can work to respond to the needs of such causes as environmental protection and recovery from natural disasters. Third, Barber (chapter 9), Seginer (chapter 10), and Whyte (chapter 8) depict youth's identity formation under conditions of war and civil unrest: Barber and Seginer discuss how the chronic threat of unrest and violence can intensify the integration of national and personal identity. Applying a comparative framework, Whyte reports striking differences in beliefs and attitudes between Catholics and Protestants in Ireland. Fourth, several countries are experiencing the collapse or diminution of the welfare state, leading to increased reliance on the private and nonprofit sectors. Some of the most extreme examples come from Eastern and Central Europe, but clearly this trend is also important to conditions in Western Europe, the United States, and Canada. Reflecting the influence of the availability of state-sponsored services, Flanagan et al. (chapter 7) report that in their study, the lowest rates of youth voluntarism occur in Sweden, which has the strongest welfare system.

Theme 5: Roles of Community Organizations, Family, and Peers

Community organizations, family, and peers play important roles in offering youth the opportunity to become involved in community and civic activities. The chapters specify the types of organizations that offer opportunities and the social processes through which parents and peers might influence youth's actions.

In terms of community organizations, schools and churches in several countries – such as Canada, Ireland, Italy, Japan, the United Kingdom, the United States, and former West Germany – are often cited as helping to organize community service. Political parties have also reached out directly to youth via local and national youth groups in such places as Israel, Palestine, and the United Kingdom. These political parties seem to recognize the importance of engaging youth at an early age and their potential contributions to political movements. Importantly, each of these organizations – schools, churches, and political parties – operates with an explicit ideological agenda, a part of which entails the activism of citizens or community members. In organizing these opportunities, they invite youth to become part of a collective tradition.

The powerful influence of the family on political development has long been acknowledged in the political socialization literature. Several authors offer insight into the process through which this influence might occur (e.g., Hofer [chapter 6]); Oswald [chapter 5]; Pancer & Pratt [chapter 2]; Whyte [chapter 8]. They report that parenting practices, values, and styles are related to youth community and civic engagement. For example, Pancer and Pratt (chapter 2) suggest that youth's engagement is related to parental practices of generosity, a congruence of parent – child values focused on kindness and caring, and a parenting style that is both demanding and responsive. Whereas Hofer's findings (chapter 6) are similar to Pancer and Pratt's (chapter 2) in explaining democratic engagement, Oswald (chapter 5) and Whyte (chapter 8) address extremism and inactivism. Oswald indicates that a power assertive parenting style or parental neglect may be related to willingness to engage in illegal political activities and right-wing extremism. Whyte theorizes that parents' efforts to protect and control the lives of adolescents growing up in Belfast may actually lead youth to feel like less competent participants in political processes.

Barber (chapter 9) and Yates (chapter 1) speak to the role of peers in political development, an area that has received far less research attention than the family: Barber discusses how for Palestinian youth, the negative experiences of parents and peers help to motivate initial activism. Once engaged, peers are described as supporting youth's actions and acting as collaborators and mentors. Yates reports on how peers can encourage each other to reflect on service experience and, thus, build a collective understanding of the meaning of service. Together, peers deliberate the broader meaning of their experiences in relation to society's moral order and political processes as well as their own present and future lives.

Theme 6: The Desire to Be a Societal Participant

An underlying assumption of the chapters is that given the proper conditions, youth possess the desire to play an active role in improving their countries. As we have already pointed out, the authors find that in many different countries youth volunteer and perform regular service.

The cross-national consideration of service and civic engagement in its variety of forms helps us to get a better grasp of youth's motivations in these activities. Although the specific theoretical orientations of the chapters vary, with, for example, Roker et al. (chapter 3) citing social learning theory and Flanagan et al. (chapter 7) presenting the sociocultural perspective of Vygotsky, several chapters make the point that youth draw upon a combination of altruistic and instrumental motives (e.g., Hofer [chapter 6]; Marta et al., [chapter 4]; Pancer & Pratt [chapter 2]; Roker et al. [chapter 3]; Seginer [chapter 10]; Yates [chapter 1]). On this issue, Hofer, Marta et al., and Seginer conclude that these two types of motives do not need to be seen as antagonistic. If one identifies strongly with the collective, then the line between doing something for oneself and doing it for another becomes an artificial construction. Barber articulates this idea as represented by Palestinian youth who see no distinction between the personal and political.

Pancer and Pratt's model (chapter 2) offers insight into the relationship between altruism and instrumentality by distinguishing between initiating and sustaining motives. They suggest that although youth may become involved in service for reasons that are understood as individualistic, sustained volunteerism tends to focus more on being an effective member of a social network.

Yates's (chapter 1) discussion of the debate over mandatory versus voluntary community service participation also pertains to reorienting the issue of motives. Whether participation in a service program is required or voluntary is less important than whether the rationale for service participation coheres with, for example, the pedagogical mission of a school or community agency. From this perspective, identity formation is seen as a fundamentally social process and service is seen as an instance of being and becoming an active member of a collective society.

Theme 7: Addressing the Nature of Society

By focusing on youth's community and civic practices, the chapters offer a grounded portrayal of society, one that operates on the level of the concrete encounters of everyday life. The message is that in order to understand society as it affects the lives of citizens and as it is abstracted by individuals into a concept of "society," we must begin by examining the activities and relationships that society comprises for adolescents. The need for this kind of grounded approach has become increasingly necessary in the modern era. As modern societies expand and become more pluralistic and technological, the task of understanding the concept "society" has become increasingly challenging. Indeed, Hofer (chapter 6) and Takahashi and Hatano (chapter 11) refer to contemporary youth as experiencing a "crisis of meaning" in trying to make sense of fragmented experiences and to find a place for themselves within a complex societal framework. They suggest that now, more than ever, service and civic participation may play a vital mediating role by helping youth to feel socially connected and to understand how different aspects of society, such as the economy or electoral process, actually work.

Theme 8: The Development of Civic Identity

The development of civic identity – a sense of who one is in relation to society and desire to be an active member in that society's present and future – is the central theme of this volume. The chapters reveal the close interconnections of political development and identity formation. As youth seek to explain and interpret their involvement in activities, they reveal how they are coming to think about and understand themselves. Youth view their motives for participation and the lessons drawn from actual community and civic experiences as significantly affecting their maturing personalities (e.g., Barber [chapter 9]; Pancer & Pratt [chapter 2]; Roker et al. [chapter 3]; Seginer [chapter 10]). Canadian care exemplars attribute service to helping them become more patient and caring. For Palestinian youth, participation in the Intifada was a double edged sword. It helped youth to feel like societal leaders, but it also yielded a sense of premature loss of innocence. Using retrospective studies of members of the Israeli military, Seginer (chapter 10) reports that adults view their military service as key to defining their adult identity. This finding matches those reported from studies of civil rights activists (McAdam, 1988) and community service participants in the United States (Youniss & Yates, 1997).

The findings reported in this volume gives us reason for cautious optimism. They highlight the competencies of today's youth in challenging, and often stressful, conditions. The portrayal of youth as active participants in enacting social change and constructing their own identities, however, should not detract from the pivotal influence of social and historical conditions. Youth can surmount great odds and make significant contributions, but it is not reasonable to expect them to become civically engaged in communities and societies that fail to support them. Family, peers, community organizations, and the media all have important roles in conveying positive messages that encourage youth to become a part of societal traditions, treat them with respect, and convey a sense of hope for the future. From within this supportive framework, youth can progressively take on leadership positions and aspire toward their ideals.

References

McAdam, D. (1988). *Freedom summer*. New York: Oxford University Press.
Youniss, J., & Yates, M. (1997). *Community service and social responsibility in youth.*
    Chicago: University of Chicago Press.

Author Index

Subject Index

Printed in the United States
83728LV00005B/259-276/A